EveryWoman's® Guide
to Sexual Fulfillment

EveryWoman's® Guide to Sexual Fulfillment

An Illustrated Lifetime Guide to Your Sexuality and Sensuality

Susan Quilliam

press
élan
A GENERAL PUBLISHING IMPRINT

A General Publishing imprint
34 Lesmill Road
Don Mills
Ontario M3B 2T6

A MARSHALL EDITION
Conceived, edited, and designed by
Marshall Editions
170 Piccadilly
London W1V 9DD

EDITOR *Anne Yelland*

ART EDITOR *John Grain*

PICTURE RESEARCH *Elaine Willis*

DTP EDITORS *Mary Pickles, Kate Waghorn*

COPY EDITOR *Jolika Feszt*

MANAGING EDITOR *Lindsay McTeague*

PRODUCTION EDITOR *Emma Dixon*

ART DIRECTOR *Sean Keogh*

EDITORIAL DIRECTOR *Sophie Collins*

PRODUCTION *Bob Christie*

Typeset in Monotype Baskerville
Originated in Singapore by Master Image
Printed and bound in Italy by New Interlitho SpA, Milan

10 9 8 7 6 5 4 3 2 1

ISBN 1-55144-130-6

CONTENTS

INTRODUCTION
DISCOVERING YOUR SEXUAL SELF

There has never been a better time to be a sexual woman. At the end of the 20th century, for perhaps the first time in the Western world, female sexuality has come into its own. We have increasing freedom to choose whether to take an intimate partner, whom to take, and when to leave. We are free to do what we like in bed, and we are increasingly aware of sex as a means to give and receive pleasure. And when it comes to the natural result of sexual intercourse, giving birth to a child, we now have a choice—and the help of advancing medical technology to support us when we do conceive, if we can't conceive, or if we conceive when we don't want to.

These radical shifts in women's sexuality are not without their problems. The sexual revolution has brought a health backlash in the form of sexually transmitted diseases and an emotional backlash in the form of partnerships that are less reliable, less long-lasting, sometimes highly pressurizing—and, in the end, far more likely to make us feel betrayed.

But we are learning to cope with creating sexual choices that feel appropriate, sexual decisions that seem wise and sexual relationships that are fulfilling. For this new age of sexuality is a new age of female sexual maturity. It is as if, prior to the social changes of this century, women were in a sexual "childhood,"

IN MOST WESTERN CULTURES, IT IS ONLY IN THE LAST FEW DECADES

1850s

1900s

• *Women were usually judged incapable of feeling sexual arousal. For a woman, sex was about bearing children and "continuing the line;" any departure from marriage, fidelity, and heterosexuality was seen as abnormal and morally and legally wrong—sometimes even a capital offense.*

• *It was finally accepted that sex might be arousing for women, but only if their husbands taught them how to be passionate. Emotionally, women were thought unlikely to appreciate sex.*

• *Sigmund Freud claimed that women envied men's overt sex organ, the penis. Women were thought to be interested in sex only because it allowed them to be mothers.*

• *In many countries, World War I altered women's place in society because of their more direct involvement in a "man's world;" this brought with it slightly more sexual freedom.*

• *Between the wars, extramarital affairs, bisexuality, birth control, and lesbianism were far more accepted in some societies; for many women, though, the status quo still ruled.*

a state of inexperience in which we had no control over our sexuality. After the liberation that came about in the middle of the century, we entered an "adolescence," in which we explored, experimented, and fought for control of our own life—often getting hurt in the process. Now, as the century turns, perhaps we are at last reaching sexual "adulthood."

This book is intended to reflect clearly and directly the sexual experience of women in today's world. It presents the essential facts, as shown by current research, about all aspects of sex—sensuality, lovemaking, fertility, and emotions. It also offers practical guidelines on how to face and negotiate the

key issues that we now encounter in our lifetime as a sexual being such as when we should lose our virginity; how we can be sexually assertive; how we should balance the demands of sexuality and fertility; and how we can maintain our right to be sexual for as long as we choose. And throughout the book, in their own voices, women tell us their personal experiences and what it really means to be a sexual woman now.

Today, women are facing a special time. We are encountering difficulties. We are suffering setbacks. We are facing challenges. But above all, we are now experiencing a possibility of passion that no other generation of women has ever known.

THAT WOMEN HAVE BEEN TRULY FREE TO EXPRESS THEIR SEXUALITY

1950s | | **1970s** | | **2000**

• *Sex researcher Alfred Kinsey's work proved that women, as well as men, took pleasure in intercourse, masturbated, and enjoyed such "abnormal" acts as oral sex.*

• *The contraceptive pill promised women sexuality without fear of pregnancy; abortion laws were eased in many countries. But this also brought great social pressure to have sex, whether it was wanted or not.*

• *The women's movement encouraged women not to rely on men for their pleasure. Researchers Masters and Johnson discovered that many women had more reliable orgasms through clitoral pleasuring than through intercourse.*

• *The increasing divorce rate and rising number of single-parent families left in its wake, as well as a rise in sexually transmitted diseases, including AIDS, caused women to question the sexual "freedom" of the 1960s and 1970s.*

• *Women developed a stronger sense of personal sexuality and moved toward increased sexual development.*

THE UNDERLYING BELIEF IN WESTERN culture is that female children are born asexual, that rather like Sleeping Beauty before Prince Charming arrives, girls do not instinctively know how to be passionate. We may know the facts of life, but in terms of sexuality we lie dormant and passive, waiting until we become women before realizing our potential.

But the fact that we may not experience passion until our early adult years does not mean that we are incapable of doing so. It is more likely to be because we may have been told so often and so firmly that we are not naturally sexual that we ignore any feelings to the contrary.

Childhood is not simply a "waiting in the wings" for sexuality and its natural result, childbearing. Rather it is an essential first act. Throughout our early years, our female bodies are busy, working to bring us to sexual and reproductive maturity. Our minds and emotions are developing continuously, building the beliefs and attitudes that will inform our enjoyment of intimacy and our success in intimate relationships. Above all, female childhood is a time to explore sexuality instinctively. We aren't waiting for Prince Charming to arrive. We are much more likely to be finding out for ourselves what being female is, what works for us sexually, and what we do and don't like.

Appreciating this, and reclaiming a sense that girlhood is a vital part of the process, is the starting point for fully integrating sexuality into life.

REHEARSING FOR ADULT *femininity is a key part of growing from girl to woman. But little girls don't only "dress up" in their rehearsals. They also observe their mothers, sisters, school friends, and teachers; they think about what they will be like when they are grown up; and they play act the relationships they see enacted around them. Like a second skin, they slowly take on the femininity, sensuality, and sexuality that are their birthright.*

BORN A SEXUAL WOMAN

FEMALE SEXUALITY IS PRESENT FROM BEFORE BIRTH

Every baby girl is born with the potential for sex. We have the potential for lovemaking—vagina and clitoris—and for childbearing—ovaries and Fallopian tubes, womb, and cervix. And in our brain is the system to release the female hormones that will trigger and regulate the sexual process. We also have an innate capacity for sensuality, the foundation on which our passion will eventually develop.

All fetuses suck their fingers for sensual pleasure. A newborn baby wriggles delightedly when stroked and sighs with joy as she fills her mouth with food. It is impossible to tell what babies experience, but many signs of sexual arousal, including vaginal lubrication, genital swelling, and pelvic thrusting, have been noted in infants. As young as four months, baby girls show patterns of building excitement followed by relaxation that are similar to those of orgasm.

Of course, small children do not have the richness of adult experience, physically or emotionally. But girls do know about sexuality, and we know it from birth: the physiological building blocks are in place, and we have the necessary psychological instincts for pleasure.

INTERNAL SEXUAL ORGANS

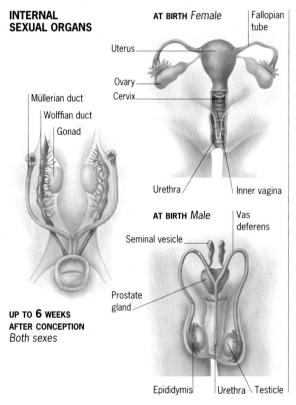

AT BIRTH *Female*

Fallopian tube

Uterus

Ovary

Cervix

Müllerian duct

Wolffian duct

Gonad

Urethra

Inner vagina

AT BIRTH *Male*

Vas deferens

Seminal vesicle

Prostate gland

UP TO **6 WEEKS** AFTER CONCEPTION *Both sexes*

Epididymis

Urethra

Testicle

EXTERNAL SEXUAL ORGANS

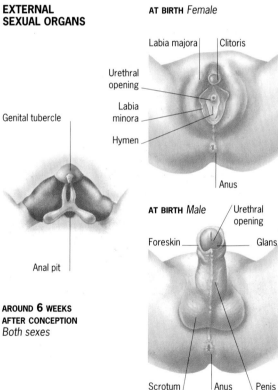

AT BIRTH *Female*

Labia majora

Clitoris

Urethral opening

Labia minora

Hymen

Genital tubercle

Anus

AT BIRTH *Male*

Urethral opening

Foreskin

Glans

Anal pit

AROUND **6 WEEKS** AFTER CONCEPTION *Both sexes*

Scrotum

Anus

Penis

GENDER DIFFERENTIATION *begins about six weeks after conception. Until then both boys and girls have a pair of gonads, which produce hormones to regulate body functions, and two sets of internal gynecological structures (Müllerian ducts*

and Wolffian ducts). After six weeks the reproductive and sexual organs move into place. In your case, the gonads developed into ovaries and moved into position in the pelvis, already carrying a lifetime's supply of eggs for childbearing. The potential

male sex organs in your Wolffian ducts withered, but the Müllerian ducts developed into your womb, Fallopian tubes, cervix, and inner vagina. You began to develop the basic female pattern of hormone stimulation, which at puberty allows you to be fertile.

Externally, differentiation also starts some six weeks after conception when the external genitals develop. These include the labia minora, labia majora, clitoris, and the outer two-thirds of the vagina, which links to the inner third developed from the Müllerian ducts.

10

YOU SHOW ME YOURS

As a girl, you were probably comparing notes with friends about your private parts by the time you were three or four years old. For while boys masturbate sooner, girls take the lead in playing "doctors and nurses," "mommies and daddies," or simply "show and tell." Little girls are particularly interested in boys' penises because penises are visible and obvious. But other girls' bodies are fascinating too: there is a magic fountain pouring out golden water (the vulva), strange buttons to be prodded and pulled (nipples), a hole to stick fingers in (vagina). The aim is knowledge rather than sensation; to explore sexual parts, and to find out how it feels to be explored in return.

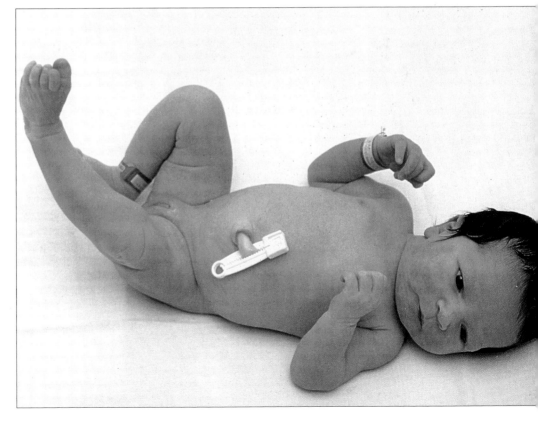

AS SOON AS *you are born, you start to build your sensuality and lay the foundations of your sexuality through your interactions with other people. Looking, listening, tasting, smelling, and above all, touching others and being cuddled and held all make you feel loved and consequently give you pleasure. Later in life, when you begin to have sexual relationships, all these sensations arouse you, and also make you feel safe and loved because they link back to your earliest memories.*

SEXUAL MESSAGES
CHILDHOOD INFLUENCES ON SEX AND SEXUALITY

Our initial potential for sex is shaped as we grow from babies into little girls. We constantly receive information from the world about us—from what we see and hear, how people react to us, how those around us react to each other. These experiences give us messages about sex which will affect us for the rest of our lives.

Some messages are directly about sex. We learn the facts of life when we ask where babies come from. We pick up from other children that sex is sometimes funny, sometimes special, sometimes dirty. Most of us do not actually see sex in action—but that makes it all the more intriguing and compelling.

But we also receive indirect messages which affect the way we approach sex. If enjoyable cuddles show us that physical expression is good, twenty years later we will be happily demonstrative in bed. If family experiences teach us that we're basically "okay," twenty years later we'll be self-confident in intimate relationships. If we see that sexual partnerships—such as those between our parents—are contented and balanced, we will be equipped for a good sexual partnership. And if we learn that childbearing is both an option and a responsibility, we will be able to make our own choices about family planning and carry through and live with the implications of any decisions we make.

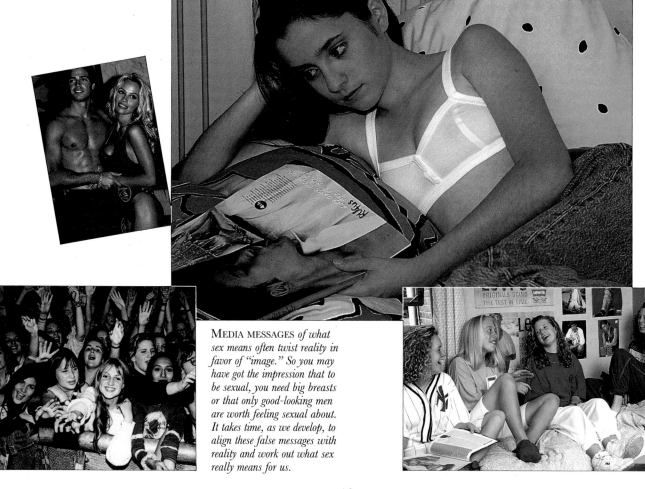

MEDIA MESSAGES *of what sex means often twist reality in favor of "image." So you may have got the impression that to be sexual, you need big breasts or that only good-looking men are worth feeling sexual about. It takes time, as we develop, to align these false messages with reality and work out what sex really means for us.*

Case history

"I was brought up by a mother who loved sex and who, even before sexual openness was fashionable, thought the best way to rear a daughter was with total honesty.

"So when at three, I asked where babies came from, she explained it all to me, simply but accurately. When a few years later, I wondered what men and women did to make the babies, she told me that, too. I was disgusted at the thought of a man putting his 'thing' inside me, and decided that I wouldn't be doing any of that, thank you.

"At 13, when I'd realized that 'that' was related to the way my stomach trembled every time I saw the red-haired boy on the bus, I asked her what it was like to make love. She gave me a tactful but nevertheless blow-by-blow account of what she and my father did. And she said it was wonderful."

MARIA

SURVIVING ABUSE

Abuse is the most harmful message a girl can receive, not only because the physical act may be disgusting, but also because an abused child may feel confusing emotions: afraid because she has been threatened; angry because she is being forced to do what she doesn't want to; guilty that she might somehow be to blame.

In adulthood, these negative feelings can be translated into sexual difficulties. A woman may be fearful of lovemaking; unable to get aroused; guilty when she does enjoy sex. Emotionally, she may be unwilling to trust in sexual partnerships or—conversely—she may find herself in unhappy relationships because she can't distinguish between partners who love her and those who abuse her.

If you have been abused in the past—even if you have only vague memories—it will help to talk to someone, preferably a professional counselor. They will not blame you or force you to relive unhappy past events. But they will help you deal with negative effects on your life now and help you fully reclaim your sexuality.

SEXUAL INFLUENCES

How did you learn about sex? A 1985 American national survey by R. Coles and G. Stokes showed that parents and teachers give the facts, but the "how to" is learned from friends and, despite its often mixed messages, the media.

REPRODUCTION	BIRTH CONTROL	MASTURBATION	SEXUAL TECHNIQUE
Teachers 50%	Teachers 37%	Teachers 21%	Teachers 14%
Parents 23%	Parents 17%	Parents 12%	Parents 9%
Friends 15%	Friends 17%	Friends 32%	Friends 26%
Media 9%	Media 20%	Media 30%	Media 32%
Doctor 0%	Doctor 4%	Doctor 1%	Doctor 0%
Brother or sister 2%	Brother or sister 4%	Brother or sister 3%	Brother or sister 2%

Note: Partners are an insignificant influence, except on sexual technique, where 17% said they played a role.

13

BECOMING A WOMAN
THE PHYSIOLOGICAL CHANGES AT PUBERTY

The shift from girlhood to fully functioning sexuality is remarkable. It happens at some time between the ages of 8 and 14, and lasts approximately three years. With natural growth, the body reaches a certain weight (about 105 lb/47.5 kg) and body fat reaches a certain percentage of weight (about 25 percent). Then, as if reassured that we now have the physical resources to cope with pregnancy, the pituitary gland triggers the release of follicle stimulating hormone (FSH), which in turn signals the ovaries to secrete estrogen, the female hormone. It is estrogen which, for the rest of our lives, influences physical health, creates emotional moods, and affects sexual desire.

In response to estrogen, the ovaries prepare to release eggs, from the store of about 200,000 in our bodies. The womb matures in readiness for carrying a child. The vagina grows and its lining thickens in preparation for intercourse and childbirth. The clitoris develops to assume its place as our main organ of pleasure.

Eventually comes the first of the menstrual cycles which, month after month, gear up the body for a possible pregnancy. The end and, of course, the beginning of each cycle, is a menstrual period. The first period, called the menarche, is the most obvious sign of approaching fertility, although in fact for about two years afterward we are probably not fertile. And along with all these physiological changes come strong sexual feelings—it is as if our bodies are begin to urge us on to what we are now ready for: sexual maturity.

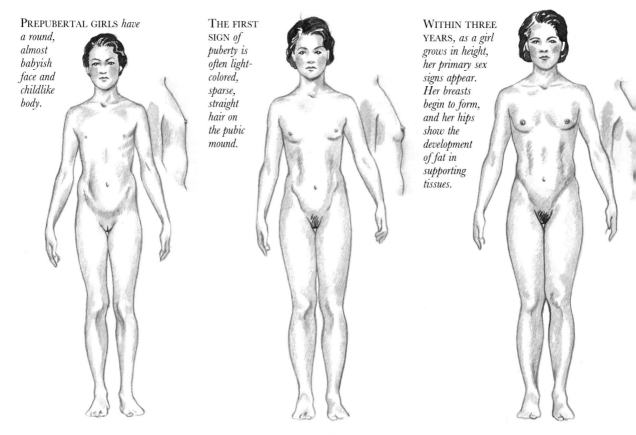

PREPUBERTAL GIRLS *have a round, almost babyish face and childlike body.*

THE FIRST SIGN *of puberty is often light-colored, sparse, straight hair on the pubic mound.*

WITHIN THREE YEARS, *as a girl grows in height, her primary sex signs appear. Her breasts begin to form, and her hips show the development of fat in supporting tissues.*

YOU WILL HAVE *up to 400 menstrual periods, during each of which you will lose 2–2.5 fl ounces (60–75 ml) of blood over 3 to 7 days. The interval between each period varies from 21 to 32 days and is influenced by your health and fitness, weight, use of contraception, and stress levels.*

Falling estrogen levels at the end of menstruation cause your brain to secrete gonadotropin releasing hormone (GnRH), which triggers the pituitary gland to release follicle stimulating hormone (FSH). FSH stimulates your ovaries to ripen eggs in their follicles; as they do, they produce estrogen which causes the womb lining or endometrium to thicken.

When an egg is big enough, and the estrogen level sufficiently high, luteinizing hormone (LH) is released. LH stimulates ovulation: the biggest follicle releases its egg, which enters the Fallopian tube, where it waits to be fertilized. The follicle that released the egg or corpus luteum produces estrogen and progesterone, to prepare your womb for possible pregnancy.

If the egg is not fertilized, high progesterone levels trigger a drop in LH and the corpus luteum decomposes. Levels of estrogen and progesterone fall, triggering the disintegration of the womb lining, which is shed in your menstrual period.

The cycle then begins again.

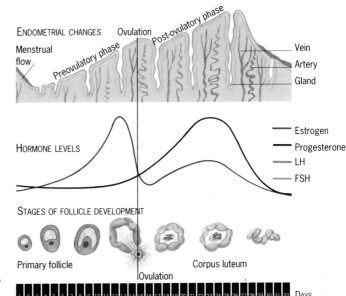

ENDOMETRIAL CHANGES — Preovulatory phase — Ovulation — Post-ovulatory phase

Menstrual flow

Vein
Artery
Gland

HORMONE LEVELS

— Estrogen
— Progesterone
— LH
— FSH

STAGES OF FOLLICLE DEVELOPMENT

Primary follicle

Corpus luteum

Ovulation

| 1 | 2 | 3 | 4 | 5 | 6 | 7 | 8 | 9 | 10 | 11 | 12 | 13 | 14 | 15 | 16 | 17 | 18 | 19 | 20 | 21 | 22 | 23 | 24 | 25 | 26 | 27 | 28 | 29 | 30 | 31 | 32 | DAYS |

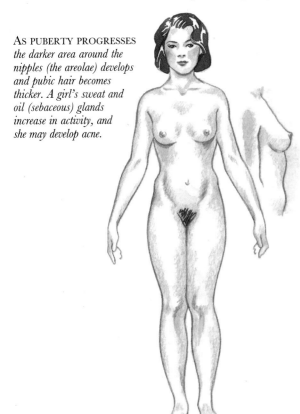

AS PUBERTY PROGRESSES *the darker area around the nipples (the areolae) develops and pubic hair becomes thicker. A girl's sweat and oil (sebaceous) glands increase in activity, and she may develop acne.*

AFTER PUBERTY, *a female's body has full breasts, a distinct waistline, wide pelvis, and rounded hips. Her face is finer, and its bone structure shows through. Her breasts have obvious areolae and the pubic hair is full and thick, forming a triangular shape. The sweat glands are now fully active, giving off a strong female odor, and her vagina is producing a slight, natural discharge.*

FIRST BLOOD

THE PHYSICAL AND EMOTIONAL EFFECTS OF YOUR FIRST PERIOD

The first menstrual period can be an unforgettable occasion. At its best, first menstruation can be a happy rite of passage. We may have celebrated our first period and welcomed its arrival, particularly if our culture sees it as a positive thing to become a fertile woman, and if women close to us have been through this crucial transition in a positive way.

At worst, we may have needed to cope alone with the blood flow, uncomfortable symptoms before the event, and cramps during it. Unaware of what was happening to us, we may have panicked—first periods have convinced many a girl that she is dying of some terrible, embarrassing disease. Even once we knew what it was, we may have worried how others would react if they found out we were menstruating.

Whatever our experience of the menarche, it will have affected our attitudes as adults. If it was laden with fear or guilt, the trauma may have left us ill at ease with our body, resentful of the monthly flow, even, some research suggests, more liable to feel discomfort and pain. But if parents, friends, or teachers gave us the hard facts and the emotional insights into what would happen, what to expect, and how normal it is, then we probably took things in stride. Such a foundation allows us to move into adult life feeling at ease with our monthly cycle and in control of the biological event that is a regular part of life.

Case history

"I thought I was prepared for my periods. We'd learned about them at school, and my mother had shown me where the sanitary napkins were and how to use them. But I wasn't prepared for the pain. Doubled up and sobbing, I hugged a hot pad to my stomach while my mother gave me warm drinks and assured me it would be better next time. But it was worse. The third month she took me to the doctor—an elderly man who, to my mother's outrage, refused to prescribe painkillers to help me cope with this 'natural' event. Next time I had my period, my mother took the law into her own hands and fed me warm gin drop by drop."

NINA

SANITARY NAPKINS *are useful if your vagina is not highly lubricated, or has a small opening, while "liners" for between periods prevent staining. Change the pad every 2 to 4 hours to prevent odor. Before self-stick pads were available, belts were used to keep pads in place.*

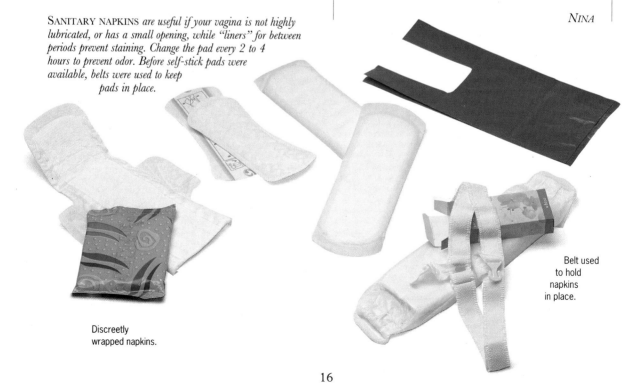

Discreetly wrapped napkins.

Belt used to hold napkins in place.

YOU MAY HAVE BEEN
USING TAMPONS *since an
early age. But if you have
never tried them, you may feel
apprehensive the first time.*

*First wash your hands,
then stand with one foot on the
toilet seat. Hold the tampon
applicator with your thumb
and middle finger where the
tube has ridges, and make sure
that the tampon cord is
hanging out of the bottom of
the tube.*

*Hold your inner labia slightly
apart and put the tip of the
applicator at your vaginal
opening.*

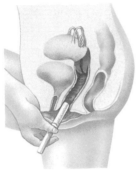

*Then push the applicator into
your vagina until your thumb
and middle finger are touching
your body. Relax, then with
your index finger push the
small tube completely up
inside the big tube.*

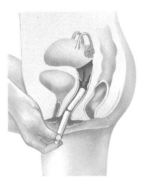

*When the tampon is in the
right place you should be
unable to feel it. Remove the
two tubes and throw or flush
them away.*

*To remove a tampon, pull
gently on the cord. Wrap the
tampon in toilet paper before
throwing in the wastepaper
basket, or flush it away.*

COPING WITH DISCOMFORT

*During menstruation, you may overproduce
prostaglandin, a hormone which helps the uterus to
contract during labor, but which also causes painful
cramps during your period.*

*Don't suffer unnecessarily. Take painkillers; do
relaxation exercises to loosen tension in your pelvis; try
using a hot pad or take a hot bath; massage your back
and stomach; ask your gynecologist for help; or get
herbal or homeopathic remedies from a pharmacy.
Professional acupuncture may also help.*

Non-applicator
tampons of
varying
absorbency

TAMPONS ARE CONVENIENT *if you
want to swim or wear light-colored or
tight-fitting clothes. They are inserted
into the vagina through an
opening in the hymen, so you can
use tampons even if you are a
virgin. Tampons are available
with applicators or without.
Over-absorbent tampons can lead to
infection, so choose one that is only as
absorbent as you need. Only use a
tampon during your period and change it
every 4 to 6 hours. Use a pad overnight.*

More absorbent
applicator
tampons for
heavier flow

Regular
applicator
tampon for
average
flow

EARLY PLEASURE

SEXUAL FEELINGS IN CHILDHOOD AND ADOLESCENCE

Perhaps as many as three-quarters of all girls masturbate before the age of 16. We build on the foundation of sensuality that has been there from birth and move instinctively to self-pleasuring. It usually begins by accident. We slip a hand down our pajamas; use the soap in the bath; rub against a toy; go horse riding; wriggle when sitting on the arm of a chair or sofa. If we are taught by a girlfriend in early adolescence, we may sit alongside or opposite her, building the pleasure together, but we are quite happy alone. If we have not done so by mid- or late-adolescence, a boyfriend may masturbate us himself and then encourage us to try alone.

However it happens, it is always remarkably effective. We touch our clitoris and rub it from side to side, or back to front. We press our legs together rhythmically. We push into a mattress or a pillow. We probably do not think of penetration since it is not relevant to what we feel: the clitoris provides all the pleasure we want. In particular, as puberty approaches, that pleasure soon turns to orgasm. And, if none of the messages we have heard or absorbed up to now has presumed to tell us the "right way" to reach a climax, we are free to discover this for ourselves and probably do so quite easily.

The sensations may be fairly mild at first but with time, as both hormones and increased sexual experience kick in, our orgasms grow stronger, deeper, and more prolonged. But left to ourselves, our natural instincts for self-pleasuring are spontaneous and effective—and regularly and reliably lead us all the way to climax.

Case history

"I remember that when I was in my crib, very young, I used to lie on my stomach with my legs apart and my feet together, and rub up and down against the mattress. It gave me such delicious feelings between my legs. My parents called it my 'frog position' and laughed. I don't think they knew what I was doing.

"Later, I'd realized that I got further if I used my hand as well, pushed down inside my panties while I bounced on my front. One day my mother caught me doing it, and this time she came to the right conclusion. Hands were slapped, voices were raised. From then on, I played at being a frog in private.

"One day when I was about nine and a half, much to my surprise, the sensations grew and grew to an overwhelming feeling. I had no idea what had happened. What I did know was that my parents would absolutely disapprove and that I had to keep my wonderful secret to myself."

JILL

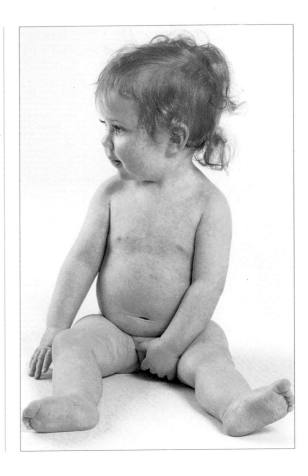

As you grew up, *you were more likely to be relaxed about self-pleasuring if your parents were, too. You were also able to touch and be touched quite happily. At the same time, you were more likely to know when you didn't want someone to touch you, because you were not confusing present uncomfortable feelings with discomfort associated with past messages of parental disapproval. Positive messages in your early years from those around you not only make you more able to say yes freely later on, they also enable you to say no with confidence.*

Negative messages

Problems can arise if we are not left to explore these feelings in our own way. However much we feel as children that masturbation is natural and wonderful, if people around us react differently, that is not the message we will get. If a parent interrupts our pleasure, then shouts or even smacks, we may get the message not only that our pleasure is wrong, but also that we are wrong to enjoy it. We then forget this message until later—probably several years later—when we begin to experience sex as an adult. And then, for some mysterious reason, we feel bad. We may be unable to touch ourselves without guilt; we might be unable to let a partner touch us without tension. And the ease with which we climax when alone disappears when we are with a partner.

BABIES *like touching their genitals from a very young age and may do so knowingly from as early as two years old, although self-pleasuring becomes more purposeful and "sexual" from about seven. At that age, in societies in which masturbation is encouraged, children do so regularly and without prompting.*

MAKING CONTACT
GETTING TO KNOW POTENTIAL PARTNERS

It is almost as if puberty compels us to make contact. Hormones drive us to look and smile at and to touch potential partners; and emotions make the thought of sex (in theory, if not in practice) wonderfully romantic. Some of us started by having experiences with other girls. We looked, cuddled, then moved on to kissing lips and touching breasts. With such behavior we wanted to experiment, to explore a mirror image of ourselves in a more extensive way than playing "you show me yours." Some of us used the opportunity to experiment all the way to orgasm; a few of us decided to stick to girls, instead of turning to boys.

When we turned to boys, what followed was often confusing. First, we may not have known what to do with a boy. Our experiences gave us no idea how to hold his penis when he asked us to, or how to react if he climaxed. (It is commonly fear of failure, rather than unwillingness, that makes women seem inhibited.)

Second, sexual contact was probably different from what we imagined or had done to ourselves. Boys wanted urgent, thrusting, "damp" activities, while we prefered the cuddles, sensual touching—even just the attention. And last, all too often everything seemed out of control. From being able to set our own sensual limits, however low or high, we were now suddenly under pressure. Everyone in the media was doing "it" all the time. Our friends claimed to have gone "all the way," even if some of them admitted later that they hadn't. A partner may have pressurized us into going farther than we wanted, as the price for his staying. If we agreed, we may have

SETTING THE SEXUAL PACE

When you are with a new partner, particularly if you are unsure of what is expected:

● Test for yourself what feels good and what doesn't, and do only what feels comfortable to you.

● If a partner asks for something new or different, suggest he (or she) tells or shows you what to do until you feel confident and skilled.

● State a clear "no" to any request that makes you feel at all uneasy, whether it is the wildest sexual variation or the safest kiss.

● Stand up to, or leave, a partner who threatens or cajoles. Be wary of tired appeals or criticisms such as "If you loved me …everyone else does it …are you frigid?"

● Remember that work with women who have sexual difficulties shows that anything that leaves you feeling uncertain or out of control (as opposed to pleasurably abandoned) is a bad idea, in both the short and long term.

FOR TEENAGERS, *bridging the gap between touching and not touching the opposite sex can be difficult. Most girls play physical games (above left); tease boys so that they are chased (and caught); mock-wrestle over some imagined insult—and emerge panting, laughing, and aroused.*

ADOLESCENT COUPLES *create their own world, oblivious of others—and of convention (above). They enfold each other, cuddle, talk in whispers. It is almost a presexual world, more like a mother and child relationship than two adults making love.*

ended up doing things to satisfy others and gain status with our peers, rather than for our pleasure.

If this "traditional" pattern sounds familiar to you, it may be interesting to note that it is changing as young women become more sexually confident. Increasingly women are negotiating a sexual pace that suits us. In particular, a late 1980s study highlighted what might be called technical virginity, holding back from intercourse with a partner and offering instead what were once seen as advanced techniques such as mutual masturbation and oral sex. This strategy not only maintains control of the situation, but it also develops sexual skill and technique, provides reliable orgasms by focusing on the clitoris, and trains a partner in sensuous pleasure. It also saves the "final act" for when we are sure that it is what we want.

THE FIRST TIME
THE LOSS OF VIRGINITY

Having sex for the first time is still a key step for most women. Sexual freedom has meant it is no longer linked with marriage and childbearing, and most of us have lost our virginity before we find our life partner (the most recent reports of Western brides estimate that only five percent are virgins). But first-time sex is still important. Many of us—particularly if we had an earlier-than-average puberty—do it because hormones drive us on. Most of us, however, do it because of its emotional significance.

First-time sex is usually seen as a sign of maturity, a step from girl to woman, a rite of passage. It marks status among peers—initial intercourse is often something done within a short time of friends' doing it. It can even be a form of revenge against parents, or a reward for a boyfriend who has stayed faithful. And still, we consider losing our virginity as a way to seal a bond with a partner. It is still a sign of love.

Case history

"I'd been out with a few boys, but he was the one every girl wanted. We'd been meeting for a while, and I'd let him touch my breasts. One night, he asked if we could do it, so we went into the woods. I lifted my skirt and pulled my panties to one side. He nuzzled my neck, went inside me, moved around, then collapsed. I didn't even know that was it. I didn't see him much after that."

DEBBIE

MANY WOMEN *say that they were emotionally disappointed at the loss of their virginity. Sex was more urgent than loving; they didn't feel more of an adult woman; they felt* guilty; *and afterward he left. But most women go on to have happy sexual relationships— the key to sexual fulfillment is knowledge, built up with a partner you trust.*

COPING PRACTICALLY

● Make sure your partner knows you're a virgin; if possible, talk through your concerns with him beforehand.

● Give yourself the right setting, with privacy and lots of time.

● Use contraception: it's a myth that you won't get pregnant the first time.

● If you've never used tampons, you are likely to have a tight vagina. Stretch your vaginal opening beforehand by inserting first one finger, then two, then three, and pressing down.

● Choose a position that lets him enter you easily. Spread your thighs wide, maybe with a pillow under your hips.

● Use saliva or KY jelly on his penis to make entry easier.

● Hold his penis and position it to go inside you; this will help you feel in charge and let you take things at your own pace.

● As he enters you, push down slightly so that you don't tighten your vaginal muscles.

● Don't expect to climax the first time—it takes practice.

Case history

"We'd been going out for about seven months, and we'd done a lot, orgasmed lots of times. One night my parents were out, and it seemed right. I lay on the rug, and he came into me gently, and then we just stayed still and looked at each other. I didn't come, but I knew I probably wouldn't the first time. I was so happy the next day that I couldn't stop smiling."

LARA

THE HYMEN

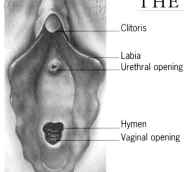

Clitoris

Labia
Urethral opening

Hymen
Vaginal opening

The hymen is a fold of skin across the entrance to the vagina. Found only in humans and horses, it seems to have no real biological purpose. A woman born with a closed, or "imperforate," hymen (left) may need to have it broken when her periods start to allow the blood through.

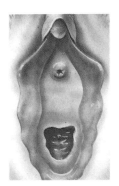

A woman who has not had intercourse may or may not have an intact hymen. You can be born with a partial hymen, or stretch it through exercise (left). If it has not broken before, it will break—and bleed— when you first have sex. Don't let anyone accuse you of not being a virgin if you do not bleed the first time you have sex. Virginity means not yet having had penetrative sex, not having an unbroken hymen.

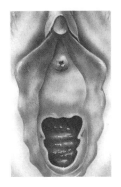

Childbirth stretches the vaginal entrance and the muscles of the vagina, although exercising after childbirth tightens the muscles again. The vaginal entrance of a woman who has given birth (left) is larger than that of one who has not.

2 THE SEXUAL WOMAN

REALIZING OUR SEXUAL POTENTIAL involves awareness of body and mind. Elegantly designed both to make love and to make babies, our bodies also have in-built vulnerabilities. They suffer the stresses and strains of the monthly cycle of preparation for pregnancy. And they are prey to all kinds of illnesses of the sexual and gynecological organs. But, as important, our bodies are also vulnerable sexually because they may simply refuse to operate, or cooperate, if we (or a partner) have no idea "which bit is which," or are not in touch with their real needs.

The mind affects sexuality by linking it to our feelings about ourselves, our relationships, and even the society in which we live. Our minds need as much care and attention as our bodies, to create healthy beliefs about sex, develop self-knowledge, create good decision-making strategies, and cope effectively with sexual difficulties.

It is a challenge, as an individual woman in today's world, to integrate both sexual body and sexual mind, so that they work together, successfully, confidently, and pleasurably.

A WOMAN CAN be sexual alone. You experience sexual feelings spontaneously as your body responds to arousing sights and as your hormones change during your monthly cycle. And you can create sexuality by choosing to arouse yourself mentally or emotionally, or by touching yourself and masturbating. This knowledge that you do not have to be dependent on someone else for sexual fulfillment frees you to choose when and how to express your sexuality.

KNOWING YOURSELF
YOUR SEXUAL AND REPRODUCTIVE ORGANS

From the web of pelvic nerve endings that make orgasm possible to the ingenious structure of internal organs that enable fertilization and pregnancy, a woman's body is a complex, incredibly intricate, and finely balanced system. As with so many such systems, the more we know about it— what each part is, what it does, how it works—the more pleasure and fulfillment we will get from it.

External genitals

The mons veneris (literally, Venus's mound) is fatty tissue covering the pubic bone; this cushions your genitals during intercourse—and can be a source of great pleasure because of its numerous nerve endings.

The labia majora, or outer lips, are large, dark folds of skin that start at the mons and continue down the side of the external genitals. The labia minora, or inner lips, are paler, hairless membranes surrounding the openings to the vagina and the urethra, through which urine passes.

The clitoris is the female sexual organ most sensitive to sensation and the only human organ designed purely for pleasure. It has the same basic blueprint as a penis, which develops from it in the womb; like the penis, the clitoris has a root within the pelvis and a glans hidden by a thick "hood" of skin.

The vaginal opening may be partly closed by the hymen. Within the opening, toward the pelvis, lies the urethral sponge; down toward the anus lies the perineal sponge. Both areas are sensitive and stimulation there may give you pleasure, although beyond the first few centimeters the vagina itself is not highly sensitive.

The reproductive organs

On either side of the womb (uterus) are the ovaries which produce eggs (ova) each month. Connecting the ovaries and the womb are the Fallopian tubes, through which eggs pass on their way to the womb and within which they are normally fertilized.

The womb receives the fertilized ovum and contains it until you give birth. The cervix, the lower end of, and entrance to, the womb, is the exit through which a baby passes during birth. Pressure on it can also turn you on.

A BREAST THROUGH LIFE

The breasts contain milk-producing glands separated by fatty tissue. If you breast-feed, milk passes through a duct and out through your nipple, which is surrounded by the darker areola.

Your breasts are unique: adult breasts vary in size and shape from woman to woman more than any other part of the body. Most women's breasts differ slightly: your left breast, for example, may be smaller than your right.

When you are pregnant, under the influence of estrogen and progesterone, milk reservoirs develop behind the nipple. As a result, the areola darkens in color. Your breasts may also become lumpy, show enlarged veins, and be sensitive to touch.

When you are breast-feeding, your breasts are full and heavy, as milk is produced in response to your baby's sucking and carried along ducts to your nipples. Secretions from the areola help to protect the breast from soreness and dryness.

The milk-producing glands remain throughout your fertile years, but the hormonal changes of the menopause cause them to shrink and the fat cells to increase. This may have the effect of making your breasts smaller.

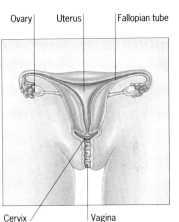

Ovary   Uterus   Fallopian tube

Cervix   Vagina

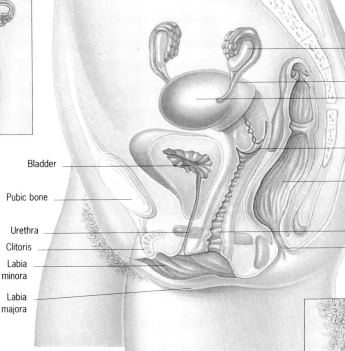

Ovary

Fallopian tube

Uterus

Cervix

Rectum

Bladder

Pubic bone

Vagina

Urethra

Anus

Clitoris

Labia minora

Labia majora

YOUR INTERNAL REPRODUCTIVE ORGANS *change with sexual feelings, your monthly cycle, and key life events, such as illness and pregnancy. The illustration above shows how the ovaries, Fallopian tubes, uterus, vagina, and cervix "fit" together. The illustration right locates the reproductive organs in relation to the other major internal organs in the lower torso.*

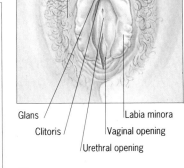

Labia majora   Mons veneris

Glans   Labia minora

Clitoris   Vaginal opening

Urethral opening

THE EXTERNAL GENITALS, *or vulva, alter constantly in ways no other body parts do. The labia open and close and the clitoris hardens as they fill with blood during arousal, and change in color under hormonal influence, such as during pregnancy and the menopause.*

SELF-EXAMINATION

Having a close look at your genitals may help you to feel more at ease with them. For an external examination you need a long-handled mirror. Your initial reaction may be that your genitals are untidy, rough, or an odd color, but be reassured— every woman's genitals look erotically "primitive."

    To examine your internal genitals you will also need a speculum (available from a well-woman clinic), lubricant, and a small torch. Lubricate the speculum, relax, and place it in your vagina in the closed position, then open it and click it until it locks. Focus the light and adjust it and the mirror until you can see inside yourself. You will see the walls of your vagina and your cervix and may also notice natural mucus or secretions.

KNEEL *with your knees wide apart, or lie down with your legs spread, knees bent, and feet wide apart.*

YOUR MONTHLY PERIOD
COPING WITH MENSTRUAL PROBLEMS

Only 100 years ago, women had about 40 menstrual periods in their lifetime. Today, in the Western world, we can expect to have 10 times that number. Healthier lifestyles bring on menarche up to eight years earlier and scientific advances mean fewer pregnancies and spells of breastfeeding. Because of this, we may struggle with menstruation in a way our great-grandmothers did not have to.

If we do find it difficult, our negative feelings are likely to be about the practicalities: the inconvenience, the mess, the limitations on wearing certain clothes, and the premenstrual symptoms such as depression and weight gain. But periods need not be hard to cope with, regarded as "days out" from normal life. The development of hormone treatments has meant that period problems can often be alleviated, while the ubiquity of tampons gives us greater freedom to wear and do what we like while bleeding.

Cultural norms, too, are more relaxed. Menstruating women used to be discouraged from even washing their hair, let alone exercising or making love. Now we can do as we please—doctors even suggest that having an orgasm during menstruation may help to reduce or relieve cramps.

And we are starting to talk openly about the positive aspects of menstruation. Having a period is proof of both overall and gynecological health. It is proof of not being pregnant—if we don't want to be. And, perhaps most importantly, it's a reminder of womanhood, and so a way of keeping in touch, on a monthly basis, with our sexuality.

Period problems

Usually linked with fluctuations in the hormones that trigger monthly cycles, problems concerning periods include: the absence of periods, amenorrhea; pain during periods, dysmenorrhea; heavy periods, menorrhagia; infrequent periods, oligomenorrhea; and over-frequent periods, polymenorrhea. Hormonal imbalance might be caused by over- or under-production of a particular hormone; by taking the contraceptive pill which alters hormone levels; and, in older women, by the menopause, when hormone levels drop sharply.

Treatment for hormone imbalance usually involves taking supplements, although the intra-uterine system (IUS), which slowly introduces progestogen into the bloodstream, may help to alleviate problems *(see pp. 110–11)*. In the case of heavy periods, doctors traditionally offer surgical treatment—removing the lining of the womb or the womb itself. Be wary, however: such treatments can have uncomfortable side effects.

Menstrual difficulties can also be caused by disease or illness. Amenorrhea can be the result of certain medication, depression, or ovarian conditions *(see pp. 36–37)*, and is also linked to eating disorders. Heavy bleeding and pain can signal endometriosis, fibroids, pelvic inflammatory disease, endometrial cancer, or thyroid conditions. Go for a checkup immediately if you start suffering from any of these symptoms.

IT IS SIGNIFICANT *that almost every culture has a negative term for menstruation like "the curse." Despite 20th-century thinking that denouncing menstruation makes women feel inferior and guilty, cultural and religious taboos still surround it. Orthodox Jewish women, for example, are forbidden to have intercourse; Egyptian women do not visit friends; Korean women do not bathe; and Indian Hindu high-caste women avoid cooking.*

PREMENSTRUAL SYNDROME

If you suffer from PMS, you will identify with the research that claims that more than 150 symptoms can be attributed to it. Yet, so far, no one has tracked down a definite cause, although it is believed to be linked to hormone imbalance.

Doctors usually prescribe hormone supplements, but these do not always help; for some women, the contraceptive pill helps. You may find it better to take charge yourself and experiment with these remedies, which many women have found to work:
- Cut down on alcohol and caffeine
- Eat small, frequent, starchy meals to prevent falling blood sugar
- Take regular exercise to produce endorphins, sometimes referred to as the "feel good" hormones

- Take vitamin and mineral supplements—B_6 (no more than 100 mg a day), C, magnesium, niacin, and zinc along with evening primrose oil; you will need to stay on these for at least three months to find out whether they help
- Yoga, acupuncture, homeopathy, and hypnosis have all been reported as reducing symptoms.

ADVERSE REACTIONS

Using a vaginal tampon can sometimes trigger certain bacteria that occur naturally in the body into causing a toxic reaction. The first signs are vomiting, diarrhea, aches, dizziness, and a rash on your trunk and neck; if you get any of these, remove the tampon immediately and see a doctor straightaway. Treatment with antibiotics is simple and effective, but if left untreated toxic shock syndrome can kill.

Tampon absorbency seems to be a factor in triggering the syndrome, so choose the tampon with the lowest absorbency practical, change it every four to six hours, and wear a sanitary napkin rather than a tampon overnight.

KEEPING A MENSTRUAL DIARY *helps you be aware of your body and enables you to relieve symptoms by predicting them and taking early action. Symptoms usually start shortly after ovulation, so record:*
- *When you ovulate, if you know*
- *Physical symptoms such as fluid retention or vaginal discharge*
- *Emotional symptoms such as tearfulness or irritability*
- *When your period starts. Note the pattern of symptoms before menstruation for three months, then try—one by one— the remedies outlined above.*

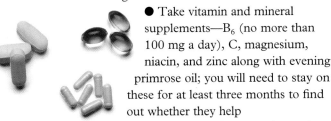

AUGUST Felt nauseous
JULY Ate chocolate
JUNE
1 Hair a mess Period started
2 Had an argument with C Cried
3 Period started
4
5
6 Period started; bad cramps
7

BODY CARE

THE IMPORTANCE OF LOOKING AFTER YOURSELF

Taking care of your body is almost second nature, and many of the things we do routinely contribute to the health of our sexual and reproductive organs.

Diet

Eating a balanced diet of a little protein, a small amount of fat, plenty of carbohydrates, and at least five helpings of fruit and vegetables a day helps create the sort of health that promotes sexual energy. But we should not assume that being healthy means cutting back on food—a body weight that falls too low can result in altered hormone levels, reduced sexual desire, and even infertility.

Certain vitamins and minerals, as well as some fatty acids, have been identified as necessary for sexual functioning. They include vitamin C, found in fresh fruit, green vegetables, and potatoes; vitamin E, found in sunflower seeds, nuts, and avocados; zinc, found in oysters, whole grains, peas, and milk; iron, found in red meat, leafy green vegetables, and pure fruit juices; and fatty acids, such as those found in oily fish and seeds. It is best to get all these substances direct from food, and eating a balanced diet makes a deficiency in any one of them less likely. Over-the-counter supplements may have a place, but it is important to follow the package advice on dosage—overdoses can cause problems.

Sleep and relaxation

Recent studies have found that women today are suffering from a marked loss of desire due to exhaustion and stress—that is, not enough sleep or relaxation. Sleep is a chance for brain and body to shut down their conscious processes and rest, while relaxation gives an instant opportunity to recover from immediate stresses. It may not be necessary to have a lot of sleep each night—estimates suggest that six hours may be enough—as long as we regularly de-stress during the day, through "cat naps," yoga, massage, meditation, deep breathing, and relaxation exercises.

A BALANCED DIET *helps maintain health and generate sexual energy.*

A diet high in antioxidants has been proven to reduce the incidence of all cancers, including cervical, breast, and other cancers of the sexual organs.

EXERCISE *for suppleness makes you lithe in bed, able to move easily and flexibly; exercise for stamina trains your body to breathe more easily, use oxygen efficiently, and keep going for longer.*

Alcohol

A small amount of alcohol may help create sensuous feelings. More than this, however, may make unwise sexual decisions more likely, as well as reducing stamina for extended passion. Long-term heavy drinking may increase arousal problems and depress both fertility and the capacity to orgasm; drinking immediately prior to ovulation and menstruation increases vulnerability to these side-effects, as does being on the contraceptive pill. Sensible guidelines are to keep intake moderate, dilute liquor with mixers, never drink on an empty stomach, and avoid binges.

Smoking

Women who smoke die sooner, on average, than those who don't. They may also be more prone to breast abscesses; reduced fertility; problems in pregnancy, often resulting in babies of lower than average birth weight; and early onset of the menopause. In addition, carcinogens from cigarette smoke can filter down into the cervix, making vaginal secretions smell unappealing and, at worst, increasing vulnerability to cervical cancer.

Exercise

A fit body raises our chances of living longer and gives us the energy for extended sex sessions. But perhaps more importantly, any exercise that encourages body awareness and pride makes us more confident sexually and better able to enjoy our own physical pleasure.

TAKING CARE OF YOUR SEXUAL ORGANS

Looking after your genitals is vital not simply to avoid infections: healthy genitals give off a natural odor specifically designed to arouse a partner, while unhealthy ones do the opposite.

● Wash your outer genitals daily with warm water and a gentle soap or cleanser that will not cause irritation or an allergic reaction.

● Wipe front to back after going to the bathroom, to avoid spreading bacteria from your anus into your vagina.

● Inner genitals clean themselves daily by their secretions, so avoid douches or sprays that can undermine this process.

● Do not put anything near your genitals— whether sex toy or your lover's body parts— that is not clean and hygienic.

● Avoid tight nylon underwear that creates moist warmth, the condition in which bacteria grows fastest, around the genitals.

● Avoid a high-sugar diet, which can affect the natural chemical balance of the vagina and make it more vulnerable to infection.

BODY IMAGE

HOW DO YOU FEEL ABOUT YOUR BODY?

Female sexuality today is inextricably linked with body image. Films and advertisements constantly present images of attractive models; and many parts of the media reinforce the belief that youth and beauty are far more valuable than experience. The message seems to be that if we don't look good, we can't expect to have a sex life.

As little girls we are at ease with our bodies. But as we grow into women, life's lesson seems to be that our worth depends on our looks. So we try to correct our imperfections. We diet, exercise, perm our hair, get our teeth capped, have plastic surgery, spend a fortune on cosmetics and a huge amount on clothes. There is nothing wrong with this if we enjoy it and it makes us feel good. But the problem is that, despite our best efforts, the vast majority of us feel that we are not good enough; we believe that the ability to be sexual and sexually attractive does depend, at least to some extent, on youth and beauty.

SEX AND STARVATION

Weight is the main body-image issue for Western women. Slimness equals sexuality. The result is that up to 90 percent of women have been on a diet at some time, and many are on a permanent diet in an effort to control their weight. The figures for anorexia (cutting food intake to starvation level) and bulimia (bingeing, then vomiting) rise every year.

The problem is that while the media may dictate that a slim image equals a sexual image, too slim a body—or slimness that is gained by controlling diet with starvation, pills, laxatives, or vomiting—makes sexuality plummet. You not only lose your sexual desire—and the energy that makes for enthusiastic lovemaking—but you may also become infertile, have pregnancy complications, or give birth to babies with physical abnormalities.

If you suspect that the wish to be thin has become more important for you than the wish to be healthy, take action. Eating disorders thrive on secrecy, so start confiding in other people and enlisting their support. Talk to your partner, your family, friends—and professional counselors. Get them to help you strike a balance between a healthy diet and feeling in control of what you are eating. Get them to help you sort out other stresses in your life which may be triggering your need to binge or starve. Above all, get them to help you realize your own powerful sexuality, whatever your shape and size.

THE EASE *you had with your body as a child can be difficult to keep: many women have frequent negative feelings about how they look. But accepting that your body is unique* (below)*, and that in any case youth and beauty are not essential to a happy and fulfilling sex life is vital in becoming and remaining a sexual woman.*

HAIR *is a secondary female sexual characteristic. Changes in color, length, and form (by curling or straightening) are all claimed to make women more sexually attractive.*

Since perfection is impossible, and aging inevitable, we seem locked in a battle that cannot be won. It may be, however, that a backlash is gathering momentum. Increasing numbers of us are starting to aim for fitness rather than thinness, to view claims by cosmetics manufacturers with scepticism, to regard older women as role models. Perhaps we are moving toward a time when sexual success will be defined by sensuality, self-assurance, and a love of passion—elements that all women can achieve throughout their lives.

CHANGING YOUR IMAGE: BREASTS

The body part with which most of us are least happy is our breasts. Breasts are an obvious signal of sexuality, so if you have large breasts you may attract unwelcome attention, and if you have small breasts or have lost breast tissue, you may imagine that you are unattractive or unsexual. Surgery can be an answer.

In breast reduction, excess breast tissue is removed and the nipple repositioned. In breast lift, stretched tissue is removed without affecting breast size. In enlargement, a pocket is formed within the breast (if you have lost breast tissue through surgery, skin and muscle are folded to create the same effect), then an implant is inserted.

These operations are not without drawbacks. All carry the risk of infection, thrombosis, or the failure of the entire procedure. Nipple repositioning in breast reduction usually makes breastfeeding impossible, and questions are being raised about the side effects of some materials used in breast enlargement.

If you are unhappy with your breasts, changing how you feel, perhaps through counseling, may be more appealing than an operation. But many women who have breast surgery find that it boosts their sexual confidence.

THE "DIET" INDUSTRY is vast (top), *with meals, drinks, pills, and creams all offering slenderness without hunger, sometimes while you sleep. Other ways of altering your basic body shape range from something as simple as wearing a different type of bra to a drastic measure such as undergoing surgery.*

FASHION dictates that there are certain areas of the female body where hair is not acceptable and must be removed (above). *Makeup alters the face slightly, masks "imperfections," and highlights "good" points.*

BREAST DISORDERS

SPOTTING BREAST CONDITIONS EARLY AND GETTING HELP

Natural symbols of fertility, breasts in Western society are also a strong and potent symbol of sexuality. And that makes it even more traumatic for us when we are affected by breast illness.

Breast cancer is the major cause of death for Western women between the ages of 35 and 55. The underlying reasons why women develop this cancer are unclear, but one likely link is exposure to high levels of estrogen. So the women at greatest risk are those who started their menstrual periods early; had the menopause late; had no children; had children late. Risk also seems to rise with age, weight, a high-fat diet, and a history of breast cancer among close family members.

The best ways to protect breasts are to eat a low-fat, high-fiber diet and avoid being overweight. Hormone supplements to keep estrogen levels low may also offer some protection for high-risk women. Finally, an appealing if unproven study from the University of Adelaide, Australia, suggests that, to increase production of oxytocin—a hormone which it is believed may protect against breast cancer—a woman should stimulate her nipples for two or three minutes twice a week.

SELF-EXAMINATION

The earlier breast problems are spotted and treated, the less likely they are to become serious. So protect yourself by regular self-examination, preferably just after your period when your breasts are naturally least lumpy.

First, standing in front of a mirror, quickly check the appearance of your breasts. Start with your arms at your sides, stretch them above your head, then place them on your hips.

Second, when soaping yourself in the shower, or lying in bed at night, put one arm above your head and check your breast with your other hand. Use a pattern of concentric circles from the armpit through the outer diameter of the breast inward. Finally squeeze your nipple.

What you are looking for in both checks are alterations in shape or feel: swellings, lumps, orange-peel skin, changes in the areola, bleeding, or other discharge from the nipple. If you notice any of these things, arrange to see a doctor as soon as possible.

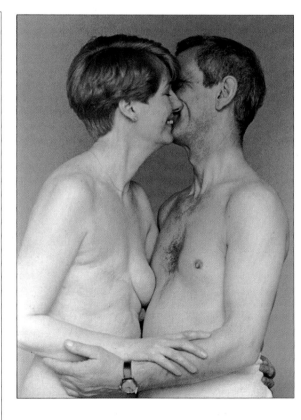

LOSING A BREAST *need not undermine your sexuality. You may feel that all pleasure is gone, but other erogenous zones will become more important and your partner should be able* *to take pleasure in the sheer fact that you are alive. Accept his reassurance; if you prefer hide in silky underwear, and lie on the side of the bed that presents your healthy breast uppermost.*

KNOWING YOURSELF — 26–27
PLANNING YOUR FAMILY — 110–11

TREATING BREAST CANCER

If you have breast cancer, a combination of drugs, surgery, and radiation may be offered.
* *Tamoxifen is a hormone drug that stops the breast producing the estrogen that may be triggering the cancer.*
* *Chemotherapy—treatment with drugs—can be used to shrink the cancer before you have surgery to remove it.*
* *Radiotherapy—treatment with high-energy rays—can be used to kill remaining malignant cells after surgery.*

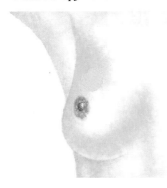

LUMPECTOMY
Depending on how big the lump is, surgery may involve removal of the lymph glands as well as the lump.

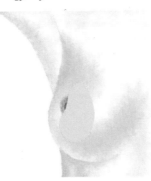

PARTIAL MASTECTOMY
This treatment involves the removal of a substantial area of breast tissue, usually including the nipple.

COMPLETE MASTECTOMY
This involves the removal of the whole breast; in an extended mastectomy the adjacent muscles are also removed.

BENIGN CONDITIONS

Most breast conditions are not fatal. Lumps may be frightening, but are often due to natural changes in the breast. Soreness may be caused by hormone imbalance, particularly before a menstrual period. Nipple discharge is often caused by inflammation of the milk ducts.

● Have regular checks. If a lump is found, a mammography (X-ray), or a biopsy (removal and testing of a section of tissue), to eliminate the possibility of cancer may be suggested. Hormone treatment is often offered for premenstrual pain and antibiotics for abscesses.

● During treatment, watch your symptoms; if they seem related to your monthly cycle, try the methods outlined on p. 29.

Case history

"We were cuddling in bed one night, and I noticed this tiny lump, just the size of a pea in one breast. I went cold. I spent three days trying to ignore it, and eventually Alan took me, almost forcibly, to the doctor. I remember going back to the specialist for the results, and knowing just by his face that the news was bad. After that some days were good, and on others I was convinced I would die. It's now a year since my mastectomy and the scarring is better than I thought it would be, although it was a long, long time before I wanted to make love. Everyone's very hopeful now."

SUZANNE

GYNECOLOGICAL PROBLEMS
INVESTIGATING ILLNESSES OF THE GYNECOLOGICAL ORGANS

Perhaps because our gynecological systems are so responsive, they are also more prone to illness than other parts of the body. The chart on the right details some of the most common gynecological conditions.

Sexual investigations

As a woman, you will have a number of gynecological examinations during your lifetime. Particularly if you are sexually active, insist on having one and a Pap smear every year, or if there are changes in your normal cycle. You will be asked to lie on a couch, possibly with your legs in stirrups, and the doctor will examine your external genitals for rashes or discharge. She or he will then carry out a bimanual examination, placing two fingers in your vagina and the other hand flat on your stomach (then perhaps one finger in your anus and one in your vagina) to check your internal

gynecological organs for swelling or growths. Finally, she or he will insert a speculum into your vagina to examine your cervix. You may find this last examination a little uncomfortable if you have not had one before *(see p. 27)*; relax as much as possible.

If anything unusual is found, you may also need:
• Pelvic ultrasound, in which a small instrument is passed painlessly over your stomach to produce a picture of your internal organs on a monitor.
• Hysteroscopy, in which a long illuminated tube is passed through your cervix to explore your womb.
• Laparoscopy, in which a long illuminated tube is passed through a tiny cut below your navel to give a view of your internal organs.
• D(ilation) and C(urettage), in which a large, spoon-shaped instrument is passed through your cervix to investigate and clear any problem areas of the womb.

SYMPTOMS OF GYNECOLOGICAL PROBLEMS

FIBROIDS
Painful urination; constipation; painful or heavy periods; abnormal vaginal bleeding; backache; pain during sex; possible infertility.

CYSTITIS AND URINARY TRACT INFECTIONS
Increased urge to urinate; burning pain on urination; pus or blood in urine.

CERVICAL EVERSION
Vaginal discharge; blood in discharge because of friction; abnormal vaginal bleeding.

OVARIAN CYSTS
Pain during sex; pain or discomfort in abdomen, particularly if a cyst has burst; swollen abdomen; disturbed menstrual cycle.

ENDOMETRIOSIS
Painful urination; painful bowel movements; pelvic pain, particularly immediately before menstruation; heavy periods; painful periods; abnormal vaginal bleeding; pain in abdomen, especially around the middle of the menstrual cycle; swollen abdomen; pain during sex; possible infertility.

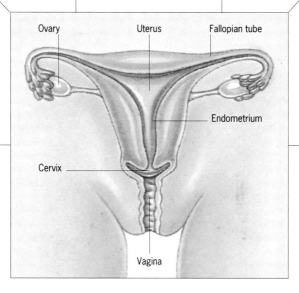

Ovary   Uterus   Fallopian tube

Endometrium

Cervix

Vagina

PELVIC INFLAMMATORY DISEASE (PID)
Need to urinate frequently; burning pain on urination; abnormal vaginal discharge; heavy periods; painful periods; too frequent periods; abnormal vaginal bleeding; swollen abdomen; pain or bleeding during or after sex; fever; nausea; vomiting; aching back and legs; dizziness; depression and fatigue; weight gain or loss; possible infertility.

GYNECOLOGICAL CONDITIONS

Condition	Causes	Treatment and self-help
Cystitis and urinary tract infections	*E. coli* bacteria travel from the lower intestine where they exist harmlessly to cause problems in the urinary tract; allergic reaction; friction and bruising from intercourse.	Treatment: Antibiotics. Self-help: Drink large amounts of water regularly; take painkillers; use hot compresses to soothe. Prevention: If you are susceptible to urinary tract infections avoid irritants such as spicy food; avoid tight underwear and slacks; avoid tampons because inserting anything into the vagina increases the risk of introducing infection; wash and urinate before and after sex; wipe from front to back after using the toilet; drink plenty of water; urinate as soon as the urge occurs to help wash away bacteria.
Cervical eversion	Lining of the cervix swells and turns outward into the vagina; can be inherited, or develop through pregnancy or using the contraceptive pill. (This condition used to be called cervical erosion.)	Treatment: No need for treatment, but have a medical check in case symptoms are due to less benign conditions.
Endometriosis	Fragments of tissue usually lining the womb become attached to the outside of the womb, Fallopian tubes, or ovaries. During menstruation, these tissues bleed and can cause scarring.	Treatment: Hormone supplements to stop menstruation temporarily so patches shrink; laparoscopy to cut away problem tissue; hysterectomy once childbearing is complete; pregnancy occasionally solves the problem.
Fibroids (hard lumps of muscle in the wall of the womb)	Excess of estrogen sometimes caused by using the contraceptive pill or taking hormone replacement therapy (HRT).	Treatment: Surgery; drugs which cause a temporary menopause; progestogen-releasing intrauterine device (IUD).
Ovarian cysts	Egg-containing follicles fail to release an egg, then become solid; in polycystic ovarian syndrome, the ovary is covered with tiny, multiple cysts.	Treatment: Removal of the cysts through laparoscopy; polycystic ovarian syndrome is treated by hormone supplements.
Pelvic inflammatory disease (various infections of the reproductive organs)	Bacteria such as *E. coli*; from surgery such as fitting of an IUD; childbirth; or through chlamydia or gonorrhea (*see pp. 40–41*).	Treatment: Antibiotics to kill the infection. Self-help: Rest, take painkillers; masturbate to increase blood flow to the pelvis. Do not attempt self-help only; always have medical examination in case infection has spread dangerously. Prevention: Practice safe sex; check before any gynecological procedure involving surgery, such as termination, insertion of IUD, or childbirth, that PID is not present—if it is, treat before the surgery, which can spread the infection.

SEXUAL CANCERS

INVESTIGATING AND TREATING GYNECOLOGICAL CANCERS

Gynecological cancers, by their very nature, strike to the heart of sexuality and fertility.

Cervical cancer

Today a routine test exists to catch this "cancer" before it starts. In a "smear" or Pap test, cells from the surface of the cervix are removed with a spatula or brush, then analysed; a "photograph" may also be taken as extra evidence. Once diagnosed, any abnormality—usually a precancerous condition—can be easily removed, often by heat treatment. For more advanced cases, surgery followed by radiotherapy can remove problem cells. There are several causes of cervical cancer: smoking, environmental pollution, stress, and low levels of folic acid have all been implicated, as have genital warts and unprotected sex. But the old myth of "nuns don't get it, prostitutes do" has been disproved: the typical cervical cancer sufferer has few partners and is certainly not "promiscuous."

IF YOU ARE OFFERED *a hysterectomy to resolve a gynecological problem, it may involve the removal of these organs.*

Ovarian cancer

Most cases of ovarian cancer are diagnosed during a routine gynecological check-up since there are rarely early symptoms. Few certain causes are known, although women who have had more monthly cycles may run a greater risk: those who started their menstrual periods early; those who reached the menopause late; and those who have never been pregnant. Treatment is mainly by chemotherapy, but surgery can be used in cases discovered before the cancer is too far advanced. Ovarian cancer is not usually diagnosed as early as cervical cancer, but new developments in screening look promising.

Endometrial cancer

This cancer begins in the endometrium (womb lining); the main symptoms are vaginal bleeding and discharge. Overweight women, older women, and those with diabetes, high blood pressure, or fibroids seem to be most at risk. There is also a hormonal link affecting women with high estrogen levels: women who have had few periods; who have not ovulated; and those who have had estrogen-only hormone replacement therapy. Treatment is by surgery, radiotherapy, chemotherapy, or hormone therapy. The good news is that, if diagnosed before the cancer has spread outside the womb, the survival rate can be as high as 90 percent.

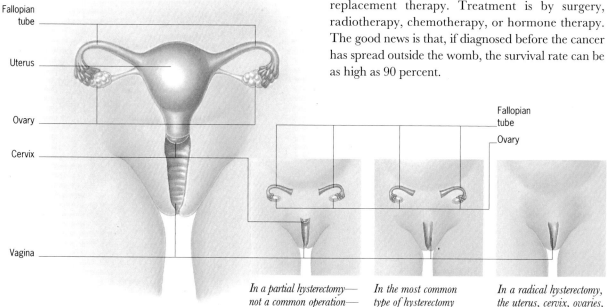

Fallopian tube

Uterus

Ovary

Cervix

Vagina

Fallopian tube

Ovary

The internal gynecological organs before surgery.

In a partial hysterectomy—not a common operation—only the uterus (womb) is removed.

In the most common type of hysterectomy performed, the uterus and cervix are removed.

In a radical hysterectomy, the uterus, cervix, ovaries, and Fallopian tubes are removed.

Hysterectomy

For treating sexual cancers, hysterectomy is often the treatment of choice. And if it is a lifesaving operation, then it is essential. But hysterectomy can negatively affect your sex life: scarring from the operation can make intercourse more painful; removal of the ovaries or the uterus may lower desire; and removal of the cervix may affect orgasm. You may therefore want to talk through the possibilities with your doctor, particularly if a hysterectomy is being suggested for a condition that is not life-threatening such as fibroids, endometriosis, PID or heavy menstrual periods. In such cases, treatments using medication are available.

If you find that a hysterectomy is your only option, you can offset negative side effects in several ways. Explore the joys of the clitoris and the G spot, both of which can potentially lead to orgasm without involving full intercourse. Consider hormone therapy to increase your sex drive. Exercise to tone your vaginal muscles, thereby strengthening your orgasms.

Above all, never accept that your sex life is at an end. The mind rules the body in many sexual matters and if you believe yourself a sexual woman, then you will be.

AT THE POINT *where cervix and vagina meet, there is a "transformation zone," where soft cervical cells meet more robust vaginal cells. The cells in this transformation zone are particularly vulnerable to developing cancer. It is from here that cells are taken during a cervical smear, to check if they are changing toward a cancerous condition.*

Columnar cells
Transformation zone
Squamous cells
Cervix

RARER SEXUAL CANCERS

CANCER OF THE VAGINA
Some women in the 1960s were prescribed synthetic estrogen to prevent miscarriage. Not only these women, but also their daughters, now seem vulnerable to cancer of the vagina. It is treated through surgery and radiotherapy, and there have recently been encouraging developments with the use of progesterone.

CANCER OF THE VULVA
This cancer may be linked to infection or irritation caused by environmental pollution. It usually affects older women, and because the first sign is often an obvious ulcer, it tends to be detected in the early stages when surgery can effect a cure.

WHEN SEX CREATES PROBLEMS
MINIMIZING THE RISK OF SEXUALLY TRANSMITTED DISEASES

Although most are uncomfortable rather than fatal, sexually transmitted diseases (STDs) are on the increase, largely because more of us are having more sex, earlier and for longer, with more partners. The risks are high: there is a one in two chance of catching gonorrhea after one sexual encounter. And women are particularly at risk—it is 17 times easier for a woman to contract HIV from a man than vice versa.

Don't confuse protection with emotion, or think that intimacy with someone you love is safe. Sex with a partner after knowing him (or her) for a year may be no safer than after knowing him for an hour, if he has ever indulged in risky behavior, or continues to do so.

USING A CONDOM

CONDOMS *are a defense against STDs. Choose latex rubber and use a water-based lubricant. The condom must be in place well before his climax, as sperm leak out in advance. After ejaculation, hold the rim while he withdraws, so that it does not slip.*

ANAL SEX

Those who like anal sex—penetration, or using hand or tongue—do so because the many nerve endings in the anus make stimulation there physically arousing, and because the intimacy of the act makes it emotionally satisfying.

But it is the highest risk sexual activity. Bacteria transferred to the vagina after anal sex can cause infection, and anal tissues are more easily damaged than vaginal ones, allowing the HIV virus into the bloodstream. Use a thick latex condom and spermicide, and wash body parts and sex toys before other forms of lovemaking.

Sexually transmitted disease	Symptoms
Bacterial vaginosis	Often symptom free; genital irritation; vaginal discharge; mildly painful urination.
Candidiasis (also known as a yeast infection or thrush)	Itching; white, cheesy vaginal discharge; pain in vagina and vulva.
Chlamydia	Often symptom free; vaginal discharge; frequent and painful urination; abdominal pain; can lead to infertility.
Genital herpes	Painful reddish bumps which develop into blisters on the genitals, vagina, thighs, and buttocks; vaginal discharge; burning sensation on urination; fever; swollen glands; herpes recurs cyclically, but symptoms may be milder after first attack.
Genital warts	Painless warts on outer genitals and in vagina.
Gonorrhea	Often symptom free; vaginal discharge; burning sensation on urination; irregular menstrual bleeding; can lead to infertility.
Viral hepatitis	Flulike symptoms; tiredness; nausea; loss of appetite; liver inflammation.
Human immunodeficiency virus (HIV)	Mild flu which comes and goes, then vulnerability to infections such as thrush, shingles, and herpes, and rare forms of cancer such as Kaposi's sarcoma.
Pediculosis (crabs), scabies	Intense itching caused by crab lice that infect the pubic area.
Syphilis	Hard, round, painless sore, which if untreated can lead to a red spotty rash, fever, loss of appetite, fatigue. Then symptoms may disappear leaving syphilis latent. It is relatively rare.
Trichomoniasis	Often symptom free; vulval itching or burning; foamy, yellow, smelly discharge.

SEXUALLY TRANSMITTED DISEASES

Causes	Treatment	Self-help and prevention (in addition to protected sex)
Sexual contact; an overgrowth of organisms in vagina; allergic reactions; may be triggered by gynecological surgery or childbirth.	Antibiotics.	Prevention: Avoid tight-fitting clothes, harsh chemicals, over-absorbent tampons, the contraceptive pill or IUD; get good lubrication during intercourse; clean genitals after sex and using the toilet.
Growth of fungus in vagina often triggered by sexual contact but can develop in women who are not sexually active; pregnancy; breastfeeding; possible link with diet, stress, oral contraceptives, antibiotics, vaginal irritation.	Suppositories, creams, or tablets; partner should also be treated.	Prevention: As for bacterial vaginosis; relaxation techniques to reduce stress; reduce intake of sugar, refined carbohydrates, and dairy foods (douching with or eating *active culture* yogurt can help, since it alters acidity levels).
Sexual contact.	Antibiotics; partner should also be treated.	Prevention: Use barrier methods of contraception; avoid the IUD; get fully treated before having gynecological surgery as this can cause the infection to spread.
Sexual contact; sharing towels; toilet seats; once contracted, can be triggered by stress, infection, tight clothing, and friction sex.	No cure; antiviral drugs relieve symptoms.	Get antiviral drugs to use at the first sign of attack; when attack happens, bathe sores in tepid salt water, take painkillers, use cold compresses. Prevention: Avoid sex from first sign of attack until sores have healed; wash after touching sores; follow care suggestions on p. 31; avoid stress; get counseling and group support.
Sexual contact; infected towels or clothing.	Removal by freezing, burning, surgery; partner should also be treated.	Prevention: Use barrier methods of contraception; genital warts are linked with cervical cancer, so have regular smears; don't smoke; eat plenty of fruit and vegetables.
Sexual contact.	Antibiotics; partner should also be treated.	Avoid sexual contact until cured.
Sexual contact; contact with fecal matter; transfusion of contaminated blood.	Antibiotics; rest.	Prevention: Avoid procedures such as ear piercing and acupuncture unless the practitioner uses sterilization.
Sexual contact, including oral sex; sharing sex toys; contact with contaminated blood; sharing needles with someone infected (NOT through kissing, sharing dishes, swimming in the same pool).	No cure for HIV; treatment for the infections that characterize AIDS.	Keep immune system healthy through good nutrition; have regular cervical smears; join support group. Prevention: Avoid unprotected intercourse, oral sex, and anal sex; avoid contact with contaminated blood, for example, through sharing needles during drug use.
Sexual contact; contact with infected towels or sheets; toilet seats.	Application medicines.	Prevention: Avoid contact with infested clothes or bedding.
Sexual contact.	Antibiotics; partner should also be treated.	Avoid sexual contact until cured—syphilis can cause miscarriage or birth defects.
Sexual contact; masturbation using same finger or device anally then vaginally; wiping genitals from back to front; infected towels or washcloth.	Antibiotics; partner should also be treated.	Prevention: Wipe front to back after using the toilet; clean sex toys; do not share towels or washcloths; avoid tight clothing.

YOUR SEXUAL MIND
ADULT INFLUENCES ON SEX AND SEXUALITY

Sexuality is not created by our bodies alone. When our fantasies about a lover turn us on—or the thought that the baby might wake turns us off—it is actually the mind that determines sexuality.

The bedrock of beliefs about sex are formed in childhood. As adults, we constantly build on this foundation as we gain experience of sex and sexuality, both first hand and through what others (partners, friends, and the mixed messages of the media) tell us. Through all these influences, we form personal sets of beliefs about the sexual world: what sex is; who we are sexually; how a sexual partner should behave; what a sexual relationship should be like.

Our beliefs may be misleading or misguided. Our particular experiences may not be representative of what most people do or think, or we may interpret the experiences of others in an inaccurate or unhelpful way. After an unhappy love affair, we may decide that all men are jerks. Conversely, a series of lovers who have cherished us may make us think "I'm always safe in sexual situations." Neither impression is universally correct; both may lead us into physical or emotional difficulties.

Every time we approach a sexual situation, our beliefs kick in, uncontrollably and—usually—unconsciously. They trigger our body to lose desire or to become aroused. They generate our emotions, as we create or undermine sexual relationships. And so, in order to really understand our sexuality, we must understand our sexual mind.

PARTNER INFLUENCES

The key influences on the sexual lives of adults are sexual partners. Each partner brings with him (or her) personal beliefs, attitudes, and approaches which—particularly if you are deeply involved—make a deep, although subconscious, impression.

Three particular messages are vital. Watch out for them and resist them if you feel they are affecting you negatively.

Criticism ~ Celebration
A partner who says you are sexually inadequate or compares you unfavorably with past lovers can make you unsure and undermine your skills ~ One who praises your sexuality will boost your confidence and ability.

Denial ~ Acceptance
A partner who insists that his (or her) way of making love is the right one, denying your preferences, instills self-doubt ~ One who accepts your ways of lovemaking confirms your instinctive self-knowledge, as well as giving pleasure.

Pressure ~ Freedom
A partner who pressures you into sexual activities causes a buildup of a backlog of resentment that blocks desire ~ One who accepts no leaves you relaxed and more likely to experiment.

SOME OLD SEXUAL MYTHS...

- *A woman shouldn't enjoy sex.*
- *If you let him sleep with you, he won't respect you.*
- *Sex before marriage is wrong.*
- *A man should always make the first move.*
- *Masturbation makes you blind.*
- *It's all right for men to sleep around, but not for women.*

...AND SOME CURRENT ONES

- *If sex with my partner isn't always wonderful, I must be in the wrong relationship.*
- *Everyone else gets more sex than I do.*
- *There's something wrong with me if I don't climax easily.*
- *Good sex isn't learned, it just happens.*
- *Orgasm through penetration is better than any other kind of orgasm.*
- *Only women who haven't got a good sex life need to masturbate.*

PERSONAL MESSAGES

Which are the various influences in your life? What messages might they have given you about sexuality and yourself as a sexual woman? Have these messages helped or hindered you? Thinking through the beliefs you have gained from each influence can help you understand more fully why your sexual self is the way it is.

Father, mother, or parent figures • Brothers and sisters
Religion and religious teachings
Culture and cultural ideas
Friends • Sex education at school
Losing your virginity • Sexual traumas
Partners • Media

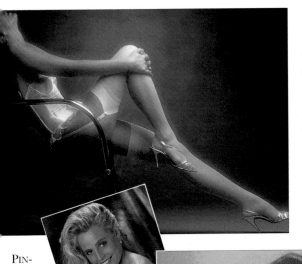

PIN-UPS *and sex clubs seem to say that it is okay to sell sex, but the idea of a woman hiring a gigolo is laughed at. And ads for perfume and underwear tell us that our role is to arouse, yet rape trial judges have stated that overtly sexual women deserve what they get. The media's messages about sex are both confusing and conflicting.*

SEXUAL PERSONALITY
WHAT IT MEANS TO BE A SEXUAL WOMAN TODAY

For centuries, there has been an ideal of the female "sexual personality"—the sort of women we should be in bed. And, because our position in society has been largely determined by men, that ideal has typically mirrored male views of appropriate female sexual behavior. In Victorian England, for example, the ideal female personality was passive in bed, "allowing" her partner to penetrate her in order to fulfill her duty as a wife or mother.

The advent of the contraceptive pill heralded a personality ideal that was the exact opposite of the Victorian woman. In the sixties, we were expected to be rampantly heterosexual, happy to have sex with any man who asked, solely responsible for contraception, and able to orgasm to order. And although this "personality" did show the relief on the part of most women that we were at last allowed sexual freedom, it was still a reflection of what men wanted us to be.

In the years since the pill, along with the accompanying social changes of the mid-twentieth century, there has been a move toward a personality template that is more in tune with what women want. Today's ideal woman is in touch with her own sexual preferences and responsible for her own pleasure, yet expects involvement from her partner.

This is still an "ideal," and we may feel resentful that even today a standard is imposed. But in the same way that current fashion is far more eclectic than ever before, so current sexuality allows us more freedom of choice than we have ever had.

THE CURRENT IDEAL OF A SEXUAL WOMAN SAYS YOU SHOULD BE

❦ *Knowledgeable*: informed about physiology and the art of sex.

❦ *Physically confident*: relaxed about your own body.

❦ *Self-aware*: sure of who you are and what you want.

❦ *Honest*: clear and truthful when something doesn't work, or you don't like what's happening.

❦ *Emotionally self-assured*: relaxed and secure both about yourself and your relationships.

❦ *Enthusiastic*: able to be positive and supportive to your partner.

❦ *Imaginative*: willing and able to experiment during sex.

❦ *Proactive*: able to take the lead in bed.

❦ *Sexually sensitive*: in touch with your body's sensations.

❦ *Responsive*: able to sense what your partner desires and offer it.

FUTURE PERSONALITY

Social attitudes worldwide are becoming more diverse with trends suggesting that in future there may be no one definition of an "ideal" sexual personality. You may soon be able to choose, without fear of reprisal, your personal:

● Orientation: whether you are straight, lesbian, or bisexual.

● Activity: being celibate, active, or alternating between the two.

● Involvement: your commitment to one person or a number of people, and whether you have sex outside relationships.

● Temperament: being active and dominant, passive and compliant or aspects of the two.

● Fertility: bearing or not bearing children, or bearing children without having sex.

DEVELOPING A SEXUAL PERSONALITY

Contemporary culture offers many resources to help you develop your sexual personality.

● For knowledge and confidence: sources of information—books, magazines, and videos.

● For self-awareness and honesty: courses in personal development; assertiveness training.

● For emotional assurance and enthusiasm: counseling to bring inner security and relationship harmony.

● For imagination and proactivity: sources of sexual fantasy and stimulation such as erotica.

● For sensitivity and responsiveness: more opportunities for practice through masturbation and having more relationships in a lifetime.

ADMITTING YOUR PREFERENCES

The sexual ideal in mainstream culture still does not accept a woman being lesbian. The media presents images of women who are heterosexual or, at best, temporarily "bi." Families and friends presuppose a woman to be straight. So what if you suspect you like women? You may find the idea threatening, since being lesbian is not an easy option. At best, lesbians are marginalized; at worst, they are persecuted.

It could be that you aren't sure about your sexuality. Most women find both genders attractive at some point, and you may not have discovered your clear preference. Or perhaps you are lesbian, but haven't yet had the support you need to accept it. Seek information and help from those who know. Contact a lesbian group, and talk to gay women. They will not try to pressurize you into joining them. Instead, they will tell you about their own process of self-discovery and support you to find out what your desires really are.

SEXUAL DECISION-MAKING
TAKING RESPONSIBILITY FOR THE CHOICES WE MAKE

The relaxation of social and legal rules that followed the advent of the pill gave women, for the first time, some power to make key sexual decisions: to have sex outside marriage, a relationship with a woman, a child out of wedlock, a termination of pregnancy. At first, it was perhaps a false liberty. Many women say that the freedom contraception gave them led them into activities they now regret. And decision making is still sometimes less than fully informed; we compromise because "I had had too much to drink . . . he said he loved me . . . I wanted to keep him."

But we are starting to take control. We are developing a clear internal sense of what is right for us, and are much more able to communicate our sexual decisions and stand by them. This is helped by a rise in skills and support: through assertiveness courses, self-help groups, information services, and helplines for all kinds of women's issues. At last we can both take decisions and assume full responsibility for our choices.

Case history

"I've known I was a lesbian since I was 15. I had my first serious relationship at college. That was quite easy; I spun my parents a lot of stories about all the boys I was going out with. When I started work I met Anna, and after a year we moved in together. The decision to come out to my family wasn't sudden; I'd thought about it for a while. I finally realized that I had to tell them—Anna and I are a lifetime partnership and they had to know sometime. I went up one weekend and just sat them down and did it. They were both upset. My Mom's OK about it now she knows I'm happy. My father still won't let Anna in the house. But I know that I made the right decision."

KATE

THE ABORTION DECISION

One of the most challenging decisions you may ever make is whether to have an abortion.

● Get information about your state's laws on abortion, and on your medical choices.
● Consider potential risks: side-effects from the procedures, complications with the anasthetic, even failure of the abortion.
● If you suspect that unconscious wishes and needs may have led you to get pregnant in the first place, explore these before you make your decision. Do you actually want to have this baby?
● Get support—from your partner, family, friends, or counsellors—to deal with negative feelings such as anger, depression, or sexual guilt. The more support you get, the more likely it is that you will make the right choice for you.

KEY SEXUAL DECISIONS

The most common sexual decisions in the course of your lifetime may be those to:
• Lose your virginity
• Admit your sexual orientation
• Have sex with a new partner
• Stop having sex
• Have premarital sex
• Have an affair
• Allow your partner to have an affair
• Forgive a partner who has an affair
• Have sex with someone else's partner
• Attend sex therapy
• Report sexual attack or abuse
• Go on the pill
• Have unprotected sex
• Get pregnant
• Have an abortion
• Be sterilized
• Take hormone replacement therapy
• End a sexual relationship

UNWELCOME SEX 50–51
SEX WITH A NEW PARTNER 92–93
SEXUAL FEELINGS 96–97
ASKING FOR HELP 148–49
WHEN A RELATIONSHIP ENDS 178–79

MAKING A DECISION

• Get as much information as you can through reading, talking to other people, getting professional help, and exploring your emotions.

• For each possible course of action open to you—to say yes, to say no; to go, to stay, and so on—answer all the following relevant questions.

1
Biological:
...benefits
...risks
...side effects?

2
Sexual:
...positive effects
...negative effects?

3
Emotional effects on:
...partner
...relationship
...other people who matter?

4
Legal:
am I breaking the law, and if so what might happen?

5
Ethical:
does it tie in with my religious, spiritual, or moral beliefs?

6
Cost:
...money
...time
...effort?

7
What would doing this say about me to other people?

8
How will I feel about myself if I do it?

• List the pros and cons for each course of action...ways to minimize the problems...ways to enhance the benefits.

• So what decision does this exploration suggest to you?

LIVING WITHOUT SEX
CHOOSING CELIBACY AND MAKING IT WORK

While women today seem to be having more sex than ever before, many of us are living without sex. First, the combination of relaxed attitudes toward relationship breakdown and predictions that by the year 2000 there will be fewer men than women creates an unwilling celibacy: we want relationships, but can't meet (suitable) partners. This leads to frustration and loneliness: we don't only need the pleasure of sex, but all the other things that accompany an intimate relationship— practical support, emotional commitment, a daily cuddle.

Second, willing celibacy—choosing to opt out of sexual intimacy—is becoming an option. We may need time to raise a child, develop a career, or recover after a break-up. We may want to explore ourselves outside a partnership, or be in an emotionally intimate relationship without having sex. But because we are expected to be sexually active, we meet new problems: self doubt that we are simply scared, social pressure from friends or family who think we are weird.

It is vital for those of us who are celibate, willingly or not, to remember that sex is not a stamp of personal validity. We do not need a sexual partner to be fulfilled and happy, nor do we need to be sexually active to be worthwhile.

PLEASURE ALONE 54–55
WHEN A RELATIONSHIP ENDS 178–79

IF YOU ARE CELIBATE *because you are not in a relationship, these guidelines may help you to make it work.*

• *See the reality as positively as you can, not as a second-rate option. There are advantages to being celibate; find out what they are for you. (Positivity draws people to you, while despondency repels others.)*
• *Build a support system of people who can provide the things that an intimate relationship includes: practical support, a "companion" for important events, a shoulder to cry on, and so on.*
• *Mix with people who accept you for who you are, rather than as half of a couple, and those who do not feel threatened by your being celibate.*
• *Build your self esteem by giving yourself treats—sensual ones like massage, emotional ones like a walk in the park.*
• *Don't abandon your sexuality simply because you have no partner. Fantasy, erotica, and masturbation can keep you aware that you are still a sexual person.*

CELIBATE COUPLES

Choosing to live celibate lives as a couple can bring you together with a mutual aim that is incredibly powerful. But it only works if both of you want it. If one simply submits, resentment builds and communication stops.

● If couple celibacy is simply a face-saving way of saying that you are heading toward a break-up, it is better to face the truth, whatever that means for your partnership.
● Be sure to offset the lack of pairbonding sex in other ways: communicate deeply, spend quality time together, plan your future to build security.

Case history

"I've been celibate for two years, since I set up my own business (I'm a caterer). I finished with Phil about a month before that—he was so unsupportive, and it was so obvious we were going in different directions. For the next six months, I was working 18 hours a day and never met anyone.

"Then one day I thought 'No partner—well that's fine, I haven't got room in my life for both work and sex anyway.' I miss the cuddles more than the passion, but I masturbate and fantasize. I've been tempted twice, once with a good friend who seemed to understand that work had to come first. Then I thought 'No, as soon as we've had sex, he'll want to see me every night.' When I've got things really going, then I'll think about a relationship. When the time is right, it'll happen."

LYNNE

UNWELCOME SEX
WHEN AND HOW TO SAY NO

The incidence of reported rape is rising: in the United States, the number surged from 17,000 in 1975 to 100,000 in 1990, and the same survey suggested that 90 percent of sexual assaults go unreported.

"Rape" conjures up images of a violent attack by a stranger down a dark alley. But most women are forced to have sex by a man they know: boyfriend, ex-lover, alcoholic husband, with the result that we are often torn between wanting to forgive and wanting to protect ourselves and other women. Family and friends may try to prevent us from reporting the attack; and if we do, we may not be believed.

Yet forced sex in these circumstances is just a fraction of the incidence of unwelcome sex. Most of us have at some time done something unwelcome with a lover—oral sex, anal sex, painful positions— or simply agreed to sexual contact when we did not feel like it. We may comply to please our partner, or because we feel it is the only way to get affection, or because a partner will be angry if we do not.

We need to move to a time where no woman (or man) should have to have unwelcome sex of any kind.

IF YOU ARE RAPED

● Call your local rape crisis center immediately for support.

● If you decide to report the attack, do so as soon as possible. Expect questioning and a medical examination; it will help if you have not bathed or changed your clothes.

● See a doctor immediately to be checked for pregnancy and sexually transmitted diseases.

● Attend specialist counseling to help you recover from the trauma.

● Get angry rather than guilty: women who get angry have been shown to have fewer long-term side effects.

● Remember that no one, under any circumstances, ever deserves to be raped.

PROTECTING YOURSELF AGAINST...

Attack while traveling

● In your car, check the back seat before entering; keep doors locked while driving.

● On a train, don't sit on an inside seat; avoid standing near groups of men; don't fall asleep.

● Don't hitchhike; accept rides only from women who you know well; carry the telephone number of a reliable cab company.

Obscene phone calls

● Have an unlisted number or use an initial to keep your gender secret.

● If you receive an obscene call, keep calm—it is not aimed at you personally.

● Pretend you can't hear and replace the receiver.

● If necessary, have your calls intercepted or get the number changed.

Sexual attack on the street

● Walk with other people.

● Walk steadily and purposefully, with your hands free, in the middle of the sidewalk.

● Avoid dark places and walking through or past groups of men.

● If threatened, yell "Fire!"—people run toward a fire, but away from rape.

● If followed, walk up to a house, preferably one with lights on, and ring the bell; if you have to, break a window to attract attention.

Date rape

● Choose neutral or public venues to begin with.

● Communicate sexual limits firmly from the start.

● Pay attention to your instincts; leave if you feel you are in danger.

ADOPTING THE RIGHT STANCE

SAYING NO *may not be enough with a determined attacker. But the way you respond to a sexual invitation can make the difference between being pressured and not.*

The "incongruent" body language (above) contradicts itself. The tilted shoulders and angled head suggest indecision, and the protective crossed arms are defensive. But the direct eye contact and smile may be read as encouragement by an insensitive partner or one who wants to believe you want him.

FOR A CLEAR NO, *you need to look assertive and confident (above). Stand tall, keep your posture balanced yet relaxed, without protective across-the-body gestures. Face directly and maintain eye contact without* smiling. *Keep your voice slow and steady—no "little girl" expressions or questioning tone. Choose a definite phrase like "No . . . I don't want to do that" and keep repeating it until the message is heard.*

THIS "VICTIM" STANCE *makes it more likely that a partner will increase pressure on you. The body language spells weakness: raised shoulders, dropped head, genital-protecting hands, nervous mouth, and timid, upward glance. Combined, perhaps, with a low, hesitant voice and such phrases as "If you want . . ." or "I'll let you decide . . . ," this stance seems to say that you have no right to make your own decisions and gives the impression that you can be pressurized into compliance.*

CHARTING YOUR SEXUAL SELF
DISCOVERING WHAT WORKS FOR YOU SEXUALLY

Sexuality is never static: it constantly moves in rhythms. The most obvious female rhythms are those of sex itself—as passion rises, peaks, then dies away—and the monthly menstrual cycle during which our potential for arousal shifts as hormones ebb and flow. But there are also other patterns.

Some of us have a daily rhythm of arousal. Just as a man may have an early morning erection because of hormonal fluctuations, our desire may vary, bringing greater energy in the morning or a need for gentle lovemaking in the evening. Equally, during the course of a calendar year, some seasons may create a need for quiet, warm intimacy; others, particularly spring, often bring a rush of lust; and some tend to induce a sexual hibernation.

Finally, key events in the year affect libido—anniversary celebrations may lead to lovemaking and times of stress such as Christmas can take sex off the agenda, while vacations often present the opportunity for relaxing and enjoying intimacy.

Being aware of sexual rhythms can allow both greater control and heightened pleasure. For if we know when and how we are likely to be aroused, and when not, we can adapt our lovemaking to suit.

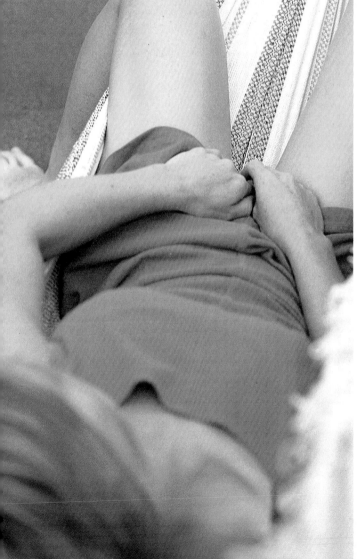

MOST OF THE TIME *you are aroused, you want to feel rather than to think. But consciously trying to chart your arousal allows you to do more of what works, or to sense when arousal dips and correct that, for complete satisfaction.*

Increased arousal is usually marked by your focus shifting from external to internal and a relaxation in the "comfort zone"—the spot in your stomach or back that automatically triggers positive—and negative— sensations. Arousal is obvious in the erogenous zones such as your lips, nipples, and genitals. Does your skin feel as if it's moving? When you are ready for penetration, is there a sudden clutch in your vagina? Do you know when orgasm is inevitable because you start to hold your breath?

AT WHAT TIMES *of the month are you most easily aroused (below)? You may find that your desire peaks during ovulation because of a surge of testosterone—this is your body's way of encouraging you to have sex at the time when you are most likely to conceive.*

You may find that you also have a peak of desire before and during your menstrual period, and if you are unwilling, or culturally forbidden, to make love while menstruating, this may result in a surge of passion once the blood flow has ceased. However, if you are suffering from stress or taking hormones, these factors may override your natural peaks of desire. Take them into account if you decide to chart your monthly levels of arousal.

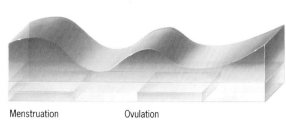

Menstruation   Ovulation

SEXUAL DESIRE

TIME

STAGES IN FEMALE AROUSAL

Excitement	Plateau	Orgasm	Resolution

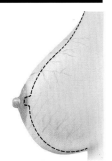  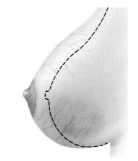 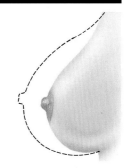

Your heart rate, breathing rate, and blood pressure rise. Your breasts increase in size, the nipples become erect, and veins are more prominent.

Your heart beats 100 to 160 times a minute. Your breasts may be 25 percent larger than normal. Swelling of the areolae makes your nipples seem less erect.

All body signs reach a peak. Your breasts remain large, with swollen areolae and erect nipples; they may also be covered by a sex flush.

Heartbeat, pulse, and breathing rate return to normal. Your breasts regain their usual size, and any flush fades as their normal color returns.

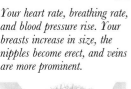 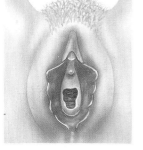 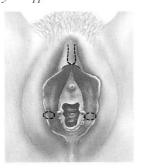 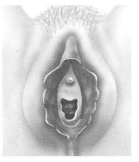 

Your labia majora flatten and open to allow the labia minora and clitoris to swell. Your vagina starts to lubricate.

Your clitoris lifts from its hood, and your labia swell; and change color to deep red. Drops of vaginal fluid may be secreted.

Your external genitals remain lifted and swollen and may feel as if they are in spasm.

Your external genitals return to their normal color; the clitoris retracts under its hood and swelling in the labia subsides.

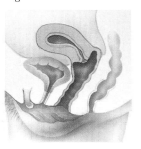 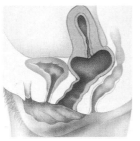 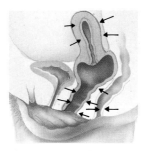 

The inner two-thirds of your vagina expand and lengthen, and the vaginal walls thicken. Your womb lifts, helping to make your vagina longer.

The outer two-thirds of your vagina swells, and your vaginal opening contracts to grip your partner's penis. The inner third of your vagina opens out.

A wave of contractions at approximately 0.8-second intervals passes through your body, affecting your vagina, womb, and rectal sphincter.

Contractions cease, and the womb and cervix tilt back to their normal positions; the vagina contracts and shortens to resume its normal size.

PLEASURE ALONE

LEARNING WHAT WORKS SEXUALLY THROUGH MASTURBATION

Perhaps as many as 70 percent of women in the Western world masturbate—single and partnered, young and old. It is one of the most powerful things we can do sexually.

We may be wary of masturbation. Women are often brought up to believe that pleasure which is focused on self and does not include a partner is greedy and wrong. We are sometimes told that masturbation will prevent us from enjoying "proper," that is, penetrative, sex. In fact, the reverse is true. Women who masturbate are more likely to be able to give pleasure and are also more likely to reach orgasm with a partner.

There are enormous benefits to masturbation. It helps when there is no partner available, and it comforts after the loss of a partner—women's rate of masturbation peaks after separation, divorce, or widowhood. And self-pleasuring involves none

of the disadvantages of partnership sex, such as the risk of catching an STD or getting pregnant. Far more importantly, during masturbation we can concentrate on ourselves without constantly checking if someone else is happy, and we are independent of anyone else for sexual release.

Masturbation has been shown to induce sleep; relieve menstrual cramps; drive away backache, headache and fatigue; and even anesthetize the pains of labor. But the main reason to masturbate is for sheer pleasure. For the vast majority of us, it's the easiest, quickest—and sometimes the only—route to orgasm.

MANY WOMEN *have a particular "masturbation position," just as many couples have favorite positions for intercourse. You need to be able to reach your clitoris easily, but also be able to squeeze together or stretch apart your legs in the way that works for you. The most usual positions are:*

• *Lying on your back with your knees bent;*

• *Lying on your stomach, with your buttocks raised;*

• *Lying on your side, sitting cross-legged propped on pillows or kneeling on all fours.*

54

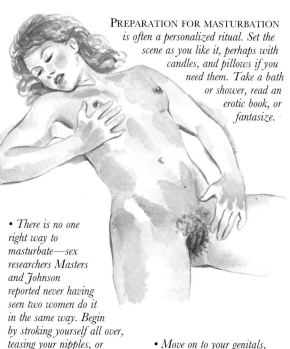

PREPARATION FOR MASTURBATION is often a personalized ritual. Set the scene as you like it, perhaps with candles, and pillows if you need them. Take a bath or shower, read an erotic book, or fantasize.

A BRIEF HISTORY OF MASTURBATION

The word masturbation is believed to derive from the Latin words meaning "hand" and "defile," which neatly sums up ancient opinions. The Judeo–Christian tradition held that anything that turned sexuality away from its "proper" job of conception was wrong—so much so, that by the 19th century masturbation was held to be responsible for a whole range of illnesses including epilepsy, heart attack, insanity, sterility, and cancer.

By the middle of the 20th century, however, wide-ranging research by sexologists such as Alfred Kinsey had clearly shown that a large number of ordinary, sane, and healthy people masturbated—and nowadays sex therapists recommend it, particularly for women who have difficulty in reaching orgasm.

• *There is no one right way to masturbate—sex researchers Masters and Johnson reported never having seen two women do it in the same way. Begin by stroking yourself all over, teasing your nipples, or stroking the inside of your thighs* (above). *Take the time to work yourself up slowly.*

• *Do you need something your vagina can "clutch" on to? Despite male fantasies, only a small minority of women do. But you may want to experiment with two or three clean fingers inserted gently.*

• *Move on to your genitals, stroking your outer and inner vaginal lips and then exploring your clitoris. Pull the hood back and lightly stroke the shaft, rubbing up and down, from side to side, or using a circular movement. If you need lubrication, lick your fingers, use baby oil, or dip a finger into your vagina and transfer your natural juices* (below).

• *Vary the pressure, speed, and rhythm with one question in mind—does it feel good?—and one aim—your pleasure. Your clitoris may get oversensitized—if so, hold back for a few seconds.*

• *When you start to feel the clitoris rise, harden, and warm to your fingers* (below), *keep going. Don't aim at orgasm, particularly if you're masturbating for the first time. Just follow your instincts.*

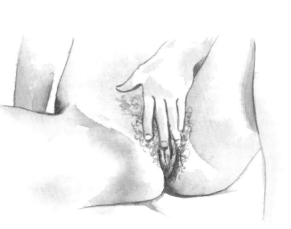

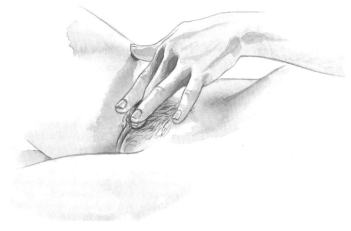

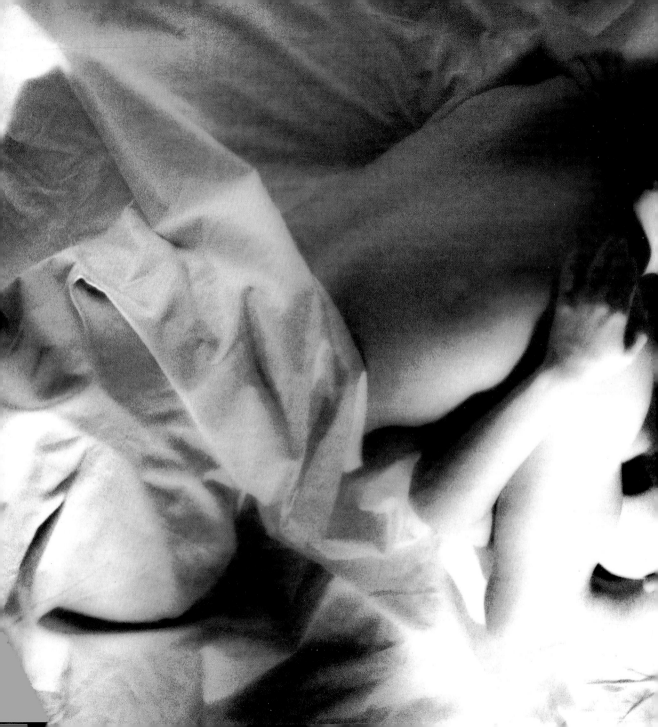

3 Making Love

AS WOMEN INCREASINGLY REALIZED THAT they could both enjoy sex and be active in giving and receiving pleasure, the time-honored notion that what pleased men was "real" sex began to be challenged. Slowly, we began to develop our own ideas of what works for us.

It quickly became apparent that our definition of sex is not always the same as men's. Women of all ages, attitudes, and sexual preferences started to say that while some parts of the sexual act were wonderful, others didn't quite work for them, and yet more could be far more amazing if they were done slightly differently.

Heightened sensuality, extended foreplay, loving affection, stimulation of the clitoris, multiple and extended orgasms...we realized that these were what we wanted. And slowly but surely, they have found their way into mainstream views and expectations about sex.

Of course what men want is crucial. No heterosexual woman would deny the importance of "straightforward" intercourse. And every woman can learn from the male approach of taking the initiative, aiming directly for pleasure, expecting to reach climax. But now that we are freer to include our own desires in lovemaking, we are also, significantly, feeling more able to take male values on board.

At the same time, we are reaching a more balanced stage in the development of human sexuality, one in which individual needs are respected, where we blend approaches and attitudes, taking the best parts from each. We're not quite there yet. But more and more, making love is not something defined or dictated by one or the other partner alone. It is a reflection of both partners' wants and desires together.

THERE IS A *particular joy in having another body to respond to. The uncertainty of what a partner may do, the delight in trying to understand him (or her), the wonder of their stroking and touching, and the emotion of feeling togetherness all make partnership sex a definitive experience.*

SEXUAL ETIQUETTE
THE UNSPOKEN GUIDELINES OF SEXUAL INTERACTION

Because sexual freedom is so new, there is as yet no definitive code of conduct. Whereas many activities such as eating, traveling, or chatting have their own etiquette—those unspoken rules that let us interact without offending others—sex is different. Society has only just learned to deal with sex openly, so we are still setting the guidelines—and, since each of us has only a limited number of experiences from which to learn, we can still be wrong-footed. We can feel nervous that we shouldn't do certain things or, alternatively, act confidently only to find that others feel threatened by our behavior.

In an attempt to map out some of the current ground rules, here are a few of the emerging norms of sexual etiquette today.

Eye to body: Aroused couples begin by "scanning" each other's bodies. Men often begin with the body and work up to the face; women tend to start with the face, then check the body. Partners then build trust through eye contact, eye movement, and speech.

Hand to forearm: The first touch is usually to a less intimate part of the body.

CHECKLIST

In the lead-up to sex, you probably won't check all these points one by one. But some checks are essential with a new partner; others need updating at regular intervals, even in a long-term relationship.

● Admit if you are a virgin. If you suspect he (or she) is, be tactful but supportive.

● Tell your partner if you are having your menstrual period; have tissues or a towel ready in case of staining.

● Suggest a shower or bath beforehand. This preempts worries, for both of you, about personal hygiene.

● Make sure that the sheets are clean and that there is no evidence of previous sexual activity.

● Give warning if you react badly to a specific touch or act: For example, if your breasts are ticklish.

● What about roommates or neighbors? Is it okay to wander to the bathroom naked, to make noise when you climax?

● Be clear about the need for sleep; whether it's acceptable to stay the night; what protocol needs to be followed in the morning.

THE ETIQUETTE OF PROTECTION

It is not only polite, but also essential to insist on safe sex. You may feel a partner will be insulted if you suggest using a condom. He may or may not be—but it's your body, and possibly your life on the line. And, even if you are sure of him, he may not be sure of you.

Rather than producing a condom suddenly at the crucial moment, however, it is tactful to give warning. Comment ahead of actual penetration that you will expect to be using one, that you do so as a matter of course. If you're on the pill, don't trumpet the fact—the focus of the discussion then shifts away from the general issue of sensible protection and on to the more threatening one of "does either of us have an STD?"

Be responsible for having a condom handy. The standard reason for not having one in your bag is that a partner might complain that you were easy, but someone on the point of having sex with you can hardly do that.

THE ETIQUETTE OF TOUCHING *is a natural part of human physiology, and there is a priority order in which to touch that lets you both feel safe. Of course you ignore it if you know each other well and are both overwhelmingly aroused—you may go from a glance to penetration in a single step. But moving too quickly through the stages can make even a long-term partner feel threatened; moving too slowly can send signals of disinterest.*

Mouth to mouth: Kisses usually move through various stages of intimacy, from closed to open mouth; from lips only, to using tongues to parallel the sex act.

Hand to upper genitals: Touching breasts is usually the next move. Once this point is passed, there is a high chance of moving through the other sexual stages— mouth to body, hand to lower genitals, genital contact, oral sex.

Arm around waist: This begins to bring the partners' bodies into full contact.

Hand to head: Marks a shift to deeper emotional feeling.

Case history

"I hate the early stages of a relationship. Everything is unclear—practically as well as emotionally—and I don't know when I'm putting a foot wrong. I remember being furious at a comment reported to me by a lover that his roommate thought I was 'too old to be wandering around in just a bathrobe.' Mind you, I get equally annoyed at partners who don't respect my privacy. If they sleep over, they are guests and shouldn't take things for granted, even once the relationship is established. They shouldn't make breakfast for just themselves; take a shower without making sure no one needs it first; presume that I'm on the pill; or jump me in the middle of the night so that I wake up to find they're already halfway there without me!"

LIBBY

SCENE SETTING
CREATING THE RIGHT MOOD FOR SEX

Setting the scene for sex is not a case of soft lights and sweet music. Creating the right ambience is about switching the emphasis, using time, place, senses, and mood to shift concentration from normal day-to-day concerns on to the experience of lovemaking.

If we don't make sure that the atmosphere is right for this shift, we never get fully involved in what is happening. We may find it difficult to contact our physical sensations and may be unable to focus on the passion and follow it all the way to climax. But if we set the scene effectively, we have a far better chance of moving from the external world of work and worries into the internal world of passionate sensation.

EARLY IN A RELATIONSHIP, meeting in a public place (above right) *can give you a sense of relaxed safety. Offset* *the distractions of being in public by choosing somewhere you can sit closely, with activity so that you talk, touch, and* *interact. When you return home* (below), *it may be best to begin on the sofa: moving straight to the bedroom can be too much* *too soon. Reduce interruptions or distractions, both physical and mental, so that you can focus on each other completely.*

CHOOSING THE TIME

Timing can make or break sexual success. If you make love when you're not in the mood, because you feel you should, then you build up a backlog of unhappiness that can kill desire. But if you choose times—of the day, month, or even year—when you are eager for sex, you will reinforce your own pleasure. Most couples make love in the evening, but you may well have more energy in the morning, or need the pressure-free mood of an afternoon.

Equally, particularly in long-term relationships, be open to changes of schedule to offset boredom. Resist a regular routine—unless the ritual turns you on. Resist, too, the temptation to say no to unusual timings—the early hours of the morning, the middle of a working day— until your body has had a chance to decide. Respond as passionately as possible for a slow count of 30. If you still think it's the wrong time, say so. If not, carry on.

ENGAGING YOUR SENSES

SIGHT: Unlike most mammals, humans identify potential mates by what they see. Men's brains in particular respond to visual input, so to arouse him, use classic visual "triggers" such as a glimpse of naked flesh. Remember too that low light encourages sitting closer, communicating more personally, touching rather than talking. Dim the lighting or use candles.

SOUND: Both genders are aroused by sound, women slightly more than men. Sound and music are particularly erotic if they mirror the pulsing rhythms of lovemaking to orgasm; voices are arousing, particularly if you lower the tone and volume, as happens naturally when making love. Sexual words are erotic— but only if they're acceptable to both of you, and are neither too crude nor too "medical."

SMELL: Personal or room perfumes may be arousing because they smell sensual or because they trigger arousing memories. But don't be shy of letting your own natural body odors stand alone. They contain pheromones. One study showed that women who sprayed pheromones on their breasts at bedtime had sex more often than a control group.

TASTE: Strictly speaking, taste plays little direct part in arousal. But some foods are so delicious that they wake up the senses; others are so romantic that they set the scene. And tasting a lover's sweat or vaginal secretions can also be exciting due to pheromones.

TOUCH: The kinesthetic sense has the most direct effect sexually. Arouse yourselves in advance of lovemaking by dancing, sports or having a massage. Try experimenting with a variety of kinesthetic sensations—such as velvet, a warm bath, whipped cream—to surprise your nervous systems into being more receptive and sensitive.

KNOWING HIM

MALE REPRODUCTIVE AND GYNECOLOGICAL SYSTEMS

We love men, but they often seem strangers to us during sex. To begin with, their physiology is different, and regardless of how much we know about "which bit does what," these differences make the whole sexual experience something more instant and urgent for them than it is for us. But, equally important, their life experiences seem to give them a completely different outlook on what it means to make love with a partner.

From the start, men are under pressure to perform, to take responsibility, and to be unemotional. In terms of lovemaking, this can all too often mean feeling pressured to get—and maintain—an erection; being compelled to assume responsibility in bed; and therefore, perhaps, feeling unable to get involved. The result can be misunderstanding, with women wanting men, but also judging them to be sexually uninformed, uncaring, or uncommunicative.

But in the same way that things are changing for us, so they are beginning to change for men, too.

They are starting actively to resist the pressures on them as we are increasingly coming to understand something of what those pressures are. And we are claiming sexual equality over both our choice of partner and of how we make love—of timing, activity, and position.

There is still some way to go for many of us. We need to be ready:

• To allow men the right not to perform if they don't feel like it (typically we are more outraged by a man's lack of erection than he is allowed to be by our strategic "headache")

• To take the initiative and share the responsibility in sex (we characteristically hold back from action for fear of failure)

• To allow men a full range of emotions (even if that means they'll sometimes complain or appear vulnerable).

In short, we need to be ready to really know our male partners—and accept them regardless.

THE PHASES OF MALE EXCITEMENT

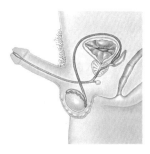 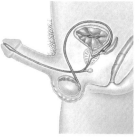 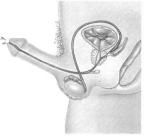 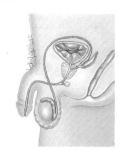

During the excitement phase—which can be as early as three seconds after arousal begins—a man's penis becomes engorged with blood, which causes the tissues to swell and the penis to become erect. His testes partially elevate, his nipples may swell, and his skin flushes. His heart rate, blood pressure, and breathing rate increase.

In the plateau phase, immediately before orgasm, his coronal ridge increases in size, and the glans turns purple. A few drops of lubricating fluid—which may also contain sperm—may flow out. His testes swell by up to 50 percent and move closer to the body, ready for ejaculation.

Orgasm is inevitable once seminal fluid is propelled into the urethral tract. Within a few seconds, regular contractions of his pelvic muscles and urethra make him ejaculate; the spurts match the contractions of a woman's vagina, approximately once every 0.8 of a second. (With training, a man can orgasm without actually ejaculating.)

In the resolution phase, as his heart rate, blood pressure, and breathing rate all return to normal, the blood flows out of the penis, which softens. His erection subsides, and the testes descend to their usual position. At this point, he is in his refractory period and cannot become aroused again for a while.

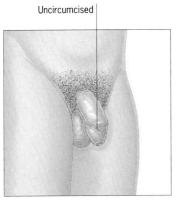

Uncircumcised

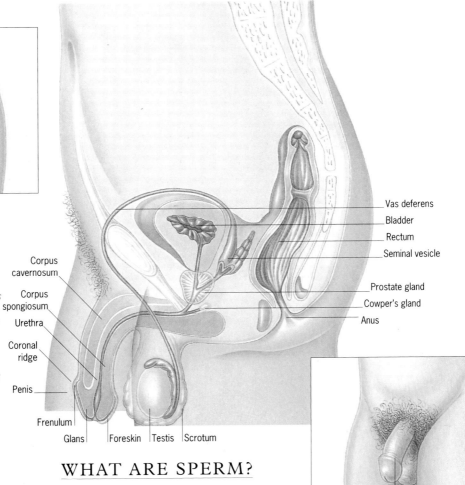

Corpus
cavernosum

Corpus
spongiosum

Urethra

Coronal
ridge

Penis

Frenulum

Glans   Foreskin   Testis   Scrotum

Vas deferens
Bladder
Rectum
Seminal vesicle

Prostate gland
Cowper's gland
Anus

Circumcised

THE MALE PENIS *is made up of three cylinders of spongy material. When a man is aroused, the larger two—the corpora cavernosa—fill with blood and create his erection. The third cylinder—the corpus spongiosum—contains the urethra through which urine is passed from the body.*

• *An average unerect penis is 3½–4 in (87–100 mm) long; most erect penises are 5–7 in (125–175 mm) long. (He may worry about size, but smaller organs typically grow comparatively more in length when they get erect.)*

• *The corpus spongiosum broadens at the head of the penis to form the glans; the coronal ridge separates the glans from the body of the penis; connecting the two is the frenulum, a thin strip of tissue.*

• *The root of the penis extends into the pelvis. Below is the scrotum, a pouch of loose skin that contains the testes, smooth oval structures that produce sperm. Their position shifts up or down to keep sperm at the optimum body heat, according to his temperature, arousal, and emotions.*

WHAT ARE SPERM?

Mature male sperm cells (spermatozoa), which fertilize a woman's egg, are 0.0002 in (0.005 mm) long and have a head, a cone-shaped midpiece, and a whiplike tail to propel them along. Throughout a healthy man's adult life, his testes produce sperm at the rate of about 1,000 a second—30 billion per year. Sperm then pass into the vas deferens, where they mix with fluids from the seminal vesicles and prostate gland to make seminal fluid (semen). At ejaculation, seminal fluid travels through into the urethra and out of the tip of the penis.

Sperm can be capable of fertilization up to eight days after ejaculation. A typical ejaculation contains between 200 and 400 million sperm; between 10 and 20 ejaculations contain enough sperm to populate the earth.

• *The foreskin, loose skin at the top of the penis, folds over to cover the glans. Some cultures remove it for hygienic reasons; this removal—circumcision (above)—is a religious ceremony for Jews.*

• *Men may also have a G spot, a point inside the anus where pressure stimulates the prostate, resulting in orgasm.*

PERSONAL PATTERNS
DIFFERENCES IN AROUSAL BETWEEN MEN AND WOMEN

For far too long women had no sexual guidance. Now it seems that wherever we turn we are told how to make love. But the danger in setting standards, ideals, and rules is that we ignore the real secret of sex—that there is no one right way. Every person has an individual pattern of arousal, particular turn-ons, personal preferences, favorite ways of gaining pleasure. And so with each partner, we need to relearn sexual skills from the start. His (or her) particular physiology and how it affects what he does and doesn't like needs to be considered. His level of sex drive, and when and why it fluctuates must be gauged. We should learn about his background, attitudes to sex, hangups, vulnerabilities, and fantasies. And it is important to be able to read his signals so we know his pleasure and meet his needs during lovemaking.

Having learned all this, there is a final step we should take. We need to give ourselves the same respect we give our partners, enjoying our own patterns as much as those of our partner. As women we should feel justified in going for what we want in bed, even if it is different from what he wants. A partner needs our encouragement to meet our particular desires, in the same way as we are willing to meet his.

TYPICAL SEXUAL PATTERNS

HIM	YOU
A man's normal level of desire is constant, but he is easily aroused and easily deflated.	Your desire varies, and is slow both to build and fade.
He feels sex as a release of energy.	You need a build-up of energy before release.
He needs direct, often rapid, stimulation.	You need indirect stimulation, that touches, moves away, and returns.
His sensations and ultimate satisfaction are focused on his penis.	You feel arousal throughout your body.
He climaxes most easily from the enclosing warm moisture of penetration or oral sex.	You need penetration and oral sex as part of a wider repertoire.
His orgasm is usually reliable and straightforward.	Yours is more subtle, variable, and sometimes unreliable.
His orgasm is the end of arousal for a while.	Your orgasm can be simply the beginning.

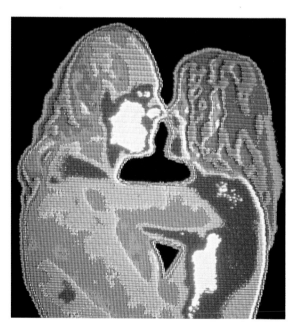

YOUR BODY HEAT *rises as you become aroused. In the image both faces and her upper body (shown red) have already responded. As arousal increases, heat builds up in the lips, breasts, and genitals. Other signs include a sex flush, sweating, rise in heart rate and blood pressure, tension in the muscles and nerves, an open mouth, full lips, and a change in voice tone. In women, the nipples harden, clitoris hardens and swells, the vagina lubricates, and its outer lips draw apart. In men, the penis hardens and swells, the testicles rise, and nipples swell.*

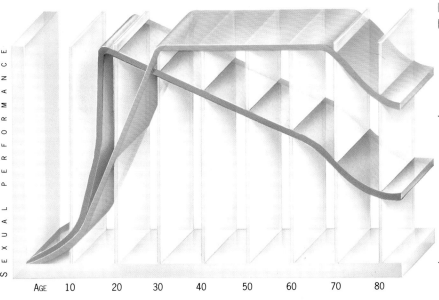

Female
Male

THE PEAK OF SEXUAL PERFORMANCE *in men typically occurs in their late teens, after which they may find it progressively more difficult to get an erection and ejaculate. Even so, a third of men in their eighties are making love as often as before. Your sexual capacity, which is based more on learning than on sheer physical reaction, builds until your thirties, then plateaus rather than dips. Your desire may wax and wane because of fluctuating hormones, but you may have the same orgasmic potential at 80 as at 60.*

PATTERNS OF AROUSAL

Male response
Typical female response
When she is quickly aroused
When she has multiple orgasms
When she doesn't reach orgasm

TYPICALLY, A MAN'S *sexual pattern features fast arousal, which leads quickly to the peak of orgasm, followed by a sharp de-arousal. You are typically more slowly aroused than he is but your pattern may vary more. Sometimes you will reach orgasm fairly quickly,* followed by swift (yellow) or slower de-arousal (green), and at other times you may have multiple orgasms (pale green). Or you may become aroused but not reach orgasm (red), either struggling to reach the plateau or reaching it but then hovering there without resolution.

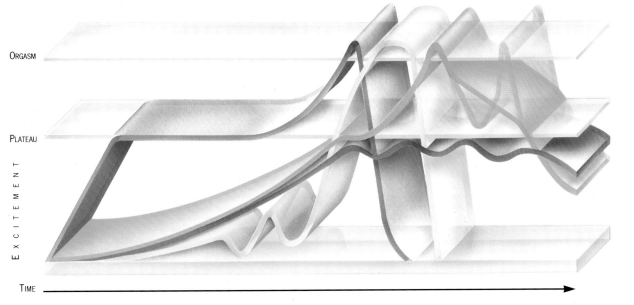

ORGASM

PLATEAU

EXCITEMENT

TIME

SEX ZONES

THE BODY AREAS WHERE TOUCH IS MOST AROUSING

Erogenous zones have something of a reputation as "magic buttons." We tend to think that, once pressed, they will excite no matter what. But as with all things sexual, mood is everything—the most erogenous of zones remain unresponsive when we are tired, anxious, or in a bad mood.

Primary erogenous zones are responsive because of their physiological structure. They are abundantly endowed with nerve endings and, when touched, engorge with blood and swell slightly, becoming extremely sensitive. They also expand to give more surface area to be pleasured. Genitals are obvious primary zones—but so are many areas on the body's periphery such as lips and ear lobes. In particular,

any part where a dry area of the body meets a moist area is likely to be a primary erogenous zone.

Secondary erogenous zones are sensitive because of their mental or emotional associations. These can sometimes be quite unconscious and are often unexpected; sex researchers Masters and Johnson found some women who orgasmed when a partner simply rubbed the small of their back. Women—whose nervous systems are more influenced by the part of the brain governing the emotions than men—have far more secondary erogenous zones than they do: areas that are sensitive because a past lover adored them, because they were the focus of an erotic book or video, or because they feature largely in a personal fantasy.

IN A WOMAN *the breasts, especially the nipples; inner thighs; perineum (between the vagina and anus); clitoris and buttocks are obvious erogenous zones. In addition, some women are aroused by touching of the ears, particularly the lobes; mouth, lips, and tongue; neck; navel; armpits; face, especially the forehead, temples, eyebrows, and eyelids; insides of elbows and backs of knees; and the small of the back.*

IN A MAN (right) *the genitals are the most obvious erogenous zone, but the following are particularly sensitive: the area just behind the root of the penis; the area between the penis and anus; the anus itself; testicles; the glans and the frenulum. For him other potentially erogenous zones include the shoulders; palms of the hands; top of the back and base of the spine; chest; and mouth, lips, and tongue.*

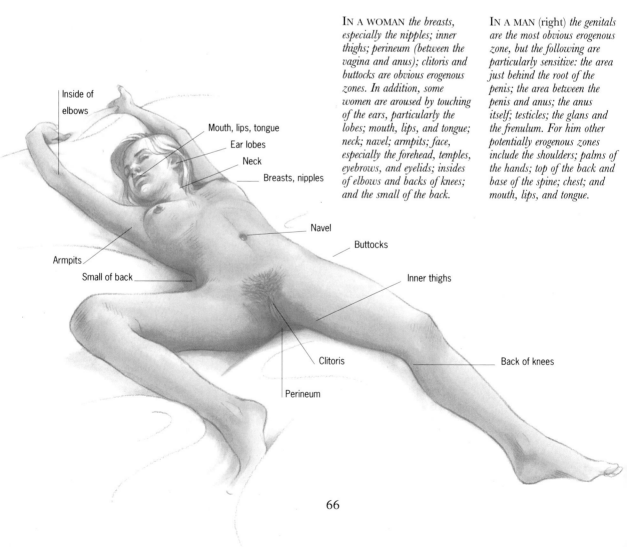

Inside of elbows

Mouth, lips, tongue

Ear lobes

Neck

Breasts, nipples

Navel

Buttocks

Armpits

Small of back

Inner thighs

Clitoris

Back of knees

Perineum

| CHARTING YOUR SEXUAL SELF | **52–53** |
| KNOWING HIM | **62–63** |

TRACING
EROGENOUS ZONES

You may find it interesting—and arousing—to identify where you and your partner are particularly sensitive. Begin by "tracing" your own zones, perhaps while masturbating or by taking the time to explore yourself. Gently and slowly touch those parts of your body you can reach, and start to get a sense of what works and what doesn't. You may discover and want to communicate to your partner, for example, that one side of your clitoris is more sensitive than the other, or that stroking the soles of your feet tickles at first, but is then arousing.

To do this with a partner, set the ground rules first: a sensuous atmosphere; any no-go areas; no lovemaking until you've both finished. Then take it in turns to lie down, relax, and be explored. When you are the toucher, use your hands slowly and methodically over your partner's body, experiment with different kinds of touch, and don't miss any area, however unlikely it may seem. Encourage your partner to respond in a way that shows what he or she is experiencing and to what extent—giving each body area a murmured "mark" out of ten is one approach.

Repeat this at regular intervals. Erogenous zones change, particularly at different times of the month.

YOUR MOUTH *is designed for arousal. It is a primary erogenous zone—the sensory area of the brain that receives input from the lips and mouth is enormous compared with that of almost any other part of the body. When you kiss, your lips engorge with blood, the nerves become extremely sensitive and the surrounding sebaceous glands produce* chemicals *that signal arousal. Your mouth is also a secondary erogenous zone. Years of feeding have taught you that this is a part of your body that gives you pleasure. You have only to see something arousing to automatically open your mouth slightly and you may even unconsciously lick your lips, as if you were preparing for a kiss.*

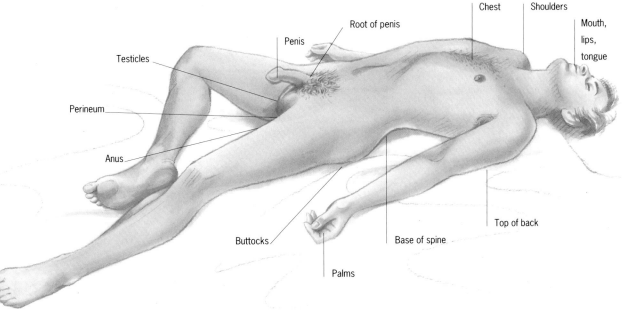

TOUCHING AND KISSING
THE IMPORTANCE OF SENSUALITY

Few women are ever touched and kissed enough. Of course, sometimes we like pure "quickies," particularly at the start of a relationship when the hormones are overflowing. But as a prelude to sex, or as a daily "fix" between one sex session and the next, we like to make physical contact in a far less focused way than by simply heading straight for the genitals.

We love being touched by hands, lips, and any other part of a partner's body. We love being kissed almost anywhere. We love to snuggle in private. We may even love to cuddle in public, overtly pushing conventional barriers and daring to kiss a little more passionately or touch that bit more audaciously.

For most of us, sex is wonderful and orgasms are amazing. But more than one piece of research has shown that if asked to choose between cuddles and orgasms for the rest of our lives, 90 percent of us would choose the sensuality rather than the raw sex.

How and where to touch

Touch is the most compelling human communication. It calms babies when they can't understand what is being said and controls children when they misbehave. So to adults, touch may not only be arousing, it can also be reassuring, calming, loving— and sometimes even a little worrying or alarming. It's important, even with a long-term partner, to go carefully, taking a lead from him (or her) as to where it is good to touch, moving from less erotic to more erotic; beginning with light touches then making them more urgent; and moving from comforting strokes or pats to more playful tickling or pummeling only when you have built a level of trust together.

What kissing means

When kissing, we offer our mouths and receive a partner's mouth in return. In addition to being a wonderful gesture of trust, it allows us to gather information, to find out more about a partner through smelling odor, tasting saliva, feeling warm breath. Again, it's important to be guided by what your partner seems to like, holding back from too much passion until you have built a level of confidence and, equally, not letting yourself be pushed farther than you want to go. Use your tongue when you are sure that that is what you both want. Then move from soft to harder, dry to moister, shallower to deeper kissing. And only then begin to experiment gradually with lips, teeth, and tongue— nibbling, biting, sucking, licking, and blowing.

Case history

"The best sex I've ever had didn't involve intercourse at all. He was much younger than me, only nineteen, and a virgin; I told him from the start that I was engaged back home. But the first night, we were down on the beach and he asked me if he could see me undressed, because he'd never seen a woman naked before. So I stood in front of him, kept looking at him, and took my clothes off one by one. He stood there mesmerized, then he stretched his hand out. I pulled back, but he said 'I just want to touch.' And, would you believe, for four consecutive nights, we just lay in the sand, and he ran his hands over me, so lightly I could hardly feel them. It was like being made love to by feathers, or the wind, or the sea."

CHARMAINE

UNDRESSING for the first time can be a crucial point in intimacy. You may both feel insecure about your appearance: women typically worry about breast and stomach size, men about chest and penis size and firmness of erection.

• Avoid a gap between dressed and undressed; keep touching and kissing to focus on arousal rather than nudity.

• Act particularly lovingly if a worried look suggests that your partner may be insecure.

• If you are concerned about something like a scar, mention it early to avoid tension.

AS THE RELATIONSHIP develops, you may want to make undressing more playful or even risky.

• Taking only some clothes off, or having one of you dressed while the other is undressed, creates an interesting interplay between skin and material.

• Undressing each other fully from head to foot can make you both feel nurtured and cared for.

• Playing the stripper to arouse each other may take on an air of the forbidden, which often tends to make undressing more erotic and exciting.

PLEASURING A WOMAN
BRINGING A WOMAN TO ORGASM BY HAND OR MOUTH

There are some women who do not like being pleasured, that is, having a partner stimulate their genitals with the hand or tongue, or both. We may have ethical objections, be wary of having our genitals touched at all, or think our partners resent pleasuring us—even though studies show that they typically love both the experience and seeing us overwhelmingly aroused.

But most of us love it. It gives us unpredictable and uncontrollable sensations that no other kind of lovemaking achieves and is often a guaranteed way to orgasm. Perhaps the crux, however, is that being pleasured represents time for us. As women brought up to focus outward and to others, we often find it

difficult to let go and focus inward on ourselves. It is hard to let others give to us without feeling guilty that we are not giving something back. Being pleasured lets us do this. For a while, we are the center of attention and our partner's emotional focus, and can concentrate on feeling good and nothing else.

If you pleasure a woman by hand—or want to give a partner advice on pleasuring you—these guidelines may help.

TEACHING A PARTNER

A partner may be happy to pleasure you. But he (or she) may not know how. A man may base his responses on his own preferences and will need re-education. Offering this will let a partner give you far more pleasure in the long run—surely what you both want.

● Most partners' typical mistake is stopping too soon—men in particular are guilty here. Reassure both of you, as you ask for more time, that the average woman can take up to 10 times as long as the average man to climax through foreplay.

● Variation is important. What feels right one day (or one minute) can feel wrong the next. If you don't like giving constant redirection, remember that it often takes several sessions for a partner to learn your preferences.

● Many partners go too hard, too fast, with too much urgency and too regularly, above all as you get aroused. Ask him to hold back if he starts this sort of treatment; reassure him that you like it, but need things gentle. Otherwise you will never climax, will be sore the next day, and will be wary of masturbation in future.

• Start with the least erogenous zones and work inward.

• Customize your fondling of breasts and nipples; some women get nothing from breast stimulation, others orgasm; some like it soft, others hard.

• When moving to genitals, don't head straight for the clitoris. Use your hand to close her outer lips, then massage directly.

• The clitoris gets sensitive (above), particularly once the hood moves back. Use plenty of lubrication—saliva, baby oil, or her own fluid transferred with a finger from her vagina.

• "Something in the vagina" gives a feeling of fullness, but many women dislike it. Don't use anything that might get stuck — clean fingers with trimmed nails are best (above). Try shallow penetration toward her stomach, hitting her G spot, or slide right in and gently nudge her cervix.

• What she needs at orgasm may vary, so be prepared to switch movements as she comes.

• She may want to be cuddled afterward, however briefly.

GIVING ORAL SEX TO A WOMAN

STIMULATION FROM A TONGUE *has several advantages, offering warmth, softness, and good lubrication. You'll need to have built a level of trust beforehand, because your partner may be worried about how she smells; wash together first if necessary. Don't bite, suck hard, or give oral sex if you have a cold sore that could infect her. Never blow air into her vagina as this can cause an air embolism, which can kill.*

• *Lick her labia, back and forth, to lubricate her and make her receptive.*

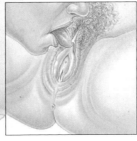

• *Try licking or sucking her clitoris, using a firm or soft tongue; use a downward movement from root to tip, or a flicking movement from side to side.*

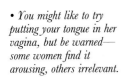

• *You might like to try putting your tongue in her vagina, but be warned— some women find it arousing, others irrelevant.*

• *Her perineum, between her vagina and anus, can be very sensitive – but don't put your tongue in her anus and then lick her other genitals, or you may transfer infection. When she comes, be careful; she could arch her pelvis upward— painfully—into your face.*

PLEASURING A MAN

USING HAND AND MOUTH TO BRING A MAN TO ORGASM

Men luxuriate in being pleasured for all the same sensual reasons as women. And, just as we can relax into not having to give, a man can relax into not having to perform. He can allow us to take control and assume responsibility.

Why then, are women typically less generous in this matter than men? Some of us perform manual and oral sex; many of us offer the latter in particular as a sign of love and a gift of passion. But we can also act shy, finding the whole issue a little off-putting, or just too difficult. Admittedly, if our oral pleasuring is successful, we will end up with seminal fluid in the mouth. But perhaps our unwillingness lies a little deeper. When we stimulate our partner by hand or mouth, we take charge; if he doesn't enjoy it, it is our fault. We may not feel altogether confident of our skills—if we do, however, we are much more likely to perform oral or manual sex and enjoy it.

If we can build confidence in our own skills, we can begin to change. By starting to enjoy giving pleasure to a partner, we may also begin to revel in learning how to do it well. We can reach a stage where we are proud of our skills in bed, as well as our sexual power and achievement in creating intense pleasure for a partner.

GIVING ORAL SEX TO A MAN

Oral sex is his chance to relax and simply not try. Your tongue is soft, warm, and lubricated; your mouth contains the same kind of moist membranes as your vagina; and your mouth muscles offer varied pressure and movement.

● Your main block to giving good oral sex may be a natural "gagging reflex," triggered by the pressure of the penis against the back of your throat. The way around this is to make sure you control the depth of penetration. Lie him on his back so he can't suddenly thrust into you; start off with shallow penetration; and gradually relax your throat muscles as you allow him in deeper.

● The glans is the most sensitive area; try kissing the tip, or flicking your tongue across the frenulum.

● The most direct way to arouse is to plunge the penis in and out of your mouth, with added help from your hand to provide friction. Try giving the frenulum extra pressure by pressing your tongue into it with each thrust.

● Nibbling the penis itself can be arousing, but don't bite the glans. Cover your teeth with your lips when plunging, particularly if you're aroused to the point of losing control.

USE YOUR TONGUE *to lick his penis, or nibble it gently.*

PAY PARTICULAR ATTENTION *to the highly sensitive glans and frenulum.*

MOVE HIS PENIS *into and out of your mouth, as deeply as feels comfortable.*

PLEASURING A MAN BY HAND

What you think he likes may not be what he actually does like. We often fall into the trap of being too slow, too gentle, or too indirect. If possible, get him to show you what he does—then follow his lead.

● Experiment with different ways of holding his penis: with both hands, one hand, just a few fingers, with your saliva-wetted palm cupping the glans.

● If he's uncircumcised, check whether he wants his foreskin held forward or back.

● Try cupping or stroking his testicles with one hand. Don't squeeze because that can be incredibly painful; for the same reason, it is wise to let go as you (or he) start to get really aroused.

● Most men like up-and-down movement, but preferences about speed and rhythm differ; start slowly, add some variety into what you do, and ask for feedback.

● What he likes will probably change as he reaches a climax; he may want you to stop as he starts to orgasm or carry on until he has come.

● After orgasm, he will be very sensitive, so if you keep holding him, steer clear of the glans.

LETTING HIM COME IN YOUR MOUTH?

Many women like swallowing a man's semen. They like its taste and feel and the sense of intimacy. Objectively, the only reason not to is if he has an infection. If that is the case, you should use a condom for oral sex, anyway, for your own protection.

But just as many women hate swallowing semen. They hate the taste, loathe the sensation, and feel it is an intrusion of the worst kind.

If you don't like it, get him to warn you when he's coming or learn to read the signs—the penis rising and becoming even harder; his breathing changing; the head of the penis darkening; a few drops of warning fluid seeping out. Remove his penis from your mouth, continue pleasuring with your hand, and let the seminal fluid slide onto his stomach or into a tissue. If you are subtle enough, he may not even notice.

MANY MEN LIKE *a firm up-and-down movement along the length of the shaft.*

STROKING, *cupping, or gently squeezing his testicles can also be arousing.*

USE AS MANY FINGERS *as feels comfortable and vary both speed and rhythm.*

THE AREA *at the base of the penis is particularly sensitive, so stroke or fondle that, too.*

ON TO PENETRATION

SIGNALING YOUR READINESS FOR INTERCOURSE

For most heterosexual women, intercourse is the ultimate sexual experience, but it is not the peak of physical sensation: masturbation and oral sex can give us as much raw pleasure, sometimes more reliably.

Intercourse is unique in that it is about closeness: a partner inside us, moving as one, feeling him ejaculate. The emotional experience is one of unity, as we together perform a unique and binding act. And so, while sex in general may be fun and wild, intercourse sometimes fills us with awe. In this we agree with men. They see intercourse as being "the real thing" because for them it is the most natural and direct way to reach a physical climax. We see intercourse as being the "the real thing" because for us it is the most natural and direct way to reach an emotional peak.

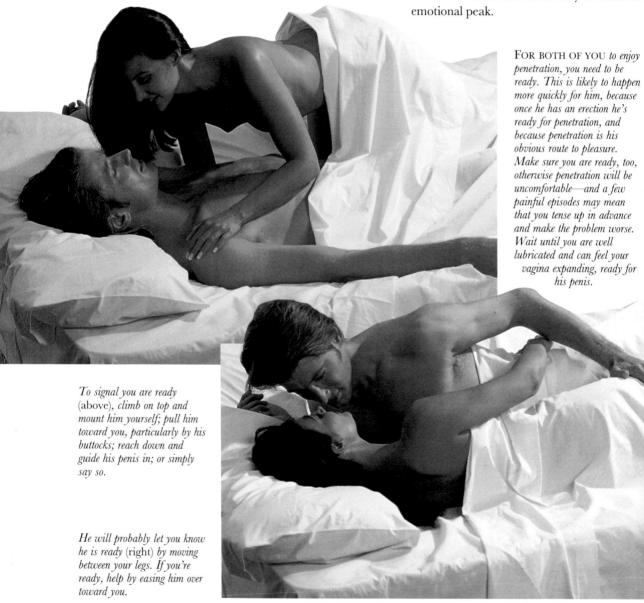

FOR BOTH OF YOU to enjoy penetration, you need to be ready. This is likely to happen more quickly for him, because once he has an erection he's ready for penetration, and because penetration is his obvious route to pleasure. Make sure you are ready, too, otherwise penetration will be uncomfortable—and a few painful episodes may mean that you tense up in advance and make the problem worse. Wait until you are well lubricated and can feel your vagina expanding, ready for his penis.

To signal you are ready (above), climb on top and mount him yourself; pull him toward you, particularly by his buttocks; reach down and guide his penis in; or simply say so.

He will probably let you know he is ready (right) by moving between your legs. If you're ready, help by easing him over toward you.

Case history

"I like everything in sex. But there is nothing to beat that moment when a man goes inside me, that 'aah' when he slides into me, and we both sigh. With a new lover, it is always a turning point; I'll often do everything else for several dates, until I'm sure that intercourse is what I want, because it is so special. I feel we are really communicating, picking up signals from each other, moving together. Then, I love him coming in me, that rush of liquid that hits right inside me. I always feel much more in love with someone after we've had intercourse, even if things have been going wrong beforehand. And I always feel appalled if he rejects me afterward. How could he, after what we've just done together?"

YVON

If you need to slow him down, pull back and make eye contact, or deflect his penis with your hand or mouth. To speed yourself up, add lubrication to your vagina with saliva or KY jelly, or ask him to pay more attention to your genitals.

MOVEMENT, SPEED, AND RHYTHM

There are so many variations in lovemaking that it's worth finding out what you like most, and guiding a partner toward it.

● There are two main types of movement: thrusting, when a partner moves in and out; and grinding, when he moves his pelvis in a circular motion. To encourage a shift from one to the other, use your hands on his thighs, or buttocks, moving him in the way you want.

● Different speeds evoke different sensations. Fast, when you are in the plateau phase, can tip you into orgasm—but won't be so good early on when too much pumping can leave you dry. To alter the pace, use your hands, thighs, and body to join him at his rate, then gradually slow or speed up until you are comfortable.

● Most men prefer a regular rhythm. But right after penetration, you may need to stop and start because too regular a sensation can numb the nerves. It's difficult to alter a man's rhythm with body movements; if you bring him to a stop, he may complain. Describe to him the advanced Eastern technique of pausing fractionally during intercourse to introduce an element of surprise, and persuade him to try it out in your lovemaking.

SEXUAL POSITIONS
CHOOSING A POSITION THAT FEELS RIGHT FOR INTERCOURSE

Positions mean different things for women and men. For men, whose focus of arousal is in the penis, a change of position brings a whole new sensation—in the penis. A new angle brings a different type of turn on, often focused on those few inches only. For women, a shift of position gives a changed relationship. Of course we enjoy the different sensations that a twist of the body or new stimulation against the wall of the vagina give. In particular, we

like differences in depth, as one position lets the penis just nudge against the entrance, while another allows it to plunge right inside.

But position for women is far more about connection. We love the missionary position because it gives a face-to-face view. Being side to side allows lots of body contact. One position is favored because it makes us feel close to our partner, and another hated for making us feel used.

So for many women, constant shifts of position are an unnecessary extra. Lovers who want to impress us with their advanced technique may shift position with every thrust. But women tend to prefer one or two favorites, positions that typically allow us to feel close, bonded, loved, and that reflect not a love of sensation, but a need for connection.

FOR DEEPER PENETRATION when you are in the missionary position, stretch your legs up and rest your calves on his shoulders (left). For greater stimulation, clasp your feet around his neck.

THE MISSIONARY POSITION (above) *is so traditional that some of us feel apologetic for liking it. It does make it difficult to feel in control, as he is literally on top, setting the pace. It also blocks any direct touching of the clitoris and makes it likely that he will climax quickly. But it's also a very intimate position: you can see and kiss each other, and run your hands over his body. It gives you support for your back and* *can also provide clitoral stimulation if he stretches your genitals on the way in and out. You can also try closing your legs so that his penis is "caught" in your vagina, for added stimulation.*

WOMAN ON TOP *is a favorite for many women, but it won't work if you are wary of being looked at or of taking the lead in sex. If you can overcome these feelings, though, it has many advantages. You can set the pace and the depth of penetration, get extra stimulation on your clitoris, and allow him to lie back and relax. You are face to face, able to touch and stroke each other, and can take things slowly, which is useful if he sometimes can't keep control. Try altering your angle by leaning back or forward, lying down with your legs bent underneath you, or turning around and doing it all with your back to him.*

CHANGING POSITION

The right position simply feels good. It is relaxed—or full of arousing tension—but never uncomfortable. But most intercourse positions sometimes become "wrong" for a variety of reasons: you start to feel uncomfortable; sensation fades; you need more or less depth; you need more or less friction; you become sure you won't climax; he gets too aroused too soon.

If you want to change, think ahead. Work out as few moves as possible to get you both from the position you are in to the one you want to be in. Then signal the change to him by interrupting the flow, stopping movement, then murmuring directions. To keep penetration intact as you move, pull his buttocks toward you with your hands, or wind one leg around his waist to make sure he doesn't slip out.

If he suddenly stops absolutely still, it usually means not that he wants to change position, but that he is about to climax. Stop moving, too, unless you are ready for him to do so.

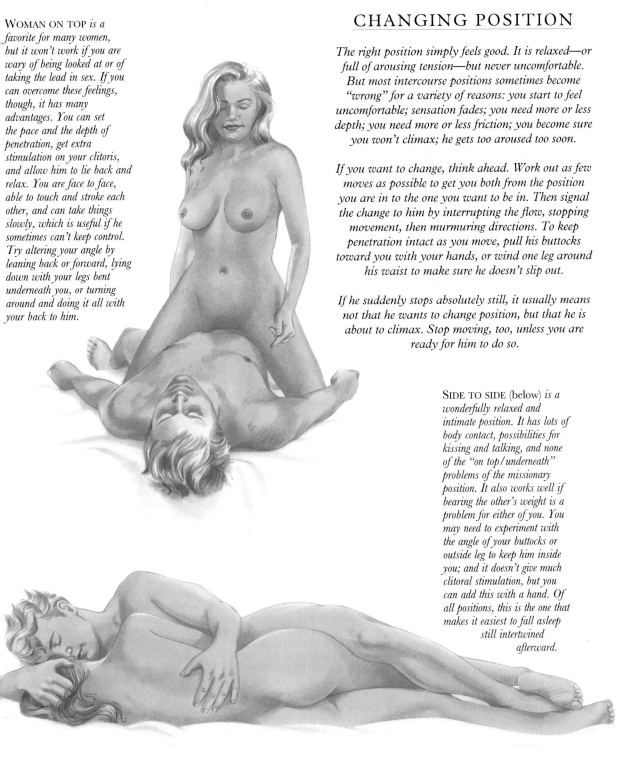

SIDE TO SIDE *(below) is a wonderfully relaxed and intimate position. It has lots of body contact, possibilities for kissing and talking, and none of the "on top/underneath" problems of the missionary position. It also works well if bearing the other's weight is a problem for either of you. You may need to experiment with the angle of your buttocks or outside leg to keep him inside you; and it doesn't give much clitoral stimulation, but you can add this with a hand. Of all positions, this is the one that makes it easiest to fall asleep still intertwined afterward.*

USING THE CLITORIS
THE IMPORTANCE OF CLITORAL STIMULATION IN FEMALE ORGASM

When a man wants to climax, he reaches for his penis, the main pleasure organ of his body. A woman's "penis equivalent" is the clitoris, her principal pleasure organ. There is some debate about whether all female orgasms are due to clitoral stimulation, but most of us do get our orgasms like that—either directly, or because we have intercourse in a way that stimulates the clitoris indirectly.

Because intercourse—penis into vagina—is the best way to make babies, for thousands of years it has also been assumed that it's

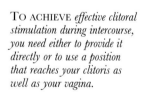

the best way to ensure orgasms. That, after all, is true for men. But the clitoris is nowhere near the vagina, and so for many women, penis into vagina is not the most obvious way to climax. Yet, even now, many of us still think that we are wrong if we don't climax through thrusting alone. And men can still sometimes accuse us of frigidity if we don't.

The fact is that, physically, women are much more likely to climax through clitoral stimulation. And this has two implications. First, there is no need for any woman to feel inadequate if she cannot reach orgasm through penetration. And second, for the many women who find orgasm difficult, the realization that this is almost certainly not due to neurosis or immaturity, but to a simple misunderstanding of physiology, may well be the most important sexual realization of their lives.

TO ACHIEVE *effective clitoral stimulation during intercourse, you need either to provide it directly or to use a position that reaches your clitoris as well as your vagina.*

• Direct stimulation has to be done by hand, either yours or his. The secret here is that the more space between you during intercourse, the better. So in the missionary position, it is possible but squashed. With woman on top (right), or facing each other with your legs entwined (center right), it is extremely easy for either of you.

• Other positions, such as rear entry or any of the variations on the starfish in which your legs are entwined, allow him to help (above), or you to stimulate yourself discreetly (far right) if you are not comfortable being obvious.

• The best intercourse position for getting clitoral stimulation without hand help is the missionary, though you may need to experiment until you get the angle right. If he pushes his body above you by resting on his elbows, or rests his weight on you, it may press the right spot.

CLITORIS OR PENIS?

The clitoris is your only body part devoted entirely to pleasure. It develops in the womb from the same organ from which the penis develops if a fetus is male. As a result, the clitoris parallels the structure of a man's penis, the tip of a huge pelvic system of nerves, muscles, and blood vessels. When touched, the clitoris too fills with blood and becomes erect, the tip pulling back from the hood and emerging like a glans from its foreskin. And, just as stimulating the penis results in climax, so stimulating the clitoris fills your whole pelvic region with waves of sensation.

INVOLVING A PARTNER

If you are worried about your partner's possible response to including clitoral stimulation as part of intercourse, try any of these "solutions."

● You can stimulate yourself without explanation to your partner. You'll need to be fairly secure in your ability to arouse yourself and make sure you can always reach your clitoris easily.

● Try to encourage your partner to give you stimulation without explanation. Give a clear positive response every time he accidentally touches your clitoris during penetration, so guiding him to do so deliberately. This may take time, and feel a little like dog-training, but may work if your partner feels threatened by direct requests.

● With a partner who can handle such requests, point out that your clitoris is the equivalent of his penis—he wouldn't expect to climax if you just squeezed his balls! Then experiment: when it feels good, make it really clear how much it turns you on.

• Alternatively, try positions that stretch your outer genitals and so stimulate your clitoris. In particular, experiment with shifting the position of your legs as he moves, perhaps by putting your knees down on the bed or using a pillow under your buttocks to push your bottom up toward the ceiling.

ORGASM

WHEN WE EXPERIENCE THE ULTIMATE SEXUAL SENSATION

As arousal peaks during lovemaking, and you pass the excitement and plateau stages, increased blood flow to your genitals draws them apart. The entrance to the vagina swells as if to clasp the penis. You move into orgasm.

Contractions—typically between 3 and 15 starting at 0.8-second intervals—spread from the circle of muscle near your spine and around your rectum, through your lower abdomen and womb, into your vagina. Your clitoris, breasts, nipples, and areolae swell, your heart can beat up to 150 times a minute and your breathing can reach 40 times a minute. Some women even spurt clear fluid—similar to a man's seminal fluid—from the G spot in the vagina.

In sex, orgasm is the ultimate high. Yet female orgasms are in danger of becoming the equivalent of the male erection. If we don't have one every time, our partner can feel a failure; if we never have one, we can feel invalid. We must defend our right not to orgasm: to take our time; to enjoy cuddles; to claim our identity as sexual women even if we've never climaxed.

At the same time, it would be foolish to say that it doesn't matter if a woman who wants to orgasm isn't doing so. Given a chance to explore, masturbate, and experiment with clitoral stimulation, we should claim the right to find our way to easy, reliable orgasms.

DIFFERENT CLIMAXES?

● Freud identified two orgasms: those triggered by stimulation of the clitoris and those triggered by the penis in the vagina. By the 1970s, sex researchers Masters and Johnson said all orgasms were triggered by clitoral stimulation, either directly or indirectly by the pressure of a thrusting penis. Women themselves now claim several different kinds of climax—most clitoral, some through pressure on the G spot or pressure on the cervix by finger or penis.

● Is there a "best" orgasm? Freud favored intercourse orgasms as the sign of love, saying clitoral ones were "immature." Masters and Johnson reassured women that clitoral orgasms were physiologically normal. Nowadays, even though lesbian relationships show that true intimacy does not have to involve intercourse, we far too often assume that only penetrative orgasms are "the real thing."

● In fact, all orgasms are the real thing. It doesn't matter how you climax, as long as you do and you enjoy it.

WHY FEMALE ORGASM?

It is obvious why, in evolutionary terms, a man has orgasms. A climax pushes sperm out of his body for fertilization. But it has never been as clear for women. Is it a biological mistake? A way to keep us with our partners and so provide a stable situation for childrearing? Or a way to keep us flat on our back and make it more likely that sperm won't drip out of the vagina?

New research suggests that female orgasm, like male climax, also helps fertilization. In addition to ballooning the vagina, allowing sperm to reach the cervix, orgasm tilts the cervix, causing it to dip into the seminal fluid with each contraction, thereby helping the sperm up into the womb.

Case history

"Alone, I bring myself off very quickly. With my husband, it's slow and intense. Because it's someone else doing things to me, there isn't the control—but there's an immense sense of excitement. If he uses his fingers, then I feel stretched, like a piece of elastic, until I suddenly snap, quickly, sharply, almost painfully. If it's his tongue, that's more gentle—he can keep me there for hours, and when I do come, it's almost like melting. If he's inside me, it's very deep, as if the whole of my insides are exploding. However I come, I always yell and yell!"

TANYA

AND AFTER

THE PHYSICAL AND EMOTIONAL AFTERMATH OF SEX

For many women, the end of sex is only the midpoint of lovemaking. Because we often put physical contact into the context of a relationship, the moments after sex itself may well be some of the best moments of the whole experience.

Sometimes we feel physically fragile, needing to protect our bodies in general and our sexual parts in particular. At others we are invigorated and more than ready to be aroused again. We typically feel emotionally close to our partner and eager for some further sign of that closeness through face-to-face contact, talking, and cuddling. We do need support, even reassurance; we may want to be held and nurtured; we may want to be listened to or talked to.

IT'S GOOD *if you and your partner react similarly after lovemaking, whether that is wanting to move, sleep, or talk. But you may have different needs. Having manufactured and expelled all those sperm, a man will probably need to rest. Sleep hormones affect men much sooner than they do women, so if your partner is male, he may want to doze for a while. But some, usually younger, men have a rush of energy and want to get up and keep moving or have sex again.*

• If your partner is active and you want to talk or snuggle, suggest a bath or meal after sex, so that he (or she) can be busy and you get your wish to spend more time together.

• If he usually gets sleepy and you want to move around, try changing your routine to morning lovemaking, when he is less likely to need rest afterward.

• If he gets dozy and you want to talk, curl up with him, try to have at least a few words, then wait until he wakes up for more conversation.

If we cannot get this because our partner is unwilling or unable to add the extra dimension, the physical pleasure begins to drain away sooner rather than later, and the event may start to lose its magic. But if we can get what we need emotionally as well as sexually from our partner, then the whole experience becomes rounded, complete, and fulfilling.

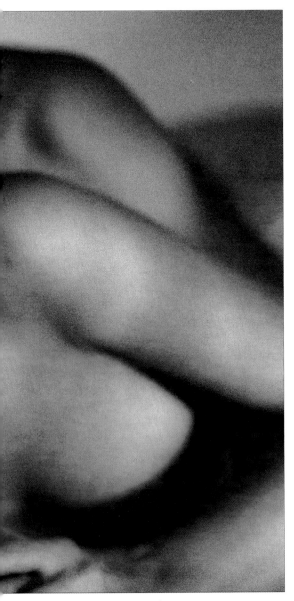

IF YOU HAVEN'T CLIMAXED

If a man doesn't reach orgasm, he may have what is sometimes known as "blue balls." Blood swelling the pelvic tissues does not flow away, causing a throbbing ache. Women feel this, too, in the vagina and clitoris. It is uncomfortable, but if left to itself your body will return to normal. But what if you want to come as well?

It is obviously unfair to insist aggressively that a partner brings you to climax if you don't get there by the time he (or she) does. But it is more than fair to ask for some support; even the sleepiest partner can cuddle you while you bring yourself to orgasm. This may get him aroused again, and he may start joining in. Or once you have climaxed, you can fall asleep in each other's arms.

If all else fails, you do have the option of leaving the bedroom to orgasm elsewhere while your partner recovers—though in all honesty, most women find this at best a compromise.

RESOLUTION STAGE FOR WOMEN

Once your orgasm is over, blood starts to flow back from the aroused areas and your body returns to normal—or almost normal.

● Five to ten seconds after orgasm, your vagina, womb, and labia start shrinking to their normal size. Your clitoris returns to its normal position and your labia minora to their usual color.

● Five minutes after orgasm, the tension in your muscles has faded, and blood pressure, heart rate, and respiration have returned to normal. Your nipples and areolae start to return to their usual size.

● Up to half an hour after orgasm, the cervix remains open to receive sperm. The head of your clitoris resumes its normal size, although if you have just failed to reach orgasm it can stay erect for several hours, presumably in hope!

While you may be uncomfortably sensitive, particularly around your clitoris, it is possible for you to have another orgasm almost as soon as you want.

4 SEX IN RELATIONSHIPS

A CASUAL OBSERVER OF TODAY'S POPULAR media might conclude that sex has become an issue independent from relationships. The headlines shriek of casual sex and orgies, while spiritual leaders bemoan declining family values and ever-rising divorce figures.

In fact, the issue of satisfying sex within the context of a relationship is probably being taken more seriously now than ever. In the distant past, pleasurable sex and marriage were often regarded as unconnected—sex was for procreation and not much more. But once women could have sex without fear of pregnancy, sex was often approached as if it was solely for pleasure, with little or no emphasis on commitment or relationships.

Now that unprotected sex has again become risky, neither procreation nor pleasure alone is good enough. Women are thinking, analyzing, and worrying about intimate relationships more than ever before: at least 70 percent of the subject matter in areas of the media aimed at women is occupied by questions on relationships and sexuality. As changing economic and social factors make us less likely to stay in failed or failing relationships, we place increasing emphasis on achieving an ideal partnership, based on shared interests and lifestyle, and sexual empathy. In theory, at least, such an ideal is more achievable now than at any time in the past, with the result that most of us are refusing to settle for less than a fulfilling sexual dimension within a satisfying relationship.

TODAY'S WOMEN *no longer simply want a provider for themselves and their families, or a compatible sexual partner to the exclusion of emotional stability. We may insist on having pleasure, but we are now more certain that long-term pleasure is best had when sex is part of a relationship, and we often end liaisons if there is no real compatibility.*

CHOOSING A PARTNER

WHAT ATTRACTS YOU TO NEW POTENTIAL PARTNERS?

In sex, we are told, good looks are what count. "Gentlemen prefer blondes...handsome men get the girls"—and the message is that only the beautiful deserve sex, and only the good-looking ever get it. In fact, that is not true: looks turn people on, but they are only the starting point for choosing a sexual mate.

When meeting someone new, both men and women make an initial judgment within seconds. Everyone is possible, until we start to eliminate. Admittedly, we do rule out first those whose looks don't attract us or those outside our preferred age or weight range, for example. But we also eliminate over-attractive people, preferring those of similar looks to our own.

When we first see someone attractive, we simply glance at them. Then we glance away, then look more closely. A woman scans from face to body to face; a man usually concentrates much more on the body—which may account for the impression that men are more interested in body than mind.

Then we start to scan the face more closely (see illustration right). A normal scan lasts about three seconds, but if we are particularly fascinated, this may stretch to five seconds, alerting the other person to our interest. If we go on to gaze at other people, however, the original target may shift from feeling flattered to feeling rejected.

Then, as we talk, we judge further on personality. We each have a personal template, created throughout our lives, of the sort of character we are attracted to: fun-loving or serious, relaxed or dynamic. If a possible partner does not fit that template, we eliminate him (or her); we need to feel at ease with someone before moving on to make love.

We then start sending interest signals. Of course, if the other person has already mentally crossed us off his own list, there won't be any response. But if he approves, we'll begin to use conversation to explore attitudes; use body language to check whether he behaves—and even smells—right; perhaps even use references to sex to test openmindedness.

Certainly, conventional attractiveness matters—good-lookers stay on the "yes" lists of more people for longer—but both women and men make sexual choices on far more subtle criteria than looks alone.

DOES SEXY DRESSING ATTRACT?

Some body parts quite simply arouse on sight. Breasts, buttocks, legs—the more a woman reveals, the more she turns men on. So a low-cut dress, tight jeans, minuscule skirt, or bright lipstick will certainly get attention.

But each gender interprets that kind of dressing differently. Women rarely see it as sexual encouragement; attention is all they want until they have got to know a partner. Unfortunately, some men think it's a direct invitation to instant sex—then either get irritated when it's not or steer clear of what they interpret as over-availability.

However you dress, you shouldn't be subjected to comments or actions you don't want. But the sad reality is that too sexual an image may lead to unwelcome attention.

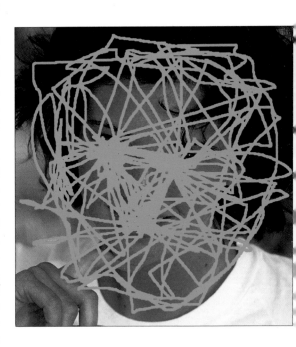

WHEN YOU LOOK *at a new potential partner, your eyes trace a pattern of movements over his (or her) face. The white lines indicate a typical pattern. Although your eyes* cover his whole face, 75 percent of your attention is focused on the eyes and mouth since these are the parts that you search for clues to his personality and character.

YOUR SEXUAL MIND   **42–43**
SEXUAL COMMUNICATION   **94–95**

MYTH AND REALITY IN CHOOSING A PARTNER

What do men (or women) ideally want in a sex partner? Both genders have their suspicions about the other. But these suspicions are only correct if ideals are under discussion. For a real-life sexual partner, both men and women tend to choose someone very different from the ideal that they lust after.

The female view of men's ideal woman

The male view of women's ideal man

The reality that both sexes usually choose

According to women, men want to have sex with a woman:
• Who is tall
• Who is slim
• Who has blonde hair
• Who has large breasts
• Who has long shapely legs
• Who has come-to-bed eyes
• Who has a pouting mouth
• Who wears red lipstick
• And who is young.

In reality men choose partners:
• Who are about (4½ in) 11–12 cm shorter than they are
• Who are well rounded
• Whose hair color is often unimportant
• Who have medium-sized breasts
• Who have a good complexion
• Who are younger by only two or three years
• Whose personality is as important as their looks.

According to men, women want to have sex with a man:
• Who is tall
• Who has broad shoulders
• Who has well-developed muscles
• Who has a hairy chest
• And who has a large penis.

In reality women choose partners:
• Who are about 6 in (15 cm) taller than they are
• Whose shape is unimportant—muscles are often a turn-off
• Whose face and eyes show character
• Who have a good complexion
• Who have well-shaped hands
• Who have a low, soft voice
• Whose penis size does not count
• And whose personality is more important than their looks.

FIRST SIGNALS

THE BODY LANGUAGE OF SEXUAL INTEREST

We use code to signal our need for sex. Despite our advanced verbal skills, sex is still something that humans are sufficiently insecure and embarrassed about for us not to state our intentions openly—at the start of a relationship at least.

Instead, we use body language. We rely on a "civilized" version of the coded signals we have used for thousands of years—well before humans had language—to tell others that we are generally available for sex; to indicate our interest in a specific individual; to receive answering signs of interest; and to chart the progress of our relationship toward sex.

But we still need to be wary. Body language isn't the whole story—we need words to negotiate

sexuality, express fully our emotions, and add detail to our nonverbal signals. Equally, body language can lie: we may send out the messages of sexual availability nonverbally even if that is not the message we wish to convey.

Nevertheless, understanding nonverbal signals can be crucial—at a conservative estimate, 93 percent of communication happens nonverbally, and the percentage is likely to be even higher in the early stages of a relationship when we are nervous about using words to express our real desires. And of course, once we move into the bedroom and the words die away, body language becomes an even more important part of a sexual relationship.

YOUR BODY LANGUAGE *becomes more focused and overt once you have identified a prospective partner. If he (or she) is in turn attracted, he will signal this nonverbally in the same way.*

The come on: This shows that you feel good in his (or her) company. You use the signals of ordinary attraction, but they are magnified. You may move close, smile, or laugh—often in an exaggerated manner— or let your voice drop and soften so that the two of you naturally focus on each other.

The back off: To keep his interest, you may then seem to "back off," so that he will want to regain your attention. You may turn away from him slightly, block your body or face with a raised hand or crossed arm, glance away in another direction, and dim your smile.

AVAILABLE OR NOT?

If you feel available for sex, your body language will show it. You will unconsciously "display" your personal attractions: your muscle tone will improve, your eyes will shine, you will stand straighter, pull your stomach in, present your best side. You'll "preen," improving your appearance by patting your hair or fiddling with your jewelry (a man will straighten his tie or adjust his watch strap). You'll go for easy accessibility, sitting where you are sure to be noticed, looking around to make direct eye contact, aiming gestures toward potential partners. And you'll do all this unconsciously if you want to be available.

You can use these behaviors deliberately to attract partners, but take care. Since most such signals are involuntary, adopting them consciously can be too obvious, particularly after a few drinks. It is better to relax and allow your natural body language to surface.

Signaling unavailability is easier, because unnatural body language puts others off. So don't display or preen; deliberately avoid eye contact; tone down friendly signals such as smiles. Put up barriers, literally, by sitting behind a table or, metaphorically, by crossing your arms over your chest. This will be a total deterrent.

The block: To make sure that no one intrudes, one of you may "block," stretching out an arm or leaning forward to show others that you are a pair. The block can also reclaim a prospective partner's interest.

The promise: You may then offer a promise. You will draw his attention overtly to sexual possibilities by touching yourself, opening your mouth slightly as you listen, brushing against him, or even eating your food in a way that parallels sexual movements.

MOVING TO SEX

PUTTING LOVEMAKING CLEARLY ON THE AGENDA

Women are currently taking a much more obvious and active initiative in raising the sexual stakes—we feel more at ease in offering a first kiss, in wooing a partner with words or gestures, in saying directly that we'd like to go to bed. We like partners to make a move because it shows they are interested, but we don't need to wait for them to take the lead.

So, in many ways, classic "seduction"—plying a woman with a few drinks, buying her presents, putting emotional pressure on her—has become far less typical. If women go to bed with men now, they are usually conscious of what they are doing. If we get drunk and regret it in the morning, we usually accept responsibility rather than complain that we were manipulated. And we no longer feel obliged to sleep with a potential partner who buys us a lavish meal—we often insist on splitting the bill in any case.

Seduction in reverse, however, is becoming more common. Now we occasionally manipulate potential partners into bed—by arousing them too far or getting them a little drunk—when that isn't, emotionally, what they want. In the morning, we realize we did it for the power game and may regret our action.

The ideal has to be that moving to sex is always a choice and that neither gender pressures or manipulates to gain what should only ever be given willingly and freely.

TACTFUL REFUSAL

There are kind and less kind ways to refuse a sexual invitation. Any eager partner will also be nervous and, therefore, to some extent vulnerable, however brash his (or her) exterior.

● Say no early: As soon as he drops a hint or makes a move; if you get unclear messages; if you feel uneasy in his presence. The longer you delay, the more difficult it will be.

● Don't be pressed into giving reasons. You risk being so vague that he'll try to argue you into a corner or so specific that you'll wound.

● Don't say no and then offset the rejection with a friendly cuddle that leaves room for misplaced hope.

● If pushed, get assertive: Keep repeating the statement that you don't want sex; stay calm; be clear; remain polite but firm.

● Remember you have the right to say no to sex, or a specific act of sex, at any time, however far advanced your relationship with someone.

MAKING THE FIRST MOVE is not a question of "jumping" your partner. Instead, use body language that lets you take things slowly and reassuringly.

An "excuse contact"—a touch with a reason other than sex—will allow you to save face if it isn't returned. If he does return the touch, he is interested. If not, he is not, although it is worth repeating your maneuver three or four times to be sure. If you make the first move, keep checking for wary reactions in a partner.

The way he leans back slightly (left), his tense shoulders, and serious expression should warn her he is not comfortable with her touch. She should hold back to see if he is merely thinking things through or is genuinely unhappy with the possibility of more contact.

As she holds his hand, his thoughtful expression and pull away (below) show reservation and wariness, while his hand to mouth gesture signals he wants to say something but is holding back. She should now give him a chance to say whether he wants the intimacy she is offering and, if not, be generously kind rather than angry or hurt.

In a friendly situation (left) there are no sexual overtures. Mutual smiles, eye contact, and leaning forward are signs that both are enjoying themselves without any feelings of unease.

SEX WITH SOMEONE NEW
WHAT DO YOU EXPECT WHEN YOU SLEEP WITH A PARTNER?

W hat does having sex actually mean? Now that pregnancy is no longer the inevitable result of sex, and social change has separated sex from marriage in many instances, the whole issue has become unclear. And so while even a few decades ago there was some consensus, now as we approach every sexual event, we each have an individual idea of its significance and importance: a one-night stand, an affair, the seal on a friendship, the start of something special.

By the morning it may be all too apparent that what we wanted is not what we are getting. The experience may have been less good than we hoped. It may have been so good that we find ourselves becoming emotionally involved—whether that was the intention or not. And, of course, we may realize that our partner's idea of what sex means is simply not the same as ours. Such mismatches in expectations may become clear at once, or—if we have sex

with the same partner again—they may take a while to surface; in both cases they are hurtful.

We are more likely to avoid disappointment if we are aware of both our own sexual needs and those of our partner, either because we've known him (or her) previously, or because we have been honest beforehand. The better we know ourselves and our partners, the fewer nasty surprises we are likely to have when we wake up in the morning.

Case history

"With my first partner, we had it sorted before we got to bed. We were both young, in love, and knew we'd stay together—we thought forever. So there was champagne and hugs of celebration, knowing we had lots more chances. After the divorce, I got a real shock. I hadn't expected true love, but the first man I slept with confessed in the afterglow that he was screwing two other women. He hadn't felt 'close enough' to tell me that before. Later I had a period of 'kiss 'em and run,' sleeping with men and then losing interest; it may have been revenge, but I think I just wasn't interested in stability. My current partner is an old friend; he'd had a bad relationship and needed reassurance one night. I thought it was just for fun, he thought otherwise. We've decided to give it a go."

MARGARET

CLASHES OF EXPECTATION *in a new sexual relationship are best solved by talking through misunderstandings at the time. If you can do this, there is a chance that you might be able to retrieve the situation. If you cannot manage to break the silence, the relationship will almost certainly fail.*

CHECKING EXPECTATIONS

It's unlikely that you will check every expectation before you have sex. Even after the event, having a "where are we at?" conversation may seem too assertive or hint that you're insecure. But you can be aware of your own aims, pick up cues as to your partner's, and check mismatches between the two. This will enable you to make more informed decisions not only about having sex, but also about getting emotionally involved.

● How will sex affect our relationship, in the short term and in the long term?
● Will we see each other again?
● How much time will we spend together?
● How will we now see our relationship; how will we describe it to friends and family?
● Will there be any change in how we interact with each other: can we be more or less romantic, more or less affectionate, more or less casual, more or less argumentative?
● Will there be any change in our emotions; will we feel less or more for each other?
● Are we still able to see people of the opposite gender just as friends?
● Are we still able to have sexual relationships with others?
● How much time will we now spend with friends, and whose friends?
● Will we be introduced to each other's family?
● Will there be any change in our loyalties; will we now see each other as more important than friends and family?
● Will there be any shift in our financial arrangements: who buys dinner; whose names are on the bank account?
● Will there be any shift in our living arrangements: who stays over with whom; whose clothes are kept in which closet; whose names are on the mortgage or lease?
● What would change any of the above expectations, for the better or for the worse: stopping sleeping together; falling in love with each other; getting pregnant?

SEXUAL COMMUNICATION
GETTING ACROSS YOUR WANTS AND NEEDS

On one hand, women love to communicate about sex. We like to talk about it with close friends, swapping stories and gathering information. We love to talk about it with partners, arousing each other and exchanging fantasies. On the other hand, sexual communication can be difficult. When the conversation turns to delicate matters, we get embarrassed. When we need to negotiate about differing needs or ask for something a partner hasn't offered, we feel self-conscious. If our partners won't talk when we want them to, we feel resentful.

In short, when we are sure that we will be accepted, we tend to open up and talk clearly and honestly. But when there is an emotional threat, we close down, feeling vulnerable and defenseless. Our underlying belief is that good communication is worthwhile, and painful or non-existent communication hurtful. We believe that good communication means good sex, and vice versa. And so the bottom line is that the better communication we have, the better our relationship appears; and, of course, the poorer our level of communication with our partners, the worse our relationship can seem.

TELLING A PARTNER *what arouses you in bed can be difficult. Women often feel that they are not allowed to have needs or are worried about their partner's response.*

• *Ask for what you want at the start of a sexual relationship. It gets harder to ask every time from then on.*

• *Begin telling your partner what you need as soon as you feel in the least dissatisfied, rather than waiting until you feel negative.*

• *Don't assume that your partner doesn't want to meet your needs; he (or she) may be embarrassed, he may not know what to do, or he may be scared of doing it wrong.*

USING THE RIGHT WORDS

Sexual communication can be difficult simply because the vocabulary sounds awkward. Many sexual words can seem too medical, too vague, too rude, too crude. The following are some common ones. You and your partner may want to find alternatives for them, more informal terms, pet names, or even code words that have nothing to do with sex. It is important to find a mutual vocabulary, words you both feel comfortable using.

Penis, testicles, breasts, nipples, clitoris, vagina, cervix, erection, ejaculation, orgasm.
Man masturbating, woman masturbating, penetration, manual masturbation performed on penis, oral masturbation performed on penis; manual masturbation performed on clitoris, vagina; oral masturbation performed on clitoris, vagina.

• *Never blame, nag, accuse, shout, or order your partner around. Instead be encouraging when you like what he is doing.*

• *Make your request positive; ask for more of something, rather than complain that your partner is failing.*

• *Make your request specific. In this way your partner will know more precisely what to do.*

• *Use body language to show him what you want, with enthusiastic sounds and movements.*

• *Move his hand to where you want it, or use your own hand and let him feel exactly what you are doing.*

NEGOTIATING ABOUT SEX

You won't always agree with a partner about every aspect of sex. Typical points for discussion often include how, when, and where to make love; what kind of protection to use; fidelity, and monogamy.

● Set aside time when you won't be interrupted; agree also a time when, if you get stuck, you will talk again.

● Start by expressing what you each want, then the reasons behind that. Keep going until each of you has clearly understood the other's point of view.

● If something really disgusts you, don't agree to it. Equally, don't ask your partner to give way on something objectionable to him (or her).

● Identify where there is overlap in your wants, an area where there is some way to meet both your needs at once.

● Explore what would happen if each of you gave up something important. Explore what you can offer to each other in return for flexibility. Allow yourself both to offer without resentment and accept without guilt.

● When you've got agreement, write it down. Agree to check progress after a specific number of days or weeks.

SEXUAL FEELINGS
THE IMPACT OF EMOTIONS ON YOUR SEXUALITY

Sex can make us feel highly emotional. First, sex is so important that it magnifies all our emotions. When sex goes wrong, it can seem like the end of the world; when sex goes right it is wonderful. Second, sex is so overwhelmingly physical that it puts us in touch with our body's sensations, the ways in which it

responds when we are emotional. So if we feel a warm glow of safety—or a churning sensation of fear—during sex or even in association with it, we are twice as likely to register that emotion than if we feel it while calculating a shopping bill.

But it's not only that sexuality creates emotion. Emotion in turn creates—or blocks—sexuality. If we feel secure, we are more able to be aroused. If, on the other hand, we feel afraid, we turn off. And if we block our emotions completely—perhaps because our relationship is too painful to handle—we can lose desire for our partner altogether.

Women can have sex without any discernible emotion—but we can't make love like this. And although the occasional episode of pure physical pleasure is delightful, making emotional and therefore passionate love is, for us, what sex is really about.

YOU WON'T OFTEN *see extreme displays of emotion – fear, anger, grief—in a partner. But it's useful to be able to spot toned-down versions of these emotions—anxiety, annoyance, disappointment—since they form the foundation of most couples' everyday interaction.*

Fear (above left): *Full fear is often marked by a sideways gaze as if to spot an intruder, blood rushing to the major organs, protective gestures, and a panicked tone. Anxiety shows in a quick sideways glance, paling skin, hand-to-face gestures, and an uncertain tone.*

Grief (left and center left): Full grief is characterized by tears, a flushed face, sobbing voice, and heavy posture. Lesser emotions like disappointment might be revealed by a gleam of moisture in the eye, reddened nose and eyes, slumped shoulders, and erratic breathing.

Anger (below): A wide-eyed gaze, twisted expression, violent gestures, and a loud voice are the characteristics of anger. Approaching annoyance is revealed by a direct or averted stare, frown or pursed lips, sharp, irritated gestures, and a varying voice tone.

COPING WITH YOUR OWN EMOTIONS

First, recognize the inner signs your body uses to alert you to an emotion.

● Anger or irritation may bring a rush of energy in your stomach or chest, a faster heartbeat, dry mouth, and a rise in the tone of your voice.

● Grief or regret may cause a heavy feeling in your stomach or upper back, warm prickle around your eyes, choking in your throat and nose, and a shaky voice.

● Fear or anxiety may create butterflies in your stomach, tightness in your shoulders or stomach, and a racing heart; your voice may also drop.

If you can express your emotions once you identify them, you are more likely to feel in control more quickly. But while a partner may find it easy to handle the expression of "soft" emotions like worry and sadness in a sexual context, "harder" ones such as anger may be more difficult. If you need to put your feelings on hold, change your physical state by moving around and breathing deeply and slowly, and change your mental state through some simple mind task such as counting the number of flowers on the wallpaper. Finally, explore what your emotions mean. To what problems are they alerting you about sex or your sexual relationship? What can you do about that?

WHEN YOUR PARTNER IS EMOTIONAL

If your partner is angry, take time out from each other—about 20 minutes—to calm down. If he (or she) is anxious or sad, get closer—touch, the most basic form of human support, will automatically give comfort.

When you're ready for words, let your partner talk first. Being listened to lowers stress levels and reduces negative emotions; what people need to know most is that someone recognizes how they feel. To find out more, ask questions, get answers, help your partner explore what's going on.

Finally, take action. Talk through possibilities, offer solutions. If your partner knows that there is an answer to the problem that's caused the bad feeling, the emotion itself will fade much more quickly.

97

PARTNERSHIP PATTERNS
WHAT DO YOU EXPECT OF A RELATIONSHIP?

The pattern of our sexual relationships has changed in the last 50 years. Our grandmothers looked forward to at least token lifetime monogamy in a marriage, tied in with shared home and income, and most of the responsibility for child rearing and running the household.

Today, we often put these more formal aspects of relationships on hold for several years. And during that time, some of us may experience both heterosexuality and lesbianism; we also typically practice serial monogamy, with occasional excursions into polygamy. Very few women nowadays have had only one partner, unless they are too old to have become involved in the sexual revolution or too young to have moved on from their first love. Even so, most of us don't have hundreds of lovers, usually fewer than ten. In time, we choose one to live with, although not necessarily in wedlock, and—perhaps—start a family. But, again unlike our grandmothers, we may have to choose a new partner as increasing numbers of us divorce.

It is not simply that we have more partners than our grandmothers did. Our partnerships are also of a different kind. With some lovers, we expect affection and good sex—and are happy that commitment is irrelevant to the relationship. With lovers we commit to, however, through marriage, cohabitation, or parenthood, we expect far more than our grandmothers did. They typically used their wide system of relatives and friends to share the burden of daily needs or occasional crises. We see our sexual partners as almost sole providers of these things—particularly as we may live far away from our families and on the other side of a huge city from our friends.

And so we probably demand more of intimate relationships than any generation of women has ever done. Today, as before, we ask that serious sexual partnerships provide financial support and a setting to raise our children. But we also want continuing passion, practical assistance, sensuality, emotional support, fidelity, friendship, orgasms—and love.

CASUAL SEX

The term "casual sex" has a checkered history. Indulging in it used to be something only men set out to do—sex without emotion. But since the sexual revolution, women too have discovered the joys of pure pleasure. Now many of us have had at least one casual sexual experience, often a one-night stand.

At present, however, both genders are having second thoughts. Sex is seen as more dangerous since the arrival of HIV, so we are all more wary of whom we sleep with. And there is a backlash against permissiveness; we prefer to feel at least some emotion for a lover, if not actual commitment. But if we like a potential partner, we may still sleep with him despite the fact that—or maybe because—it is likely to be a one-time event.

There are unspoken ground rules to casual encounters: practise safe sex; do not sleep with a man who has a partner already; do not do it if you are already committed. But given that these rules are followed, women are now almost as likely to have casual sex as men are.

Case history

"I suppose I'm lucky to live in an age where I can be openly lesbian. But I still get surprised and upset when someone passes an unkind comment, or takes a while to catch on to the fact that Lynsey and I are lovers, not just roommates.

"And then there's the other side; people think it's great being a lesbian because 'you must understand each other so well.' But sometimes we get into difficulties because we are so similar; neither of us is very proactive in sex, for example, so sometimes we miscommunicate about whether we want to make love or not. When it happens it's great; we both respect each other's bodies and are very honest with each other in bed. And now I orgasm easily for the first time. I have to say that sex with Lynsey is nothing like it used to be with my husband!"

JENNIE

WOMEN AND MEN *have different values in sexual partnership. A study based on the work of sociologist J.A. Lee showed that sheer lust, or passion, is less important for women than for men; that men find both passion and an element of fun or playfulness romantic in women; and that women value down-to-earth traits—such as practicality, selflessness, and friendship—in a lover.*

AS RECENTLY AS *30 years ago, a woman was not expected to be overt about her sexual needs. Today, however (left), many surveys suggest that it is almost as usual— and as welcome—for a woman to introduce sex into a relationship, regardless of the duration of that relationship, as it is for a man.*

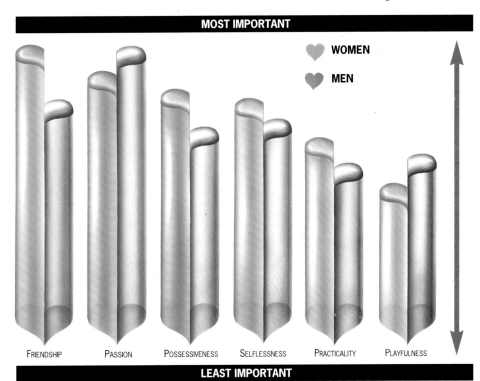

MOST IMPORTANT

♥ WOMEN

♥ MEN

FRIENDSHIP   PASSION   POSSESSIVENESS   SELFLESSNESS   PRACTICALITY   PLAYFULNESS

LEAST IMPORTANT

SEXUAL PAIRBONDING

HOW SEX ACTS AS A CONNECTING FORCE BETWEEN PARTNERS

Sex is a binding force. For women especially, sex involves compatibility. When we go to bed with someone, it is usually because we are attracted to and like them. We have a basic affection before we turn back the sheets. Then, we sleep together. If sex is successful, or if we sense that it could be in the future, we are overwhelmed with pleasure and unable to imagine being able to gain such intense feelings from anyone but our partner. This motivates us to stay.

Our partner may feel the same. If so, he (or she) signals how much he needs and loves us. These are irresistible messages, forging another link in the chain. As we get more involved, sexual pleasure encourages us to spend time together to exchange ideas, check compatibility, blend thoughts and feelings. And as we mesh mentally and emotionally, we mesh physically. Sex is the ultimate experience of body language "matching;" after it, couples tend to copy each other's

gestures, expressions, and accents; parallel each other's heart rate and blood pressure; even develop similar physical weaknesses. We also feel much closer.

In time, bonding may be eroded by incompatibility, it may build a partnership, or it may result in the ultimate binding force of a child. But however long or short the relationship, however deep or shallow the feelings, sex does bring us together with a partner. It is an undeniable source of connection.

SEX MAY ORIGINALLY *attract you, but it may not keep you together. Friendship, compatibility, and mutual goals all help, as does whether your families integrate. Being part of a larger social structure makes you more motivated to create a good relationship because your families expect it and will be disappointed if you do not. It also gives you more support when things get difficult or you have trouble adjusting to each other, when you go through transition points such as having a baby, and when you face crises. A tight family structure can offer advice, emotional comfort, and practical support.*

IS LOVE A DRUG?

Research suggests that "love" is not simply a feeling. For the survival of the human race, the aim is to get you to stay with a partner and have children—by flooding your body with particular physiological sensations.

At first, during initial attraction and falling in love, phenylethylamine—a chemical like an addictive drug— gives you uncomfortable "withdrawal symptoms" if you are separated from your partner. The aim is to pairbond you in the first months of your relationship. Once your partnership has stabilized, enkephalins—hormones which lessen your experience of pain—help you face challenges such as setting up home or raising children.

Finally, if the relationship becomes settled, endorphins—chemicals which help you feel content and peaceful—make you want to stay with your partner long term.

IF YOU MOVE *into commitment, sexual desire tends to fade. It's as if nature decides that you should now concentrate on raising—rather than making—children. The graph shows a sexual dip as couples start a family and a plateau while children are home. Then desire may rise again, but also often dips,* especially if you believe sex to be inappropriate in old age.

Emotional satisfaction does not follow the same pattern, which suggests that you can be happy in a partnership even if sex declines. Contentment hits a low when the children are young. But in old age, it reaches a peak that is higher than when you first got together.

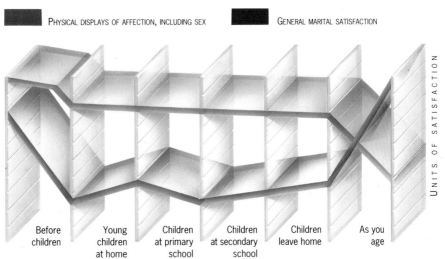

■ PHYSICAL DISPLAYS OF AFFECTION, INCLUDING SEX   ■ GENERAL MARITAL SATISFACTION

UNITS OF SATISFACTION

| Before children | Young children at home | Children at primary school | Children at secondary school | Children leave home | As you age |

MORE THAN TWO
BEYOND THE TRADITIONAL RELATIONSHIP

The idea of sharing sexual partners can be highly arousing. We imagine the pleasure of one partner, doubled—with ourself as the center of sexual attention. We get excited by the forbidden nature of "three in a bed." When it comes to reality, however, things are usually different. Of course, there are media stories hyping what fun it is to have a group orgy. But often, "more than two" is fraught with difficulty.

The scenario of two men and one woman often happens when a man wants to show off his female partner to a friend. He encourages, she complies; it could be fun. But the physical side tends to be disappointing. The additional man doesn't know how to turn her on, and the men vie with each other to "perform." She feels degraded and questions if she had to say yes in order for the relationship to survive.

Two women and one man is more likely to happen accidentally, perhaps after a party where two women friends and the partner of one are staying together overnight. Physically, this scenario has more chance of success; the women succeed in pleasing the man, and they may find surprising delight in pleasing each other. But emotionally, it can end in disaster. The women get competitive; one person is left alone and unhappy.

In wife swapping, both partners agree to be sexually available, usually at a party with other couples. Perhaps they want variety, a boost to a flagging sex life. The arrangement is that emotional loyalty stays within

COPING WITH JEALOUSY

When is sexual jealousy reasonable? If a partner clearly breaks the relationship rules, jealousy can be a useful danger signal, forcing you to face the issue and to reaffirm that you see each other as sexually more important than anyone else. (If you can't do this, then you and your partner need to reassess the relationship.) It is much more difficult when what is happening is unclear; for example, if each of you has different ideas of what is unreasonable behavior or if you suspect that the other is behaving badly. Again, you must communicate your feelings; jealousy often arises from not having come to an agreement about the ground rules.

Sometimes, jealousy is unreasonable. It may be a replay of some childhood event, when you desperately wanted to be loved by someone, so tried to keep them from paying the slightest attention to anyone else. If you know that jealousy comes from your own insecurity rather than your partner's actions, you must build your self-esteem. Ask your partner to help you understand that he (or she) really cares for you. Begin to trust him— and trust you are lovable enough to keep him.

Case history

"There were three couples; four of us had been at school together. We'd had a lot of alcohol to drink and were playing cards, then strip poker. Somehow, we ended up picking cards for who should sleep with whom. I looked across at David, we both nodded. The next minute I'm with Peter, whom I've always fancied, David is with Tanya, and we all go off upstairs.

"I have to say that the sex was amazing. I love David, but I've been with him for so long that there's nothing more to find out. Peter wanted me so much. After about an hour, we realized that we could hear voices, so we went downstairs. Everyone was a bit embarrassed and still a bit drunk but, amazingly, we carried on as if nothing had happened. Afterward, David said it was okay with Tanya, but nothing special; I didn't tell him how much I enjoyed Peter.

"Peter rang me once at work, but I said no. I wouldn't want to start anything with him. It was superb sex, but that was all it was."

VIKKIE

the couple; only the physical activity of sex is shared. Surveys show that these arrangements can be satisfying if everyone sticks to the rules, but if partners from different couples get emotionally involved with each other, the end result is usually relationship breakup.

In "open" relationships, both partners believe that they can't meet each other's every need; other relationships are necessary for complete satisfaction. The rules specify total honesty and no emotional involvement, but unlike wife swapping, each partner finds a lover individually, through normal social channels, and meets for sex in private. A 1986 study showed that, though increasingly rare, open relationships are as likely to flourish as "closed" ones—as long as partners share their common belief in relationship openness. However, if one partner becomes disillusioned, the whole thing falls apart.

SWITCHING PARTNERS can work as long as all those involved are in agreement about the rules. When one pair disregards them, they may hurt their emotional partners.

THE ETERNAL TRIANGLE
LIFE WITH, THROUGH, AND AFTER AN AFFAIR

Study after study suggests that the number of extramarital liaisons is increasing. And that does not apply only to men: female infidelity rates are rising perhaps even more steeply than those of males. This means that, as women, we are potentially involved and affected in three ways: as the tempted partner, as the other woman, and as the betrayed wife.

Affairs occasionally arise from pure lust: opportunity and desire—perhaps fueled by alcohol—come together, followed by regret in the morning. More usually, however, an affair happens because something needs to change. Our primary relationship may be breaking down, and one of us begins to look outside the relationship. Or we feel our single life is stagnating, so we look for love interest, even though the man is married. For the participants, at any rate, an affair seems to offer not only excitement but also new possibilities, even the chance of a fresh start.

And while some affairs linger for years, or result in the destruction of three people's lives, in some cases there is positive change. If the affair goes well, allegiances shift and a new stable partnership forms. If the affair doesn't work out, the straying partner may return home with renewed commitment. But although they achieve change, affairs bring pain. Whether we are the betrayed partner, other woman, or the one who strays, we always suffer when an extra person turns a relationship from a couple into a triangle.

WHEN YOU HAVE AN AFFAIR

If you are having an affair and are ready to explore the issues, ask the following questions.

● What needs to change in your life? Do you suffer from a lack of confidence, a lack of sex, a lack of affection? Can you change this by carrying on the affair but staying with your partner? Or do you need to leave your partner in order to get the life you want?

● What has your affair taught you about what you want? Are you having an affair to compensate for your primary relationship, but nevertheless realize that you still value it? Or has your affair convinced you that you need to leave?

If you realize that your loyalty has finally swung away from your primary sexual relationship, you may want to begin the process of ending it. And if you realize that you are still loyal to your primary relationship, take care not to lose it. Nothing remains the same: your lover may rock the boat, your partner may find out. How can you get what you need in life without having this affair?

WHEN YOUR PARTNER HAS AN AFFAIR

If you discover that your partner has been unfaithful, you are likely to feel totally betrayed. Most women do; most threaten to leave. But far fewer actually do leave—they tend to blame themselves or try to sort things out. It is also true that few partners leave if an affair is discovered, so if you want him (or her) to stay, he probably will.

You will both need to decide, through counselling if necessary, whether your relationship can be rescued. Can you forgive and forget? If not, you may have to part. If you do try again, remember that an affair happens because something needs to change. Whatever that is—something in your partner, something in the relationship, even something in you—it must change. If it does not, the same situation will happen again. The good news is that many couples who survive an affair say their relationship is even stronger than before.

BEING THE OTHER WOMAN

If you are having a sexual relationship with a man who is already partnered, it is wise not to be too optimistic about your future together.

He is almost certainly sleeping with you because his primary relationship is unhappy and because he cares for you. But most affairs do not break up men's existing relationships; if they do, it usually happens within the first few months. If nothing happens within a year, he probably won't leave his family.

If you can accept this, either because you feel he is worth it or because you want a part-time relationship, continue the affair. If not, end it or give him an ultimatum. In both cases, you will probably lose him, but at least you will achieve a resolution and can start getting on with the rest of your life.

THE STABILITY *of triangular relationships relies on lack of communication. If no one talks about what is happening, things remain the same. Whatever your place in the triangle, if you want things to change bring them into the open. Something will shift, although that may not be the change you want.*

5 SEX FOR A FAMILY

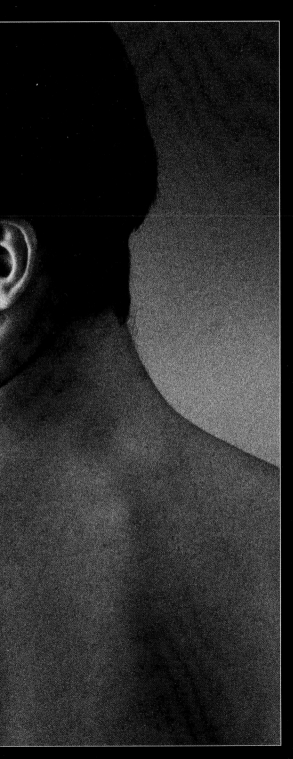

TODAY, WHEN SEX IS SO FREELY AVAILABLE, and so often enjoyed, we can tend to see it as only for pleasure. The vast majority of references to—and books and films about—sex, concentrate on that aspect alone, that sex is about giving and receiving mutual delight.

In fact, though sex between sensitive partners has presumably always been wonderful, up to recently that wasn't its prime aim. The pleasure of sex was an inducement to keep us doing it, and so propagate the species. Heterosexual sex, in terms of the human race, has always been primarily designed for making babies.

Most of us forget this most of the time and lose ourselves in giving and receiving love. If we are heterosexual, we take precautions, plan our family, and when the time comes to have a baby, we make love with a sense of surprise that this is what we have to do in order to conceive. If we are not heterosexual, we make love, plan our family, and then work out ways in which to conceive without intercourse. And after we have conceived, we return to our pleasurable but non-fertile lovemaking—until menopause removes the possibility of childbearing, although not the possibility of sexual pleasure.

But perhaps we could benefit from a small reminder of what sex is meant to achieve biologically, simply to make us even more aware of how wonderful a process it is. The whole, amazing "fit" of two bodies together, the wonderful dance of man and woman together can surely be seen by all of us as even more superb because, as well as creating pleasure, it also creates human life.

FOR MANY COUPLES *having a child provides a living reminder not only of the power of their sexuality, but also of their feelings of love for each other. And while a baby can rarely create a strong bond between two people where none exists, it can certainly enhance an existing one, focus your attention onto each other and your family, and give you the strength to face life's problems.*

PLANNING YOUR FAMILY
BARRIER AND RHYTHM METHODS OF CONTRACEPTION

We are the first generation of women to have thoroughly reliable contraception and that also makes us the first women to be able truly to choose whether to have children or not, and when to have them. We may, therefore, be completely unaware of what life was like before.

Prior to the introduction of the pill in the 1960s, every act of intercourse was potentially an act of fear. Contraception meant barriers and no spontaneity, or studiously monitoring body signs and avoiding intercourse for several days every month; and the only option for many women was constant child-bearing and—often—an early death.

And because of this lack of awareness, we can take things too lightly. We take advantage of this age of sexual freedom while failing to use the very contraception that made that freedom possible. In fact, a frightening 80 percent of women, according to some surveys, have had sex without taking precautions at a time when, as sexual women, we've never had it so good.

HOW TO USE A DIAPHRAGM

 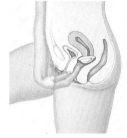

Insert your diaphragm, with spermicide, no more than two hours before intercourse. Place spermicide inside the diaphragm and spread some around the rim. Hold the diaphragm by the rim, squeeze the edges together, then squat and slide the diaphragm inside, as you would a tampon.

Check the diaphragm is tucked behind the bone at the entrance to your vagina, and that you can feel your cervix through the rubber. Leave it in place for six hours after intercourse in case any sperm manage to survive. Then hook your index finger behind the rim, dislodge it, and pull outward to remove.

HOW DIFFERENT BIRTH CONTROL METHODS WORK

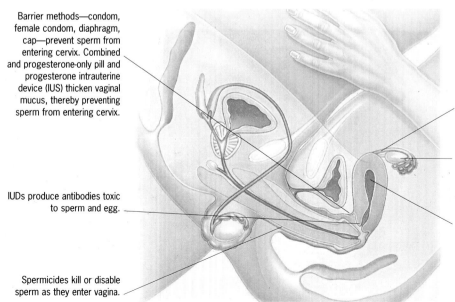

Barrier methods—condom, female condom, diaphragm, cap—prevent sperm from entering cervix. Combined and progesterone-only pill and progesterone intrauterine device (IUS) thicken vaginal mucus, thereby preventing sperm from entering cervix.

IUDs produce antibodies toxic to sperm and egg.

Spermicides kill or disable sperm as they enter vagina.

Estrogen methods (combined pill)—alter the action of Fallopian tubes so that egg and sperm don't move effectively. Sterilization blocks Fallopian tubes so eggs cannot travel from ovary to womb.

Estrogen methods (combined pill)—stop ovulation. Rhythm methods aim to avoid intercourse during fertile period.

Progesterone methods—pill, injectables, implants, progesterone IUD (IUS)—prevent lining of womb from thickening enough to nourish an embryo.

TYPES OF CONTRACEPTION

When making your contraceptive decision, alone or with a partner, work out which of these factors are important.
Note: None of these methods damages fertility; those indicated ★ are acceptable to religions that forbid contraception.

Type of contraception	Availability	Comfort and ease of use	Failure rate	Health/side effects	Outside help	Protection against STDs	Responsibility for use
Condom: latex sheath	Cheaply from pharmacies and drugstores	Needs buying; unspontaneous; easy to put on but awkward to take off; may leave a "wet patch"	2–10%—you may forget; can slip off, tear, and let sperm through	None unless you are allergic to material or spermicide	No	Yes	Him
Female condom: polyurethane sheath	Cheaply from pharmacies and drugstores	Needs buying; unspontaneous; difficult to insert; visible; uncomfortable	15%—you may forget; can slip off, less likely to tear than male condom	None unless you are allergic to material or spermicide	No	Yes	You
Diaphragm: latex or plastic barrier	Available through doctor	Needs forward planning; messy; needs to be used with spermicide, which may dull sensation	2–19%—may slip, get dislodged, develop holes	Can produce cystitislike symptoms, possible allergy to spermicide	Needs fitting and training for insertion; refitting if weight changes	Some	You
Cap: small latex or plastic cap	Available through doctor	Needs forward planning; messy; needs to be used with spermicide; unsuitable for some women	2–13%—may slip, get dislodged, lose its fit as cervix changes shape	May irritate cervical tissue and cause abnormal smears	Needs fitting and training for insertion	Some	You
Spermicide: chemical jelly, cream, pessaries, foam, film	Cheaply from pharmacies and drugstores	Needs buying; messy; can make oral sex unpleasant	3–18%—not highly effective alone	Can cause allergic reaction	No	Some	You
Rhythm method★: charting and avoiding fertile times	Kit from pharmacies and/or training course	Ill health or medication may affect physical signs; rules out sex for several days a month; some methods involve training	2–24%—you can misinterpret signals or ovulate early and so get pregnant	None	Some methods involve training	No	Shared
Withdrawal★: man withdraws before climax	Free	Man does not climax inside you	16–23%—sperm can easily leak before ejaculation	None	No	No	Him

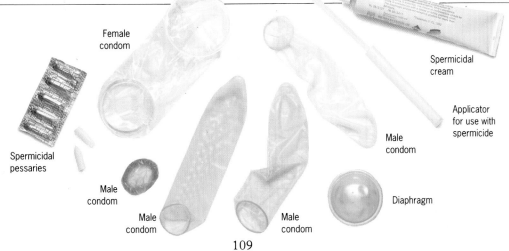

Female condom

Spermicidal cream

Spermicidal pessaries

Applicator for use with spermicide

Male condom

Male condom

Male condom

Male condom

Diaphragm

PLANNING YOUR FAMILY
CHEMICAL AND SURGICAL MEANS OF CONTRACEPTION

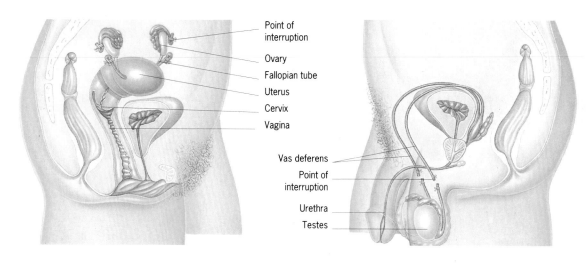

Point of interruption
Ovary
Fallopian tube
Uterus
Cervix
Vagina

Vas deferens
Point of interruption
Urethra
Testes

STERILIZATION AND VASECTOMY *are usually used by couples who have completed their family.*

• *Sterilization* (above), *in which the Fallopian tubes are cut or blocked, is effective immediately, and most women report that they are satisfied. But it is such a dramatic step* *that you should consider it carefully, talking the decision through with your partner, your doctor, and if possible with other women who have had the operation. And never go into it thinking that if you have a change of heart or circumstances, you can have the operation reversed. To all intents and purposes, you can't.*

• *Vasectomy, in which the vas deferentia are cut to prevent the sperm from being ejaculated, is a safer and cheaper operation* *than sterilization. It tends to be less popular simply because men are less prepared than women to undergo surgery.*

NEW CONTRACEPTIVE POSSIBILITIES

• *A vaginal ring that releases contraceptive hormones into your blood stream.*

• *A diaphragm that is held safely against your cervix with a suction valve.*

• *A male "pill" that instantly but temporarily immobilizes or defertilizes sperm.*

• *Contraceptive vaccines that make sperm infertile, stop sperm from penetrating the egg, or disrupt the implantation of a fertilized egg in the womb.*

• *Plugs that make both sterilization and vasectomy easy to reverse.*

WHEN CONTRACEPTION FAILS

The unthinkable happens. You've had unprotected sex; you forget to take your pill; the condom splits; your IUD comes out. There are two rescue routes, both available through a doctor or family planning clinic.

● The emergency pill gives you a high dose of hormones, preventing the fertilized egg from implanting in your womb. It consists of two doses of two pills 12 hours apart—you may suffer nausea and need to return for more pills if you vomit. The pill can be taken up to 72 hours after sex and is 95 percent effective.

● The morning-after IUD mobilizes your body to destroy sperm and also stops the egg from implanting in your womb. It's fitted in your cervix during a short medical procedure which can be done up to five days after your date of ovulation. The IUD is almost 100 percent effective, and you can use it as a regular form of contraception in the future.

TYPES OF CONTRACEPTION

When making your contraceptive decision, decide which of these factors are important. Note: None of these methods is acceptable to religions that forbid contraception; those indicated † may be viewed as early methods of abortion.

Type of contraception	Availability	Comfort and ease of use	Failure rate	Health/side effects and reversibility	Outside help	Protection against STDs	Responsibility for use
IUD†: small, usually T-shaped object	Through doctor or family planning clinic	Once inserted, does not need forward planning	1.5–5%—it may slip out	Risks include PID, ectopic pregnancy, allergic reactions; can cause heavy, painful periods; easily removed; does not affect fertility, although PID can	Needs fitting and checking	No	You
Combined contraceptive pill: hormones estrogen and progesterone taken daily	Through doctor or family planning clinic	No bar to spontaneity, but you need to remember to take it	0.5–2%—you may forget to take it	Risks include migraine, thrombosis, heart disease, cervical cancer, breast cancer; can cause depression, weight gain, yeast infections, loss of desire; can't be taken when breastfeeding; may protect against ovarian cancer and cysts, rheumatoid arthritis, fibroids, PID, and benign breast disease; can reduce period pains; does not affect fertility	Needs medical check-up and prescription	No	You
Progesterone-only pill†: hormone progesterone taken daily	Through doctor or family planning clinic	No bar to spontaneity, but you need to remember to take it at the same time every day	1–2.5%—you may forget to take it	Risks include ovarian cysts, ectopic pregnancy; can cause water retention, irregular periods; suitable for women who can't take estrogen and who are breastfeeding; does not affect fertility	Needs medical check-up and prescription	No	You
Injectable†: intramuscular hormone injection	Through doctor or family planning clinic	Once injected, does not need forward planning; effects last several weeks	0.1%	Can cause depression and irregular spotting; can stop periods; may protect against PID, ectopic pregnancy, and some cancers; does not affect fertility	Needs medical check-up and injection	No	You
Implant†: hormone capsules implanted in upper arm	Through doctor or family planning clinic	Once implanted, does not need forward planning; effects last five years	0.2–1.6%	Long-term health risks unknown; can cause weight gain, acne, ovarian cysts, headache; can be implanted when breastfeeding; reversible, but results in a conception delay once removed	Needs medical check-up and implant	No	You
Sterilization: operation cuts Fallopian tubes	Through doctor or family planning clinic; needs hospital stay	Once done, no further action needed	0.4%	No long-term health risks, but can cause infection, scarring, post-anesthetic problems; not usually reversible	Needs inpatient operation	No	You
Vasectomy: operation cuts vasa deferentia	Through doctor or family planning clinic	Once three-month "sperm clearance" period has passed, no further action needed	0.4%	No long-term health risks, but can cause local infection or swelling; not usually reversible	Needs minor operation	No	Him

CHEMICAL AND HORMONAL *methods of contraception are far more reliable than barrier methods in preventing conception, although they offer no protection against STDs. They are also less messy to use and do not affect spontaneity.*

IUD, with tube used by doctor for insertion

IUD

Combined pill

Progesterone-only, or minipill

Combined pill

Progesterone-releasing IUD, or IUS

SEX FOR CONCEPTION
THE BIOLOGY OF BECOMING PREGNANT

Most of us spend the first five to ten years of our active sex life simply making love. We de-prioritize, deliberately or otherwise, the principal aim of sex, childbearing. But then there comes a point when our priorities suddenly switch. Playing the field gives way to commitment. Career advancement becomes less important than a need for stability. Then, whether we choose it consciously or not, whether we plan our family or allow our hormones to take over, conceiving becomes vital. Suddenly, we still need to understand how sex works to achieve sensual fulfillment, but we also need to understand the mechanics of sex in order to conceive.

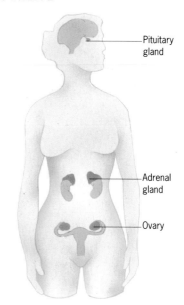

YOUR BODY PREPARES *for pregnancy each month under the influence of hormones. These chemicals are produced by the endocrine glands—chiefly the pituitary and adrenal glands—and the ovaries.*

Pituitary gland

Adrenal gland

Ovary

TESTING FOR PREGNANCY

If you think you might be pregnant, you can have a test done through a family planning clinic or pharmacy. You need to give a urine sample which will be tested for hormones only released in pregnancy. Or you can use a home kit, which also tests urine. It's best to use such a kit as early as possible; most are accurate from the day your period is due. Kits contain full instructions. Here are some helpful tips.

● If your test is negative, but you don't have a period, take another test; see your doctor within a week if your period doesn't start.

● If you do a home test and the result is unclear, repeat it; some kits contain two tests for this purpose.

● If your test is positive, see your doctor to work out your next step. If this pregnancy was not planned and you decide to terminate it, make sure you get the support you need.

● If your test is positive but you start your period shortly after, you have probably suffered an early miscarriage because the fetus wasn't developing properly or your body wasn't ready for pregnancy. This is not uncommon but if it happens you should see your doctor.

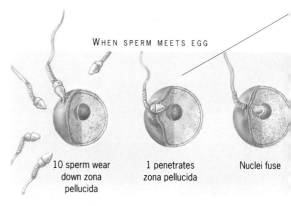

WHEN SPERM MEETS EGG

| 10 sperm wear down zona pellucida | 1 penetrates zona pellucida | Nuclei fuse |

UP TO 1 HOUR AFTER EJACULATION

Case history

"I was two weeks late. Tim was coming for the weekend, and I planned to do a pregnancy test on Saturday so that he could be there. I told him on Friday night. We'd only been together three months, but he said he'd be there whatever we decided. We went to bed and made love. I woke up to feel blood running down my leg. I always wonder if I missed my period just so I would know how Tim felt about me."

LIBBY

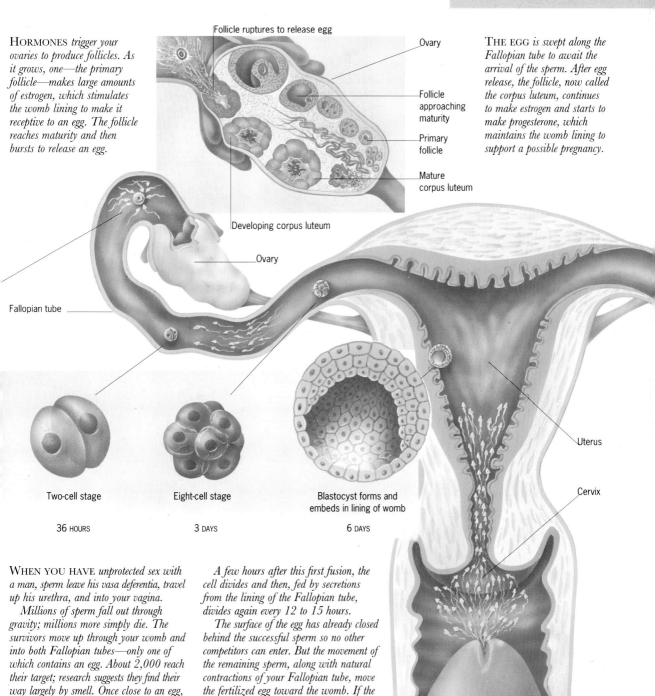

Follicle ruptures to release egg

Ovary

Follicle approaching maturity

Primary follicle

Mature corpus luteum

Developing corpus luteum

Ovary

Fallopian tube

HORMONES *trigger your ovaries to produce follicles. As it grows, one—the primary follicle—makes large amounts of estrogen, which stimulates the womb lining to make it receptive to an egg. The follicle reaches maturity and then bursts to release an egg.*

THE EGG *is swept along the Fallopian tube to await the arrival of the sperm. After egg release, the follicle, now called the corpus luteum, continues to make estrogen and starts to make progesterone, which maintains the womb lining to support a possible pregnancy.*

Uterus

Cervix

Two-cell stage

Eight-cell stage

Blastocyst forms and embeds in lining of womb

36 HOURS

3 DAYS

6 DAYS

WHEN YOU HAVE *unprotected sex with a man, sperm leave his vasa deferentia, travel up his urethra, and into your vagina.*

Millions of sperm fall out through gravity; millions more simply die. The survivors move up through your womb and into both Fallopian tubes—only one of which contains an egg. About 2,000 reach their target; research suggests they find their way largely by smell. Once close to an egg, one sperm secretes an enzyme which allows it to penetrate the egg's zona pellucida, or "skin." The sperm then sheds its tail, leaving only the nucleus, which fuses with the nucleus of your egg to form a new life.

A few hours after this first fusion, the cell divides and then, fed by secretions from the lining of the Fallopian tube, divides again every 12 to 15 hours.

The surface of the egg has already closed behind the successful sperm so no other competitors can enter. But the movement of the remaining sperm, along with natural contractions of your Fallopian tube, move the fertilized egg toward the womb. If the egg stops, it may continue to grow in the tube, resulting in a dangerous "ectopic" pregnancy. If all goes normally, the new cell implants in your womb less than a week after fertilization. You are pregnant.

113

PREPARING FOR PREGNANCY
WHEN YOU WANT TO HAVE A BABY

For heterosexual women, trying to conceive creates a dramatic change in their attitude to sex. All of a sudden, this is the real thing: it matters more than ever before whether we are ovulating, whether our partner ejaculates, and whether we feel the telltale signs of an imminent menstrual period telling us that we haven't been successful yet.

Because the act of sex becomes much more important, some women say that it also becomes much more arousing. Doing it "for real" adds an extra spice that builds passion. We have sex repeatedly, not simply to increase our chances of conception, but also because it is so exciting. Free from contraception and from the fear of pregnancy, we can enjoy ourselves as never before. On the other hand, it is easy to feel pressured to perform, to get it right. Some women find that the strain of "having to" takes away all spontaneity and that the stress of wondering whether they've conceived this time makes it hard to relax.

The secret is to enjoy a good sex life apart from aiming for pregnancy. We need to have sex not just in the few days we can conceive, and make love in positions we like, not simply those that maximize the chances. We need to choose and enjoy kissing, cuddling and foreplay—even if we know at heart that penetration is currently the essential end point.

THE DECISION to create a new life is best made together simply because the implications are so immense. It is also a decision best taken within the context of a happy and stable relationship because you need all the physical and emotional support you can get. But if you are not in a relationship and know that forming a parenting partnership with your baby's biological father is likely to lead to unhappiness all round, you may wisely decide to do your parenting alone.

ONE WAY to pinpoint when you are fertile is to buy a kit from the drug store that will identify in your urine the surge of luteinizing hormone (LH) that happens 24–36 hours before ovulation. The kit contains full directions on how to collect urine, test it, and interpret the results, although it can be expensive, particularly if it takes you some time to conceive.

CHOOSING YOUR POSITION

● If you're aiming for pregnancy, choose your position carefully. The best intercourse position is one that allows sperm to be deposited as deeply as possible in your vagina. The missionary position, with your legs on his shoulders, works well if your womb is normally placed. If your womb is retroverted (tipped backward), try supporting yourself on your elbows and knees and have him enter you from behind.

● If possible, have an orgasm, which dips the cervix into the semen, thereby increasing your chance of conceiving. When he climaxes, he should hold as still as possible, thrust deeply into you, then withdraw in a straight line to leave the semen in place.

● Afterward, lie on your back for about half an hour, with your knees up to your breasts and a pillow under your buttocks, to prevent sperm leaking out.

CONTRACEPTION FOR CONCEPTION

● If you're using barrier contraception, carry on using it until you're ready to conceive—you may well get pregnant as soon as you stop.

● You can conceive immediately after having an IUD removed. But an IUD makes you more vulnerable to infections—which can spread, particularly during birth itself. It's best to have the IUD removed, then use a barrier method of contraception until you have been tested for infections such as PID (see pp. 36–37).

● If you're using hormonal contraception, such as the pill, implants, injectables, or a hormonal IUD, you should stop about three months before you want to conceive—use barrier contraception in the meantime—so your hormone levels return to normal.

● If you find you are pregnant and still have an IUD fitted, see your doctor immediately; it must be removed to avoid miscarriage. Similarly, stop taking hormonal contraception if you find you are pregnant.

CURRENT RESEARCH *suggests you are most fertile during the five days leading up to ovulation plus the day of ovulation itself—only occasionally do you conceive after this time.*
An ovulation kit (left) will help you determine when you ovulate. You can also be trained to recognize when your vaginal mucus becomes more slippery and clear—a sign that it is able to carry sperm to the egg. In addition, keep a record of your temperature each day—your body temperature dips just before ovulation. Aim to have intercourse (or inseminate) during each cycle at this time.

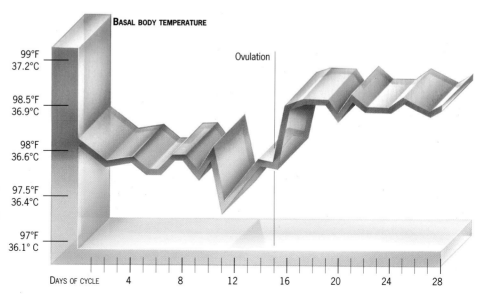

BASAL BODY TEMPERATURE

Ovulation

99°F 37.2°C

98.5°F 36.9°C

98°F 36.6°C

97.5°F 36.4°C

97°F 36.1°C

DAYS OF CYCLE   4   8   12   16   20   24   28

WHEN YOU CANNOT CONCEIVE
INVESTIGATING PROBLEMS AND LIVING WITH THE RESULTS

There are few more challenging life events than facing the prospect of infertility. Many of us happily postpone childbearing for years, but when we do want a child, discovering that it's not as easy as we thought it would be attacks our self-worth.

For most women, childbearing is important. We love children for their own sake and want them in our day-to-day lives, now and in the future. We also want them to set the seal on a significant relationship and because they give us a sense of immortality. To realize that all this is in doubt is to question everything we hold to be true. We may feel guilty: is it our fault? We may feel angry: is it our partner's fault? And we may need a great deal of courage to overcome these feelings and carry on, trying to make sense of our work, relationship, and life.

FEMALE AND MALE FERTILITY PROBLEMS

% of cases	YOU may be unable to conceive easily because of any of these problems:	Causes
50%	Fallopian tubes: eggs not traveling to be fertilized; eggs not reaching the womb after fertilization.	Blockage, perhaps through infection or previous ectopic pregnancy; scarring through endometriosis; tube compression through fibroids; surgery.
33%	Ovulation: ovaries not producing eggs; eggs not maturing; mature eggs not being released to be fertilized.	Hormonal problems, such as difficulties with pituitary gland or hypothalamus; ovaries may be affected by illness, surgery, stress, or weight problems.
10%	The womb: eggs not implanting in womb; eggs not staying implanted in womb; eggs not developing once implanted.	Some medical conditions—fibroids, polyps, internal adhesions, inflammation—affect the shape or functioning of the womb.
5%	Cervical mucus: sperm being unable to move past the cervix and up into the womb.	Too little mucus to encourage the sperm upward; mucus so thick that sperm cannot travel; the cervix produces antibodies that destroy the sperm.

% of cases	HE may be unable to fertilize your eggs because of these problems:	Causes
90%	Sperm themselves: not enough sperm; abnormal sperm.	Environmental pollution; infection; illness; injury; overheating of the testicles; injury to the testes; hormonal problems; stress or natural decline in sperm production with age.
10%	Sperm transportation: immobile sperm; blockage in tubes that carry sperm from testes; difficulty in getting an erection; difficulty in ejaculating; problems with muscles that propel semen along penis.	Hormonal or prostate gland problems; structural problems; scarring from infections.

MAKING INVESTIGATIONS

Medical investigation can pinpoint action you or your partner could take to help. But though investigations are often positive, there may be a downside: at each investigation, you may feel your hopes rise, only to have them dashed if the results are not helpful. Get as much support as possible, from each other and from others, while you keep fighting for a solution.

● FOR HIM

Hormone tests: Are his testicles producing sperm? Is hormone functioning adequate?
Sperm count: Does his ejaculate contain enough sperm?
Sperm functioning test: Can sperm penetrate your cervical mucus? Are antisperm antibodies present?
Acrosome reaction test: Can sperm fuse with an egg?
Hamster egg test: Can sperm penetrate an egg?
Surgical investigation: Are testicles functioning?

● FOR YOU

Hormone tests/endometrial biopsy: Is ovulation normal? Post-coital test: Are there any problems with your cervical mucus?

Laparoscopy: Are your Fallopian tubes clear?
Hysteroscopy/ultrasound scan/hysterosalpingogram: Are there any problems in your womb?

PROBLEMS IN CONCEIVING can deeply affect your sex life. You may find yourselves wanting to make love all the time, as if to contradict any thought that you are infertile or unsexual. Or you may lose all desire, as if the failure of your lovemaking to bring the child you want hurts so much that you never want to risk it again.

Both reactions are normal: the beliefs you had in yourselves as sexually effective have been undermined. Even if these problems are temporary and
you do eventually conceive, you need to recover from them. And this can mean feeling differently about sex. Whether you feel passionate all or none of the time, however, try to preserve other aspects of your sexuality—affection, sensuousness, physical support. Ironically, you can easily drift apart emotionally while you are trying for the ultimate sign of partnership. Using cuddles to keep you close, even when you feel separate, is an essential part of surviving.

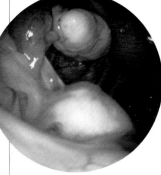

DURING A LAPAROSCOPY a tube is passed through your abdominal wall and illuminated to give a view of your internal organs. Such a procedure can reveal whether your ovaries (white), Fallopian tubes and the womb itself (orange) are healthy.

ASSISTED CONCEPTION
MEETING THE CHALLENGE OF INFERTILITY

The bad news is that we cannot rely on being able to bear children. Infertility strikes one couple in six at some point in their lives. The good news, though, is that we live in a world in which medical science can do more to solve problems in conceiving than at any time in the past. There are treatments that in a majority of cases lead to pregnancy, and medical breakthroughs each year. We have the possibility—unknown even a generation ago—of borrowing from a donor to create a child of our own. So if we do find that bearing children is not straight-forward, we have every reason to hope that we will be able to find a solution.

Problems and solutions

• If the problem is related to ovulation, hormone treatment to supplement or replace hormones that are lacking is usually offered to stimulate the ovaries, mature the egg inside the follicle, or build up the endometrium so that the embryo will survive.
• Not a great deal can be done medically about a low sperm count, although some drug treatments may help. Instead, men are encouraged to drink less, stop smoking, eat more healthily, and take more exercise.
• A "structural" problem stopping the egg or sperm from reaching the right place can sometimes be treated with microsurgery to remove the blockage.

If none of these treatments works, assisted conception may be an option. In egg implantation, eggs are removed from your ovary and mixed with your partner's sperm, then replaced in the womb (the "test tube baby" treatment). Since it carries a risk of multiple births, this is usually used only when the Fallopian tubes are damaged, or there are problems with the cervical mucus. Alternatively, your partner's ejaculate may be gathered—often from multiple ejaculations to get a higher concentration of sperm— "washed" to remove any unhealthy sperm, and then inserted directly into your womb during ovulation.

When you and your partner cannot conceive together, either because of medical problems or because you are a same-sex couple, you may want to enlist another person's help. You can use ejaculate— from someone you know or from a bank of screened donor sperm—which is placed into the vagina or inserted into the womb. Egg donation—more difficult because it requires the donor to use fertility drugs and have minor operations—involves fertilizing another woman's eggs with your partner's sperm, and then introducing them into your womb. For those women who cannot carry a baby to term, a legal solution in some countries is for a surrogate mother to do so, usually using your partner's sperm to fertilize her own egg. The issue of surrogacy may create a backlash, however, particularly if the surrogate mother wants to keep the baby.

It is important to think about the following when considering whether to involve others.
• If the egg is donated, who is the baby's mother?
• If the sperm is donated, who is the baby's father?
• What if donor treatment results in a baby with special physical or mental needs?
• What if fertility treatment gives you more babies than you think you can cope with?
• What would happen if the surrogate mother of your child demanded that she keep the baby?

Case history

"I've always known I wanted a child. And I've always known I was gay. Sally and I chose self-insemination because I didn't want sex with a man, and because we wanted control over who fathered our child, rather than using any sperm that an artificial insemination clinic dished out. The obvious thing was to ask a gay man. We contacted some through a lesbian and gay network, and then met them briefly. It was a bit like a job interview, except we asked them to have an HIV test as well!

One evening, two of them came to our apartment and did the necessary. I didn't want to know who the father was in case of later complications, so I mixed the sperm, used the syringe, and lay down for an hour. I was lucky—I got pregnant the first time. Laura is five now, and she's beautiful."

MISHA

WHEN YOU CAN'T CONCEIVE **116–17**
ASKING FOR HELP   **148–49**

MANY CHILDLESS
COUPLES *feel that the risk
of a multiple birth involved
in "test tube baby" treatment
is worth it. Where blocked
Fallopian tubes are the
problem, however, a new
breakthrough in clearing them
may make this treatment and
the attendant risks less
common. Guided by X-ray, a
tube is passed through the
vagina and cervix to clear the
blockage in the Fallopian tube.
The treatment takes less than
30 minutes and requires
neither a general anesthetic
nor a hospital stay.*

*The feasibility of freezing
freshly ovulated eggs is
currently under investigation.
This would ease the chronic
shortage of female eggs by
allowing fertile women to
donate eggs that could be used
years later. It would also
mean that if you wanted a
child but had to undergo
chemotherapy or radiotherapy,
which might make you
infertile, you could have your
own eggs frozen for use when
you were healthy enough to
consider a pregnancy. (If
your partner is facing such
treatment, he may be asked if
he wishes to have his sperm
frozen for later use.)*

NINE MONTHS

MAKING LOVE WHEN YOU'RE PREGNANT

Sex during pregnancy can seem like a bad idea—we may feel far too exhausted or nauseous for lovemaking; suffer breast tenderness; feel fat and unlovable; be drained of desire. But, in fact, making love is often a good thing to do. Practically speaking, we may want it; the fact that vaginal tissues engorge means that we may feel in a permanent state of arousal. And emotionally, sex during pregnancy not only keeps us in touch with a partner at a time when he (or she) may feel edged off center, but it also fulfils our need to be loved despite the way we feel and look.

New research suggests that having sex may be good both for us and for the baby. During lovemaking, when the womb contracts, the blood vessels fill, sending extra blood—and nourishment—to the growing fetus. So we shouldn't give up on sex because it's made us pregnant; we should continue to enjoy it for as long as we can.

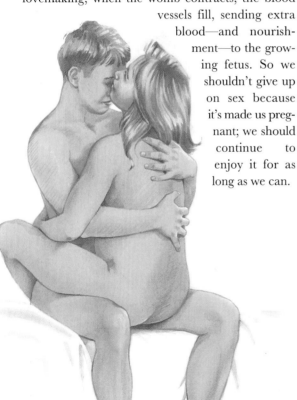

THE ONSET OF LABOR

If your pregnancy is normal, and labor imminent, you can help things along. Stimulating your cervix may bring labor on if you're almost there—the Japanese have invented a special vibrator for this purpose. But for a heterosexual couple, having intercourse works even better.

● Lie back with your head and shoulders well supported on pillows. Begin with nipple stimulation—which releases oxytocin, the hormone which triggers labor. Then move to intercourse, perhaps with your legs on his shoulders for deeper penetration. Climax if you can; the contractions may then give way to the regular contractions of labor. Once he's ejaculated, he should stay inside you for about five minutes; the aim is to bathe your cervix in the prostaglandin contained in semen, which can induce labor.

● When labor starts, masturbating to climax can act as a painkiller and help ease the contractions.

ONCE YOU'RE PREGNANT, *you may want to adapt the intercourse positions you use. All the positions illustrated here also allow you or your partner to give clitoral stimulation—this is particularly important if, as often happens, the only positions you can get into during pregnancy are the ones in which you cannot climax easily without extra "hand help."*

Remember that as your pregnancy progresses what was comfortable at one stage may not be so at another, so be prepared to be flexible.

During the first three months, there may be little outward difference in your body so you will probably still be able to manage man-on-top positions, although you may find it more comfortable to avoid deep penetration. If you are on top, or sitting on his lap (left), it is easy for you to control the depth of penetration. *These positions are also good if you are suffering from indigestion or heartburn, both of which are often associated with early pregnancy.*

But they are perhaps less suitable if you also have tender breasts, and want to avoid being touched on them.

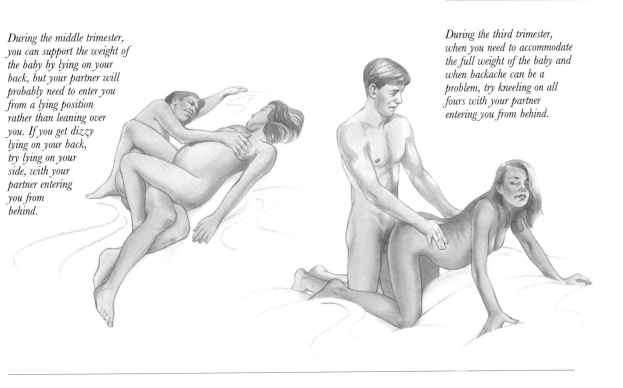

During the middle trimester, you can support the weight of the baby by lying on your back, but your partner will probably need to enter you from a lying position rather than leaning over you. If you get dizzy lying on your back, try lying on your side, with your partner entering you from behind.

During the third trimester, when you need to accommodate the full weight of the baby and when backache can be a problem, try kneeling on all fours with your partner entering you from behind.

MYTH AND REALITY

There are lots of myths about having intercourse when you're pregnant, but the facts are different.

MYTHS	**FACTS**
• The pressure and movement of intercourse will crush the baby.	The fetus is suspended in the amniotic sac that contains it, surrounded by fluid which cushions it from bumping and bruising.
• Sex might make infections travel up to the womb.	The womb is completely sealed off by a mucus plug, so intercourse won't lead to a spread of infection.
• Having an orgasm can dislodge an embryo or start labor.	If you've had a normal pregnancy, orgasm won't start labor until you're due, although you might want to avoid climax during the final month.

However, you should avoid sex:

• If your partner has an STD or an open herpes sore; avoid oral sex in this situation too.
• If you've already had a miscarriage, until your doctor gives you the all clear, usually after midterm in the pregnancy.

• If bleeding occurs; see your doctor to make sure there are no problems.
• If your waters break—the start of labor.
• If you are in pain or uncomfortable.

SEX AFTER A BABY
RECLAIMING YOUR SEXUALITY AFTER BIRTH

Until we get pregnant, sex is often a wonderful and vital compulsion. It's ironic then that on the day when the wonderful result of all that sex finally arrives in the form of an adorable baby, many women's first reaction is that they never want to make love ever again.

A good deal of what happens is physical: labor is very much a physical trauma, from which our body does not always recover quickly and easily. Equally, a good deal of what happens is psychological. We may be so wrapped up in our baby that our partner seems irrelevant. We may start thinking of ourselves as mother, rather than lover. If it has been many months since we last had sex, we may actually be shy or embarrassed, almost uncertain what to do. And we may worry that we will somehow feel different toward our partner.

Self-help guide to reclaiming sexuality

The first step on the path to reclaiming sexuality is reassuring ourselves that we are not alone. In fact, the majority of Western women go through the same post-birth decline in a desire for lovemaking. It's not a sign that we are unsexual, or that our relationship might be failing.

Taking the next step means working on rebuilding the relationship. It may seem harsh to spend even a few minutes away from a newborn, but regular "sanity time" with a partner, perhaps just a few hours a week, can build the bonds between us to the point where we want to make love.

Last, sex itself can solve the problem. There are few occasions on which we should have sex even if we don't initially feel desire, but after childbirth may be one of them. For if we haven't had sex for months, we may simply need to decide to begin again, just in order to break through the barrier of embarrassment and uncertainty. Masturbating, kissing, stroking, having orgasms all help to renew our faith in our own sexuality. Making love can do just that—remake our love at a time when, however strong it is emotionally, physically it may just be a vague memory.

When you do start to have intercourse again following the birth, take it slowly. Experiment to find a

CONTRACEPTION AFTER BIRTH

Almost from the moment you give birth, you're fertile again.

● Breastfeeding only offers contraceptive protection if you are feeding your baby on demand, as often as every two to four hours, both day and night.

● You shouldn't rely on the rhythm method until your menstrual periods settle down, when you can get accurate information about your menstrual cycle.

● The IUD, diaphragm, and cap can't be fitted until your cervix has recovered—usually in about six weeks.

● If you're breastfeeding, use the progesterone-only pill, injectable or implant, so that your milk won't dry up and the estrogen won't affect the baby.

● For short-term use, the male condom and spermicidal foam may be the best contraceptive. Use plenty of lubrication to avoid irritating your already tender vagina.

position that is comfortable and feels right. Particularly if you've had a Caesarean section, use a position that helps keep pressure off your abdomen. Placing a pillow under your hips may help give you the right angle. Lubricate well, then tighten your own buttock muscles to protect you as he slides slowly into you. Press together, but then ease your buttocks and explore the ways you can both move so that it feels best.

Examine the angle and depth of penetration and, again, experiment with different positions. Move slowly and gently; relax as much as you can and, if you want, add extra clitoral stimulation to help get you aroused. Do just as much as you want to and don't be hesitant to stop if it feels at all uncomfortable.

YOUR BODY AFTER CHILDBIRTH

After giving birth, a number of physical problems may contribute to your desire to deprioritize sex

GENERAL FATIGUE
You may need time to recover from the exhaustion of labor, and the demands of being on 24-hour call for your baby will mean that your sleep pattern is disturbed. Try to get as much sleep and rest as you can.

BREASTS
When aroused, you may ooze milk from your breasts, which may be embarrassing for you. You may also feel that it's turning your partner off. Get his reassurance that it is not a problem.

STOMACH
If labor has torn ligaments in your pelvis, or you have had a Caesarean birth, try different positions until you find a comfortable one.

ENTRANCE TO VAGINA
You may be suffering from vaginal or perineal pain, particularly if you have had cervical stitches. If this is the case, it is worth experimenting with intercourse positions until you find a comfortable one. Don't have intercourse if you are still bleeding.

BODY
Additional weight which may have crept on during pregnancy, and loose abdominal muscles which stretched to allow room for the growing baby, may make you feel unattractive. Exercise will help tone you, but in the meantime get your partner's reasssurance or cover yourself with sexy lingerie.

INSIDE VAGINA
If you breastfeed, you may find your vagina is dry because of low estrogen levels. The condition should clear up of its own accord in a few months, but in the meantime add plenty of lubrication whenever you need it and make sure you are fully aroused before penetration.

PELVIC BONE
The hormone imbalance may also give you painful cramps during intercourse. It is best to take things slowly at first and stop if you experience any pain. Remember that forms of lovemaking other than intercourse are possible, for example clitoral stimulation to orgasm. As well as building your confidence, they may also help to normalize your hormone levels.

123

SEX AND MOTHERHOOD
COMBINING THE ROLES OF LOVER AND MOTHER

As our children grow up, all kinds of factors militate against our having the rich sex life we want—too little time, too little opportunity, a wish to put our children first, guilt at thinking of ourselves. It is all too easy to say that our sex lives can wait until the children no longer need us. When they leave, it is equally easy to say that now we are past being sexual. The result is that, on average, couples who have a family make love only half as often as childless couples.

In fact, there's one very good reason to carry on having sex—our children. For if we really want to teach our children how to be positively sexual, then we need to be positively sexual ourselves. If we deprioritize sex and act as if it is unimportant, then that is the message our children will absorb. If we keep on making love and keep on enjoying it, then that's the lesson they'll learn. Above all, we need to reaffirm our sexuality because of our children, not in spite of them.

Case history

"In all honesty, it does get better. Sam, our oldest, was a demanding baby, and neither of us knew what we were letting ourselves in for. It was all far more rewarding than we thought it would be, but also far more exhausting. Sex was the last thing on our minds for most of the first year. When Lisa was conceived, we'd just about got our sex life back; but when she was three months old, she was hospitalized for a while, and that seemed to set us back again. I reckon there's some mechanism that puts sex on hold when the kids need you—and that's most of the time! I date the improvement to when they started going to kindergarten. All of a sudden, I had a few hours to myself, to think of myself and look after myself. It took a while, but I started to come out of my asexual shell. We still don't make love as much as we did before the children. But we make love more than we did a year ago."

CHRISTINE

SUSTAINING YOUR SEXUALITY

When bringing up children, you may lose track of yourself as a sexual woman. Hard work, fatigue—and a tight clothes budget—may undermine your appearance. The children themselves may view you as non-sexual, even showing surprise that you ever kiss and cuddle. By the time your offspring are blossoming as rampantly sexual teenagers, you may feel positively desiccated in comparison.

One answer is to contradict all this by giving yourself permission to keep links with your previous, sexual, self. It isn't selfish, but sensible, to indulge yourself occasionally, perhaps buying "non-Mom" magazines, or flaunting an overtly sexual outfit. More crucially, remember that sex isn't about appearance or impression. You generate sexuality inside you. You build sexuality through experience. You improve sexuality through practice. And the more you make love, the easier you'll find it to believe in yourself as a sexual being.

HAVING CHILDREN *interrupts your sex life in very practical ways. It may seem you can only make love at night when the children are in bed. You may be constantly distracted, listening for their cries. You may feel inhibited, particularly once they are old enough to find their way into your bedroom.*

• *With toddlers who naturally feel betrayed when they are not allowed access to you, you may only be able to take time out together when they are not around. Arrange regular childcare—not to go out, but to stay in with the phone off the hook and a large bottle of massage oil.*

• *Once children are old enough to understand they can't have your undivided attention, explain that sometimes you need time alone together. Put a lock on the bedroom door, and carve out time when you are uninterruptable except in genuine emergencies.*

• *By the time children are teenagers, you may feel embarrassed taking time out when they obviously know what you are doing. Remember that they need to know that some adults have a sex life good enough to prioritize. Take a "nap" on Sunday afternoons while they watch TV and try to take a weekend away once or twice a year.*

BRINGING UP SEXUAL CHILDREN
GIVING OUR CHILDREN SEXUAL AWARENESS

Our aims as mothers should be to bring up our children to be sexual beings. Naturally, we should want them to approach sex with care and take sensible sexual decisions, but at the same time we should hope that they grow to enjoy sex deeply and passionately. Touching our children lovingly not only gives them pleasure. It also sends the message that positive physical contact is good, rather than something to feel uncomfortable or guilty about—a foundation on which to build adult sexual pleasure.

Right from the start, your baby will enjoy massage as long as he or she is comfortably cradled on your legs or lying on a soft, warm rug. But obviously loving touch need not be confined to such sessions.

Helping your child to be sexual

Your honesty and the example you set in your relationships with your partner, child, and others around you are vital.

• Children learn most about sex from people they love. If you say that sex is wonderful but special, or that it's awful and painful—or behave as if it is—they will believe that and act on it.

• If you react with anger and horror at finding children doing something sexual, then in years to come, they may well come to associate sex with guilt and fear.

• If you sit children down and lecture them on the "facts of life" when you think they're ready,

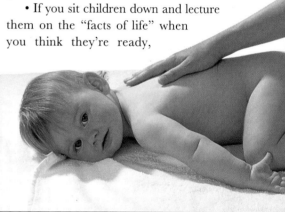

MASSAGE IS *an excellent way to teach your children about loving touch. Begin shortly after birth, settling the baby quietly in a warm room. Talk to her, hum or sing, and match your movements to the rhythm of words or music.*

While you massage, your baby may visibly relax and concentrate on the sensations. When you come to the end of the massage, don't stop suddenly but lift your hands off slowly.

As your child gets older, she may grow out of wanting to be massaged. If so, let it happen. But she may also happily want to continue, or even help massage younger siblings.

SEX EDUCATION

Most schools offer sex education. It usually covers the mechanics of what happens, plus the social skills of sex in a relationship. Lessons might include looking at pictures of the course of a pregnancy, talking about what love means, and discussing different types of contraception.

You can withdraw your children from such classes if you are strongly against them. But children who have positive sex education have proved more likely to delay starting intimacy and less likely to have an unplanned pregnancy. It is usually better to work actively with what is happening. Discuss with your child's teachers what is to be taught and when, and follow up specific lessons by discussing them at home. Offer your own beliefs about sex to complement and augment what your child learns at school.

• *Massage the baby's chest (above left), working from the center of her body out to each side with gentle strokes. Draw little circles around her navel, or use both hands to trace along her ribs.*

• *When massaging her back (above), be careful not to apply any pressure on her spine. Try stroking from her head to the base of her back, or use your fingertips to massage from the center outward.*

you're probably a couple of years too late. If you answer the questions children pose, giving them answers to what they ask but no more, they'll get what they need when they need it.

• If you feel you can do it, show as well as tell. Encouraging your teenage daughter to explore her genitals, for example, can contradict any lurking belief that she's abnormal or ugly.

• Talking ahead of time about sexual choices—for example, when to say no—will support children in being sexual decision-makers. It will also encourage them to confide in you when they have sexual choices to make.

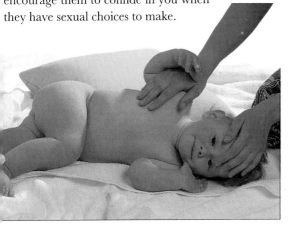

MOM, CAN WE TALK?

If your daughter or son confides that she is being abused, you may face difficult decisions.

● Avoid reacting strongly with anger or fear; she will already be upset and needs you to handle things calmly.

● Whether or not you initially think her reports are accurate, take her seriously; acknowledge her fear; do not blame her.

● Assure her that whatever is happening will stop. If necessary, keep her with you so that she feels safe.

● Get support for yourself before taking action, particularly if your child is accusing an adult who is also close to you. Ring an abuse helpline, where experts will help you to work through your feelings and decide what action to take.

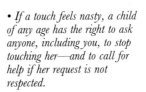

• *Cradle the baby's head (above) and stroke down from the bridge of her nose over her forehead and temples, and from her nose out to her ears. Then stroke gently down to her shoulders, arms, and hands.*

GIVING HER *a strong sense of loving touch is one of the best ways to help your child recognize inappropriate touches. But small children in particular are trusting and need to be taught a certain wariness.*

• *Give a young child clear rules of the "never go with a stranger . . . only let Mommy touch you there . . . tell me if a stranger talks to you" kind.*

• *An older child will probably understand the idea of special zones of her body that are hers alone, which others should touch only with her permission.*

• *If a touch feels nasty, a child of any age has the right to ask anyone, including you, to stop touching her—and to call for help if her request is not respected.*

• *Another useful explanation is that touching isn't secret, and that something is sure to be wrong if someone asks her to keep the fact that they touch confidential.*

• *Always stress that people who touch a child without her permission are wrong for doing it; it is not her "fault" for allowing it.*

127

6 SEXUAL TROUBLESHOOTING

UNTIL ONLY A FEW YEARS AGO, WE NEVER admitted having a sexual problem, or a partner who had a problem, or a relationship in which sex was a problem. This conspiracy of perfection was both personal—we didn't even confide in friends if things were not ideal—and cultural—the media headlined sexual success and ignored sexual failure.

Perhaps one of the most welcome developments of the past decades is the revelation that all this was a pretense. Of course, the media still hint that every woman has it twice a night, and that most have multiple orgasms. But slowly the realities of sexual problems are being revealed. Those of us who have feared for years that we are somehow imperfect if our sex life is not perfect are happy to learn that most long-term couples, heterosexual and lesbian, suffer phases of loss of desire; to realize that hardly any woman climaxes every time; and to be told that most men fail to get it up at some point in their life.

There is, however, an even more welcome development in the discovery of a solution to these problems. Sex therapy is a positive, effective, and speedy way of exploring and resolving sexual problems. It offers support to those who sense that some mental and physical blocks are impossible to remove alone and it gives results, in exercises that are being refined yearly by research and practice.

And so perhaps for the first time, we are seeing a welcome and essential honesty about the fact that sex is not always perfect. We are also seeing a way to improve matters which can, in most cases and in most situations, turn dissatisfaction into sexual satisfaction and a sense of failure into undisputed sexual success.

PERHAPS FOR THE FIRST TIME *in history, sexual difficulties are now coming to be regarded as something to be solved together. Rather than blaming or feeling guilty, couples are starting to be able to talk about their sexual problems, tackle them without embarrassment, and support each other in seeking outside help.*

FEELING WARY OF SEX
WHEN FORMER FEELINGS ABOUT SEX CREATE PROBLEMS

Making love, for some women, is underpinned by wariness. We may simply feel uncomfortable about some aspects of sex, or be unable to enjoy lovemaking at all. Or we may feel so afraid that we avoid sex altogether.

Such wariness is not deliberate or conscious. It could be rooted in childhood, when we were taught to be frightened of sexuality, or come from a single traumatic incident that has linked sex with fear.

But blocks about sex are not immovable—they shift as you go through life. And they can be altered by positive action. It helps if you are aware of, and want to change, your blocks. Try to catch yourself thinking negative thoughts and replace them with positive ones; ask your partner to teach you new ways to act in bed; or seek counseling to dissolve your fears. Whatever its origin, we all deserve to overcome wariness about sex, and to enjoy fully every aspect of it we choose.

FACTORS THAT MAY INFLUENCE YOUR FEELINGS ABOUT SEX

❦ *Having been raised by parents who didn't show their love for each other may mean you think you don't deserve to enjoy sex.*

❦ *Having been brought up with little physical affection may mean you believe it's wrong to touch your own or someone else's body.*

❦ *If you heard from your mother that her sexual experience was unhappy you may believe sex brings pain.*

❦ *Being raised in a culture that considers sex before marriage wrong may have made you repress arousal.*

❦ *Media pressure to be beautiful may mean you feel that unless you look perfect you are not allowed to enjoy sex.*

❦ *Childhood messages that you should "control yourself" may mean that you are scared of losing control in sex.*

❦ *Cultural messages that it is wrong for women to enjoy sex may have made you block pleasure.*

❦ *Childhood trauma, such as being punished for masturbating, may have made you feel guilty about sex.*

❦ *A distressing event in adulthood, such as losing your virginity painfully, may mean you dread sex.*

❦ *A previous unplanned pregnancy may mean you are now afraid to have sex.*

FEELINGS ABOUT GENITALS

Genitals can evoke strong feelings, particularly because of their association with excretion. But, in fact, the two systems—genital and excretory—are quite separate. You pass urine from your urethra, which is near to but not the same as your clitoris. You pass feces from your anus which is near to but not the same as your vagina. If you're worried you'll pass urine during sex, do so beforehand, and avoid deep penetration positions that put pressure on your bladder. (It is impossible for a partner to urinate inside you.)

As long as you wash your genitals daily, they won't smell bad to a partner. If you feel your genitals are ugly, you may want to read the "self-examination" exercise on p. 27, or get your partner to tell you how much he (or she) loves your private parts.

REGRETS OVER AN ABORTION

An abortion can be a major cause of sexual wariness. You may regret having had sex, having become pregnant, and having taken the decision to terminate your pregnancy. You may fear getting hurt like this again—so you pull back from sexual relationships.

If you do feel any of these emotions, you need to realize you did the best you possibly could, considering the person you were and the circumstances you faced when all this happened. You need time to grieve, particularly for the baby you lost. You may need counseling to help resolve your feelings of regret, anger, depression, or sadness.

But, above all, you need to think well of yourself again. Remember that most women, five years after an abortion, believe that they acted for the best—even if they were, perhaps, ambivalent at the time.

BUILDING CONFIDENCE

If you are sexually cautious because you lack confidence either in yourself—or in your sexuality, or your sexual relationship—these guidelines may help.

● Learn to like your body: Celebrate your unique features—hair, hands, eyes, breasts, legs, and so on.

● See your sexuality as normal: You are born sexual, and it is the most natural thing to be.

● Learn to trust your partner: Build your relationship so you can open up to him (or her), particularly about those parts of yourself that you fear are unacceptable.

● Learn "sexual selfishness": Women traditionally learn to put other people's pleasure first. Concentrate, during lovemaking, on your own sensations.

● Express yourself: When making love, allow yourself to move, talk, even yell as and when you want to.

● Get contraceptive confidence: Choose a method that you trust completely and are comfortable with.

● Communicate clearly: Work out, with your partner, sexual words and phrases that are mutually acceptable.

● Explore your preferences: Use fantasy, masturbation, and experimentation. Say no to what you dislike. Say yes to what you like.

FADING DESIRE
WHEN ONE OF YOU DOESN'T WANT SEX

Lack of desire is the most common reported sexual problem; both women and men feel desire slipping away. At some time or other in a relationship, one—or perhaps both—of us does not want to have sex. The reasons are as varied as our relationships—tiredness, stress, illness or medication, hormones, the relationship itself.

At a time when sex has never seemed so freely available, it is ironic that we should have so much trouble maintaining our interest. But perhaps because sex is available and we no longer have to fight for it and we don't see it as prohibited any more, we are simply unable to get excited about it. Nevertheless, there is no reason why we should settle for a life without desire. We do deserve actively to want sex as well as being theoretically free to have it.

Partnership problems

Lack of desire is often triggered by problems within a relationship. A partnership in which you constantly criticize or pressurize each other about issues—

including sex—reduces desire in the short term and simply takes away all motivation to make love in the long term.

Facing up to such problems can seem threatening; it may simply feel much easier to blame tiredness or stress for the fact that you don't want sex any more. However, if this scenario sounds familiar to you, and particularly if your desire has faded slowly throughout the course of your partnership, this may be what is happening. Once you face facts, you can start to make progress, either by deciding that this relationship is no longer the right one for you or by starting to work on improving it, perhaps by enlisting a relationship counselor to help.

IF YOU AND YOUR PARTNER'S *basic levels of desire are unmatched, there can all too easily be pressure, resentment, and anger.*

• *If you have the lower sex drive: use fantasy or erotica to stimulate; settle for hand or mouth pleasure if your male partner wants intercourse and you don't; give lots of physical and mental affection; don't always say yes or you will become resentful; don't always say no—be prepared to compromise to help offset feelings of sexual rejection in your partner.*

• *If you have the higher sex drive: avoid demanding sex constantly, or his (or her) desire will reduce even further through resentment; satisfy yourself by masturbation; be happy with cuddles or massage in place of sex sometimes; don't settle for a sexless life and then suddenly leave in frustration—come to an arrangement that works for both of you.*

IS IT PHYSICAL?

Recent research suggests that loss of desire may have a physical cause.

● Hormonal: If your desire comes and goes, especially if it is linked with your menstrual period, hormonal imbalance may be to blame. Pregnancy, giving birth, a hysterectomy, or the menopause may also affect desire. Consult your doctor.

● Illness: Most physical illnesses, even a cold, distract you from feeling sexual at all. Long-term illness can reduce desire for years at a time. Again, see your doctor.

● Medical: If your loss of desire started as you began to take medication, check whether you can alter your drug, or its dosage, particularly if you are being treated with anticonvulsants or antidepressants.

● Fatigue and stress: Both may diminish your sex drive, particularly around key life events. Rest, relax, try to reduce the work you do and the stress you are under. Longer term, change your lifestyle so you aren't always tired.

WHEN HE SAYS NO

Traditionally, it's the woman who says no but recently men have been claiming that right, too. By the mid-1980s, men accounted for 60 percent of cases of lack of desire and the figure was rising. So you may face a situation where your partner doesn't want sex. This can feel threatening—less so if he is tired or stressed, more so if the relationship is going through a bad patch.

To start with, be patient and don't pressurize. Next, talk about it: if you have a reason for his refusal, you will be able to handle it better. If low desire is constant, take action together. Support him so he is not always exhausted. Try to work together to improve your relationship. Above all, remember that desire is more likely to return if it doesn't become a source of conflict.

DISAPPOINTING SEX

WORKING TO RECLAIM SEXUALITY WITHIN A PARTNERSHIP

However much we want sex, it can sometimes disappoint. In some relationships there is a basic sexual incompatibility from the start; in others routine sex starts to pall over time. Or perhaps whereas to begin with we included a whole variety of

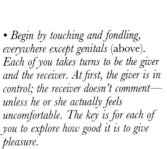

arousing sexual activities, now we pare sex to the bone and thus omit many of the essential elements.

In this situation, most of us feel powerless. Should we ask for something different after all this time? Should we opt for someone different, change partners, or have an affair? Should we keep our heads down and concentrate on what doesn't disappoint about our partnership? In fact, we need accept none of these options. It may take time, effort, and commitment on both sides. But it is possible to reclaim the sexuality within our primary relationship.

IF SEX DISAPPOINTS, *these exercises may work. They won't succeed if there is bad feeling between you, or if your relationship is over in all but name. But they do take away the pressure to perform, help you focus on your own sensations, and teach you both to please each other.*

You first need to agree to a ban on full genital sex for about a month. During this time, spend two or three hour-long sessions each week in a sensuous environment, simply exploring each other.

• *Begin by touching and fondling, everywhere except genitals* (above). *Each of you takes turns to be the giver and the receiver. At first, the giver is in control; the receiver doesn't comment— unless he or she actually feels uncomfortable. The key is for each of you to explore how good it is to give pleasure.*

• *After two or three sessions, switch the focus to receiving* (right). *Again, take turns to touch and fondle, steering clear of genitals. Now, the receiver can comment on what is good and less good, and can ask for what he or she wants. The key here is to focus on how good it is to receive.*

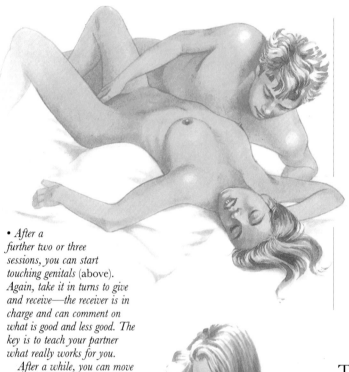

Case history

"I suppose I'm strange in that I'm committed to a partner with whom sex is not all that good. Yet I don't mind and I still love her. It was okay to start with, but it never really got better and now it is, to be frank, spasmodic. But we're best friends, we look out for each other, life with her is never dull. It all came to a head, for me, when I had a one-night stand with someone at a weekend conference. The sex was brilliant. On the way home on the train, I kept comparing her to D. Then I thought, maybe I should try to improve things. But I know that would just put pressure on us. I bought into my relationship, and I'm sticking with it. I can't have everything. I'll settle for the best I can get—which is D."

ANNE

• *After a further two or three sessions, you can start touching genitals* (above). *Again, take it in turns to give and receive—the receiver is in charge and can comment on what is good and less good. The key is to teach your partner what really works for you.*

   After a while, you can move to mutual touching, both giving and receiving.

• *After two or three further sessions, move to full genital masturbation.*

   For heterosexual couples, the next step is intercourse with the woman on top. Take turns being in charge, so that you teach your partner what works for you, and learn what works for him. After a while, blend what you've each learned in mutual lovemaking.

THE RIGHT APPROACH

You can do a lot to improve lovemaking simply by changing your ideas about the way you approach sex.

● Be realistic: Don't buy into the media's "perfect" sex, then feel disappointed because you don't have it.

● Be patient: After the first lust, there will be troughs and peaks. You need to ride out the lows and work toward the highs.

● Be willing to learn: Explore what your partner needs in order not to disappoint him (or her).

● Be willing to teach: However much in love you are, you are not mind-readers; show your partner what turns you on if he is not to disappoint you.

● Be prepared to take time: Prioritize sex over other things and leave enough time for sex not to be hurried and, particularly, for foreplay not to be forgotten.

● Be unpredictable: Try to break your routine with surprises, experiments, fantasies.

UNCOMFORTABLE SEX
WHEN YOU FEEL DISCOMFORT DURING SEX

More than 10 percent of women regularly feel discomfort when having sex, whether that is foreplay, masturbation, or intercourse. Lovemaking can be uncomfortable for many reasons—illness, disability, lack of arousal, sheer clumsiness. In the short term, it spoils the event. In the long term, however, it can create emotional blocks that initially make sex less enjoyable and eventually stop us from getting aroused at all. It's important, then, not simply to accept the discomfort, grit our teeth, and bear it. We should tackle the problem at source to make sure that sex is enjoyable, always.

The importance of lubrication

Many cases of painful intercourse are due to insufficient lubrication. When you're aroused and ready for penetration, hormones trigger your vagina into producing a kind of sweat that lets the penis enter and move easily. There are many reasons why this may not be happening. You may have a hormonal imbalance, perhaps because you are taking the pill, breastfeeding, or approaching menopause. It is also possible that you are not getting the right sort of stimulation for long enough. Or perhaps your arousal mechanism is being blocked mentally after a painful experience such as childbirth.

You can solve such problems in the short term by using a vaginal lubricant. In the long term, hormonal imbalance can be resolved by taking hormone supplements or using estrogen creams. But many such problems are caused by being rushed into intercourse before you're ready. Relax, make sure you're getting the right stimulation, then wait about three times as long as you think you need to wait before penetration.

IS IT PHYSICAL?

Painful intercourse may signal something wrong medically. If added lubrication doesn't solve the problem—or if pain is accompanied by discharge or bleeding—see your doctor.

● If you also have painful menstrual periods, the doctor may check for evidence of pelvic inflammatory disease, endometriosis, or fibroids.

● If you also have an urge to urinate, you could be suffering from a bladder infection. Pass water before and after sex; your doctor may give you antibiotics to clear the infection.

● If you feel pain only in one intercourse position, this position might be putting pressure on your ovaries. Your doctor can check for ovarian inflammation or infection; if all is clear, change your position.

● Pain when your partner thrusts deeply could be caused by infection.

● If pain starts only after intercourse begins, you may be suffering from vaginal yeast; after treatment, take preventative measures in future (see pp. 36–37).

SOME ILLNESSES *make you more tired than usual, and others can be painful. Monitor your symptoms so that you can make love when you are least tired and the pain is under control—often first thing in the* morning. *If you are able to communicate well with your partner, you can offer advice on the right way to enter you—at what angle, how deeply, how slowly—so that you are as comfortable as possible.*

WHEN ILLNESS MAKES SEX UNCOMFORTABLE

Cause	Problems	What may help
Arthritis	Pain may cause discomfort when you move; reduced mobility may make some intercourse positions difficult.	Choose your least painful time of day; ease pain and stiffness with a warm bath; take painkilling drugs before lovemaking; use pillows to support your limbs; use non-intercourse lovemaking; experiment with different positions.
Cerebral palsy	Muscle spasticity, rigidity, and weakness may make genital lovemaking difficult; you may also suffer from vaginal dryness.	Use pillows to support your limbs; use non-intercourse lovemaking; experiment with different positions; use a vibrator; use a lubricant to ease the way.
Heart disease	Tiredness may make you lose desire; chest pains may distract you from sex.	Choose your least tired time of day; ask your doctor for drugs to reduce the pain; use positions that don't tire you.
Osteomy	The osteomy bag may get in the way; you may feel embarrassed at the thought of leakage during sex.	Avoid eating or drinking for an hour or so before sex; empty your bag before sex; use positions that minimize the impact of the bag; reassure, and get reassurance from, your partner to avoid embarrassment.
Respiratory illness	Breathlessness may limit your energy and movement.	Take any relevant drugs or use an inhaler before intercourse; avoid making love near allergens; use positions that don't involve energetic movement; get your partner to take an active role.
Spinal cord injuries	You may suffer from paralysis and loss of genital sensation.	Try different positions and lovemaking that doesn't involve vaginal penetration.
Surgery	Pain in the wound may make some positions uncomfortable; loss of a limb may lower your self image.	Check with your doctor when it is safe to use the affected part; be guided by discomfort; use positions that don't put pressure on the wound.
Radiotherapy	If radiotherapy has been used to treat your genitals, scarring can narrow the vagina, making both intercourse and masturbation painful.	Use lubrication to ease the way.

IF PENETRATION FEELS WRONG

BECOMING COMFORTABLE WITH INTERCOURSE

Sometimes, penetration doesn't feel right. It may be that we simply don't enjoy it at the time. At worst, we develop vaginismus, in which mental and physical reaction to the thought of penetration is so strong that the vaginal muscles spasm, allowing nothing in. Such a reaction can be deeply disturbing. Not only does it rule out internal examinations, essential Pap smears, and the possibility of using tampons, it can also ruin our self-esteem and our relationships.

Penetration is so often seen as all-important—the words "have sex" are typically taken to mean "have intercourse". So we feel a failure, believing that we are unable to do what nature intended, feeling guilty at what we see as our illogical reaction. Our partners may feel threatened. In the short term, they are frustrated at the lack of intercourse; in the long term, they're unable to handle what to them is a crucial rejection.

Of course, we don't have to accept penetration if we don't choose to. But for so many women it is such an integral part of lovemaking that we surely should be able to enjoy it if we wish to.

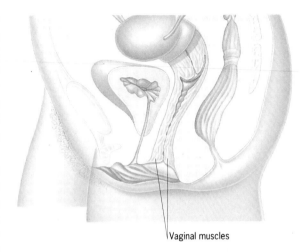

Vaginal muscles

IN VAGINISMUS, *it is the vaginal muscles themselves that go into spasm, blocking the entrance to the vagina completely. When this* *happens it becomes difficult for a penis to penetrate for intercourse, and even a small finger or a junior tampon can be impossible to insert.*

POSSIBILITIES WITHOUT PENETRATION

Penetration sometimes feels wrong because it feels compulsory. Believing that it "has to", "ought to" or "should", your body rebels and simply won't. One possible solution is to put a temporary ban on intercourse, for perhaps a month.

During that time, explore the endless possibilities of sex without penetration. (Remember that millions of lesbians have a wonderful sex life without it.) Try kissing, cuddling, stroking, massaging. Have orgasms from your partner's fingers and tongue, then return the favor. If he really needs the experience of intercourse, enclose his penis with your hands, mouth, breasts, under your arm or between your thighs.

Once you've built trust and desire through lovemaking that does not include penetration, then— and only if you want to—you may feel able to move on to lovemaking that does.

WHY DOES IT HAPPEN?

Mistrusting penetration can be put down to several things:

● You may have had uncomfortable intercourse but forced yourself to go on anyway, perhaps to satisfy your partner. After a few occasions, however, you begin to worry and tense up in anticipation.

● A single event, such as an embarrassing internal examination, sexual attack or even childbirth, could have traumatized you, with the result that your body won't cooperate.

● You may not want penetration because it's too emotionally intimate, perhaps with one particular partner, perhaps with any partner.

TO OVERCOME ANXIETY about penetration, these exercises may help. The key is to break the vicious circle of anxiety by deliberately relaxing, taking control and feeling in charge of what's happening. So it's important to do these exercises at a pace that's right for you.

• Take time alone, when you won't be interrupted. Relax first, perhaps in a bath, then use the first part of the self-examination activity on page 27 to look at your external genitals. Do this on several occasions, until it feels natural and easy.

• Next, lubricate the tip of one finger (with saliva or oil) and insert it just slightly into your vagina. Bear down. Push your finger in slightly farther; bear down again. If you sense your muscles tightening, deliberately tense, then relax them. Start to feel you have control over what's happening, that you can relax when you want to. Practise until you feel comfortable.

• Use two then three fingers, or a vibrator or dildo. Lubricate, insert the tip, bear down. Keep relaxing. Again, practice until you are comfortable. Then ask your partner to help. Get him to insert the tip of his finger while you relax. Over several sessions, if necessary, get him to insert more fingers and move them gently in and out.

• When you are ready for penetration by a penis, start with the woman on top position. Lubricate his penis well, lower yourself so the tip just touches you, keep relaxing. Do this until you feel comfortable allowing the penis inside. Keep in control, with your partner still, and you moving only the amount that feels right. As you gain confidence, you can add more movement and work your way gradually toward enjoyable mutual intercourse.

These exercises aren't the answer if your fear is deep rooted. So if you come to a halt, particularly if you're experiencing a strong physical or emotional reaction, then it's sensible to stop. Consider seeing a sex therapist who can help you work through your block.

YOUR RIGHT TO ORGASM

WORKING TOWARD RELIABLE ORGASMS IN PARTNERSHIP SEX

Of course, no woman should feel that she has to achieve orgasm in order to be sexual. At the same time, if she wants an orgasm, she should be able to. The problem is that a few of us may never have experienced orgasm, and some of us reach it only occasionally. There is no reason to accept such a situation. Every woman—and every man—can do a great deal to make sure that she has the orgasms she wants when she wants them.

Physical problems

There are various causes of sudden inability to orgasm. Illnesses such as diabetes, multiple sclerosis, kidney disease, or rheumatoid arthritis often affect orgasmic functioning, as do hormonal imbalance, perhaps caused by taking the contraceptive pill, and medication to treat such problems as anxiety, insomnia, or depression. If you suspect any of these factors are having side effects, arrange a check-up right away. Physical conditions can be alleviated, and medications and dosage can often be changed.

IF YOUR DIFFICULTY *in having an orgasm is due to lack of knowledge, practice, or experience—rather than physical or emotional blocks—these exercises will help.*

First, build confidence in your body. This might include spending time looking at yourself naked, doing the self-examination exercise on p. 27, or simply lightly touching your genitals (right).

Learn to masturbate. This is essential—if you don't learn what you need, you won't be able to include it in mutual lovemaking. Once you've learned, practice often, in different situations (below), *so that you know you can climax reliably. Try using a vibrator, which may provide the necessary stimulation.*

Then masturbate with your partner cuddling you (below). *Don't be embarrassed; most partners get incredibly turned on by watching a woman masturbate.*

For heterosexual couples, the next step is to adapt your orgasm technique for use in intercourse; you need a cooperative partner here. Start by lying back and allowing his penis just inside you, then masturbate yourself by hand as usual while you both lie still.

FAKING IT

*Should you fake orgasm? Studies suggest that more
than 50 percent of women have at some time.
Arguments rage about whether they're right to do so or
not—and, after the event, most women themselves think
that they shouldn't have faked.*

*There are several reasons for faking: it avoids
confrontation; your "orgasm" pleases your partner
(especially if he has swallowed wholesale the media
message that "women demand orgasms"); and it takes
the pressure off you to perform. The "fake it till you
make it" school of thought also suggests that by
pretending to climax, you train your body into reactions
that eventually result in the real thing.*

*But if you fake it and the relationship continues, a
partner may never learn what you need; you may
become increasingly resentful at the lack of climax; you
may feel that he (or she) should know whether you
orgasm or not and, ironically, be upset that he does not
spot the deception. And, if you eventually admit he
hasn't been pleasing you, you may lose the mutual trust
that already exists in your relationship.*

*With a new partner, it's best to warn from the start that
you don't always climax. Reassure him that it's not
his fault—but, from the very beginning, also teach him
precisely how to help. Work, together, toward your
reliable orgasms.*

MIND BLOCKS

If you can climax alone but not with a partner—
or if you used to climax with a partner but can't
now—your emotions may be blocking you.
Consider whether the following might be true.

● You find it threatening to tell your partner
the precise stimulation you need. Practice
developing your sexual communication skills.

● You feel sufficiently bad about your partner
that you can't let go and achieve orgasm. Work
on resolving your relationship conflicts.

● You are so close to your partner that you
focus only on pleasing him (or her). Aim for
climax in turns and during your turn,
concentrate solely on your own pleasure.

● You're going through a stressing phase,
maybe following bereavement or job loss. The
orgasms may return if you alleviate the stress.

● You have not had sex for a while—after
childbirth, for example—with the result that
you now "spectate," wondering how you look
or if you're doing it "correctly." Concentrate
more on your sensations moment to moment.

*Finally, move to full
penetration, perhaps in
positions such as the starfish
(below), in which you can
masturbate easily almost
without him noticing. Always
include lots of foreplay, add
enough lubrication, and
experiment with what brings
you to climax. This may*

*include intercourse positions
that make you feel in control,
angling your body in different
ways, touching yourself at
different rhythms. In time,
build your ability to climax
with more or
less clitoral
stimulation.*

PREMATURE EJACULATION
WHEN HE COMES TOO QUICKLY

Climaxing too early is one of the most common male sexual problems. If he hasn't had sex for a while or is with a new partner, it can all be over in minutes, but within weeks this problem has usually disappeared. Or he thrusts, ejaculates, and is happy—even though he hasn't satisfied his partner. Alternatively, he might reach climax at once after his erection, maybe without penetration.

In general, women are at ease with such premature ejaculation. We don't find it threatening because it doesn't seem to be an act of rejection. If a new partner does it, we might feel good that he's so overcome with lust. We even react calmly if our partner consistently reaches orgasm before we do, particularly if he's always happy to see to our needs in another way. But are we perhaps still buying into the presupposition that the male orgasm should always take precedence?

Where we do have difficulty is when he climaxes instantly. And we're right to worry. Speedy ejaculation is a sign a man is aroused; instant ejaculation is a sign that something is wrong. It means that he is physically unaware of his body's signals, perhaps because he's never learned, perhaps because he's experiencing some emotion so strong that it totally overrides the warning. This problem does need—perhaps professional—help to enable him to enjoy prolonged lovemaking, and to allow us to experience the pleasure of intercourse.

Case history

"Yes, he usually comes before I do. It's not a problem—over 30 years, we've learned to work with it. Just occasionally, we time it right and he holds still a lot, and I work hard. That's OK, but usually it's easier and happier not to struggle against nature, for him to come during intercourse and me to come some other way, some other time. I just love to let him go for it, not have to wait or worry about me, just enjoy himself. I love the look on his face when he comes."

SYLVIA

YOU CAN HELP *in a situation where he climaxes before you do (as opposed to a situation where he simply cannot control himself).*

• *Make love when he's tired so he lasts longer.*

• *Don't overstimulate him at the start of sex.*

• *Don't rush in with arousing activities such as oral sex.*

• *Have intercourse several times each session—the more he ejaculates, the longer he'll take next time.*

• *Develop mutual signals so that if he feels himself climaxing, you both stop to give him time to calm down.*

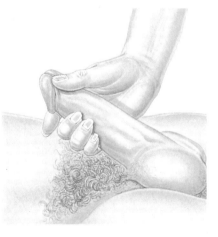

• *Also, use the "squeeze" technique. Once he has an erection and feels that he is about to climax, you (or he if he prefers) should grasp his penis firmly between your thumb and finger, just under* the head, and squeeze; after about 30 seconds, his erection will soften.

• *You can also try this technique during intercourse, if he is ready to come and you* want to prolong the session. If he is inside you, reach to grasp the base of his penis and squeeze firmly; again, after about 30 seconds, his erection will soften slightly and you can continue.

Case history

"We met at a party and within an hour, we were in bed. It was so flattering—and when he came as soon as he was inside me, I found that flattering, too. We said we'd try again in the morning. In the morning, it happened again. And again. And again. The relationship lasted a total of two weeks. I'm afraid I just couldn't take it. We never actually did it properly—he never actually got beyond the first or second thrust. Looking back now, I suspect there was something seriously wrong, something he wasn't coping with and I was too young to handle."

RACHEL

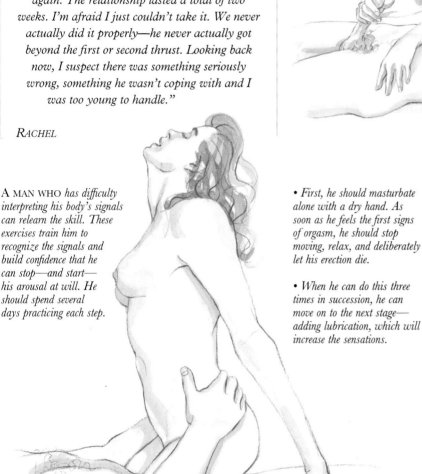

A MAN WHO *has difficulty interpreting his body's signals can relearn the skill. These exercises train him to recognize the signals and build confidence that he can stop—and start— his arousal at will. He should spend several days practicing each step.*

• *First, he should masturbate alone with a dry hand. As soon as he feels the first signs of orgasm, he should stop moving, relax, and deliberately let his erection die.*

• *When he can do this three times in succession, he can move on to the next stage— adding lubrication, which will increase the sensations.*

• *When he can do this three times in succession, you can join in. Masturbate him by hand (above)—stopping immediately he signals he's approaching climax.*

• *Next, masturbate him by mouth. Again, he must stay in charge, signaling you to stop when necessary. Practice until he has full control.*

• *Last, try intercourse, with you on top (left), stopping whenever he tells you. The aim is to be able to have intercourse in any position, with him capable of holding back as necessary.*

143

ERECTILE DIFFICULTY
HELPING TO STIMULATE AN ERECTION

Almost every man, once in his life, finds erection difficult. It's normal—often just a temporary loss of confidence. But it can damage his self-esteem and make us feel a failure, too. But if we can track down the causes, there's a great deal that can be done to help.

Coping with performance anxiety

Performance anxiety occurs when, usually after a one-time loss of erection, a man starts worrying that he will never achieve another. Worry, of course, immediately undermines his next erection, and so it goes on.

The really embarrassing thing is that women often make things worse. We feel that his lack of erection must be our fault—so we become defensive. We think it's a sign he doesn't care any more, so we become emotionally withdrawn. He then thinks we're angry, or that we don't care, and things end with the wrong results.

If you can, stay calm and loving and accept that your partner is not a machine and will occasionally have off-days. You could then try some immediate first aid. Circle the tip of the penis with a ring of your index finger and thumb, then squeeze. Offer oral sex. Ease him inside you still soft and then try moving around. If none of these work the first time, let it go. Snuggle up and forget about sex for the night. Next time, let him set the pace so he feels confidently in control, or try making love in untypical places and at unusual times—to avoid the stress-zone of bed. If over time there's still no erection, keep smiling, but gradually introduce some of the other approaches mentioned here.

IF YOUR PARTNER *has regular trouble getting an erection, try this approach:*
• *Put a ban on intercourse for a few weeks to take the pressure off. Cuddles, kisses, strokes, massages are okay.*

• *If an erection does happen, play with it for a while, then let it die away. He needs to know that he can let the erection come and go—he doesn't need to hang on to it desperately.*

• *When erections are regular, try the woman on top position, guiding him into you then moving a little. Again, let the erection die; let him concentrate on feeling the sensations, doing what feels good to him.*

144

Case history

"It started after we had Sarah. I had a really hard time with her, lots of tearing; for a few months afterward, I just couldn't bear him inside me, and we stopped having sex. Then when the scars had healed, every time we tried, he couldn't get it up.

"Our doctor suggested we try sex therapy. We talked it through, and were unsure, but it seemed worth it. We had to wait for three months—still no sex—for an appointment, and then got a woman, which didn't please Mike. But we talked about why it was all happening and realized that Mike's problem was that he'd been worried by the first few times we'd tried intercourse and I'd yelled. He didn't want to hurt me.

"The weird part was the exercises at home. It felt strange setting aside time for sex—even stranger being told to ignore erections! But it was lovely cuddling and stroking, and almost at once, Mike's erection came back, though we had to wait weeks before the therapist would let us go for intercourse. The problem's gone now—and I wouldn't panic if it happened again."

TINA

• *Only when he's confident should he go "on top" again—this position can make him feel pressured to perform. If at any time he starts losing his confidence, go back a few steps and start again.*

ALL IN THE MIND

Men have never been under as much psychological pressure as they are today, with the result that erection problems can be due to mental as well as physical blocks.

● He may be stressed by overwork, family problems, a difficult decision looming, or a sudden crisis such as unemployment or bereavement. Support him by taking the lead in bed, giving him lots of foreplay and not demanding that he perform.

● He may be wary of sex for some reason— scared you'll get pregnant, for example. Plan practical action, together, to make sure these things won't happen.

● Perhaps he is simply not attracted to women or is having doubts about his sexual orientation. If you suspect this is the problem, you can't simply ignore it. You must renegotiate or end the relationship.

● He may be sexually inhibited, usually because of some guilt or trauma. He needs understanding, support, or even therapy to resolve things.

● He may have stopped fancying you because the partnership is difficult. Sort out conflicts between you by talking them through and expressing your feelings (*see pp. 132–33*). If necessary, go to relationship counseling.

● He may have lost interest in you because sex has become boring. Try changing the time and place for lovemaking, introducing an element of fantasy or using sex toys.

● He may lack confidence, particularly if he's inexperienced or starting a new and longed-for relationship. He needs reassurance, a feeling of security, and time.

ERECTILE DIFFICULTY
PHYSICAL AND SURGICAL WAYS TO SOLVE THE PROBLEMS

IS IT PHYSICAL?

● There may be physical causes why your partner suddenly loses his ability to get an erection: low levels of testosterone; problems with the nerves that control erection; a lack of blood flow into and out of the penis. Such problems may be caused by a general lack of fitness made worse by alcohol and cigarettes; by surgery or injury; by diseases such as diabetes, kidney failure, or multiple sclerosis; by medication for depression, high blood pressure, heart disease, cancer, epilepsy.

● There are a number of solutions: surgical repair of damaged arteries and veins to restore blood flow; injections of papaverine (a non-addictive opium derivative) to create an erection; alteration of medication. (Some experts claim that hormone supplements can help; others that such supplements are useless.) So it's always worth encouraging a man to see a doctor, if only to rule out medical problems as the cause.

"Tube" fits over penis

FOR A TEMPORARY *erection, a man may buy one of the many types of penis ring that are advertised. These either encircle the penis and stop blood flowing out (above), or pump up an erection through a suction mechanism (left). These usually work, although he should avoid one that is too tight, which can stop the blood flow completely and may result in permanent damage.*

Size guide

Cone fits onto end of tube

Suction mechanism screws onto cone and draws air out to create an erection

IF YOUR PARTNER'S *loss of erection is really incurable— perhaps because the causes are physical—then he may consider a penile implant (left). This consists of one or two rods, sometimes with an inflatable tube, inserted into the penis to create a permanent erection. It's an irreversible* addition to a man's physiology, *meaning that he can never again get a natural erection, so not something to be done lightly.*

It is something a partner may, for example, do because he thinks you need him to have an erection; therefore if you don't, tell him clearly before he makes his decision.

DELAYED EJACULATION

For a few men, ejaculation is just too controlled. He takes forever to climax. It sounds as if women should welcome this, since it means that intercourse can last longer. But in fact, while delayed ejaculation makes our partners frustrated and irritated, it also makes us frustrated, bored—and sore. But there are ways around the problem.

If your partner has temporary difficulty climaxing, he may simply need more fantasy, more foreplay, enthusiastic oral sex, and an intercourse position such as man on top that offers strong friction.

But a man can also get into a vicious circle with delayed ejaculation, overcontrolling his response so he feels unable to climax at all (43 percent of men say they have faked orgasm at times when they felt it was expected of them). These exercises aim to get him relaxed with the idea of climaxing and able to let go; he should take several days to master each step.

• He should begin by masturbating alone—with fantasy, lubrication, and any kind of movement that brings him to climax. If he feels himself tensing, he should relax and focus on his sensations.

• When he's confident doing this, he can allow you into the room but not watching.

• When he can climax like this, he can allow you to watch ... cuddle him while he masturbates ... use your hand over his.

• Next, he can masturbate closer and closer to your vagina.

• When he's confident, he can enter you just at the last moment, so that he ejaculates inside you.

• Keep practicing so that he can enter you earlier and earlier, then ejaculate inside.

IS IT PHYSICAL?

If his lack of ejaculation happens suddenly, the problem may be medical. Some diseases, such as multiple sclerosis, diminish the ability to orgasm and ejaculate. Injury or surgery near his genitals, such as a colostomy or removal of the prostate gland, may well account for the problem, though since he may still be able to orgasm, the lack of ejaculation may not be too worrying. If he's taking medication for high blood pressure, the medication or the dosage can often be altered successfully. Suggest that he see his doctor if you suspect any of these conditions is causing the problem.

ASKING FOR HELP
CHOOSING A THERAPIST OR COUNSELOR

More and more of us, increasingly often, are taking the opportunities offered by sex therapy. We are realizing—and stating openly—that seeking outside help for a sexual problem is not a last resort. Sex therapy gives us support in difficult situations and enables us to explore issues that may be impossible to face alone. So by opting for therapy, we are taking control, effectively solving our problems, and positively improving our lives.

You can go to therapy on your own if you are single or if you want to work on an individual problem. If you are in a partnership, most therapists prefer both of you to attend for mutual learning and support, although you may attend some sessions separately to explore different issues.

The therapist will usually begin by taking a full "history" of your problem, considering such factors as possible medical conditions, sexual messages from

your childhood, and the current state of your relationship. Then together you'll explore these issues, with the therapist asking questions and making suggestions. You may be asked to think about things in new ways—looking back to past experiences, developing a mutual sexual vocabulary or setting sexual goals for the future.

Specifically in sex therapy, you may also be asked to do practical "homework," carrying out sensual tasks such as practicing masturbation, cuddling with your partner, or trying specific positions. Many of the exercises included in this chapter are based on tasks sex therapists suggest.

Sex therapy is uncharted territory for most people, so it can be difficult to gauge how you are doing. In particular, exploring problem areas may cause a "shakedown" in your relationship to start with. So don't worry if you find sessions challenging, or if you seem to be going backward rather than forward. Stick with it if you can. Over time therapy should bring improvement. Expect to get a gradual but steady revival of your sex life, an ability to handle problems more easily, and increasingly positive feelings about the future. If none of these is happening, you may need to find another therapist or therapy approach.

IF YOUR PARTNER IS UNWILLING

Often with sex therapy you both need to go to benefit. If your partner does not want to, these points may help to persuade him (or her).

● Most refusal is because of fear—that you will be judged, criticized, or expected to talk about distressing things. No good therapist will blame, shout, or insist. Talk through your fears together and put them to rest.

● Conversely, avoid bland reassurances. Tackling a sexual problem may not be emotionally easy, though short-term pain will almost certainly lead to long-term gain. If worse comes to worst, you can always leave therapy.

● Don't force things. If a partner genuinely isn't interested, blackmail or bribery might get him (or her) to a session, but it will not create the cooperative attitude you need. Go alone. If therapy works, your partner may eventually join you.

MANY COUPLES *enter therapy thinking it is the practical aspects of their sex life that need to change. And improving technique, or learning more about a partner's needs, can make a big difference. But if you do enter therapy, you may find to your surprise that what makes the difference to sex can be something that seems totally unlinked—anger that's never been expressed; grief over a bereavement; or even unresolved childhood memories.*

COUNSELING OR SEX THERAPY?

Individual or relationship counseling deals with more general emotional issues which may be affecting your sex life. It doesn't include the sensual exercises that sex therapy does, but involves other aspects such as talking through the problem and setting goals.

You can seek counseling to deal with:
• A trauma now or in the past: an abortion, miscarriage, sexual assault, sexual rejection.
• A personal emotional issue, such as insecurity about the way you look, or that you are without a partner.
• Relationship problems such as persistent fights or an affair.
Most sex therapists, in fact, usually suggest you attend relationship counseling before you can start sex therapy if your relationship is showing this kind of danger signal.

If you try the exercises included in this chapter and find yourself (or your partner) blocked in completing them, then find a therapist. You probably need his or her specialist help to conquer your problem.

7 · YOUR SEXUAL POTENTIAL

THERE CAN BE A DANGER IN SATISFACTORY sex. In particular, once the first lust of early sexual relationships is over and we are settled in an emotionally stable partnership, we can tend to accept what is and push to the back of our minds any thought of what could be. We love our partners, we have sex regularly, we please and are pleased. And simply because sex is satisfactory now, it can stop being something we feel we need to develop. Career, children, and day-to-day life are so obviously important that, slowly but surely, making love may easily shift to the periphery of our lives.

The danger is that the next step is that sex becomes not merely peripheral but actually ignored. Or it may simply be left static, to exist without change or development unless or until a problem in lovemaking or in our relationship makes us examine our love life and see that it needs attention.

But the best sex is not static; it changes and grows. It develops, within ourselves and within our partnerships, as we constantly update what we like and what we don't, and experiment to see what satisfies us and what doesn't. It is only by pushing the boundaries of satisfactory lovemaking that we can really reach our full sexual potential.

DEVELOPING SEXUALLY *can mean trying something different—reading erotica, using sex toys, or exploring the outer reaches of fantasy. But it doesn't have to. A simple everyday experience such as taking a shower can be an opportunity for sexual development. The mind and body alone are enough to enhance your sexual potential, if they are used with imagination, experimentation, and a sense of excitement.*

CHANGING THE BACKDROP
USING VARIATIONS IN TIME AND PLACE TO ENHANCE LOVEMAKING

As a relationship develops, it is tempting to narrow the parameters of lovemaking, keeping to traditional scenarios in time and place, and confining sex to the evening and the bedroom. But in doing so we create a situation in which we become increasingly wary of different times and settings.

Being aware of the ways we slowly and inexorably limit ourselves in time and place, and deliberately choosing to step outside these limits and change the backdrop, can be one of the most effective ways to keep our sex life fresh and interesting.

Wine

Celery

Oysters

Tomatoes

Ginseng

Spanish fly

APHRODISIACS are substances that are supposed to arouse, but many have no real impact and may have nasty side effects. Tomatoes and celery are stimulating because they look like male testicles and penis; a little alcohol relaxes, but too much dulls desire; oysters have a fishy "sex" smell; ginseng is anecdotally reputed to work, but there is no evidence that it does; Spanish fly inflames the urethra, which makes the stimulation of clitoris and penis that it induces dangerous.

IF YOU NORMALLY make love at a leisurely pace and with time to spare, try taking a quickie (left)—perhaps only partially undressed—somewhere you normally wouldn't have sex, such as in the kitchen.

WHILE LOVING, affectionate sex is a good basic diet, a friendly wrestling match (above) can arouse you both. If he wins too often, make him keep his eyes closed, or say he can't touch you above the waist.

AN INTIMATE RETREAT

Particularly if others share your living space, you may want to customize a room for sex.

● Furnish and decorate for visual and tactile comfort, and avoid reminders of the outside world, particularly work.

● Make the room soundproof, perhaps by lining the walls with curtains or throws and the floor with thick rugs.

● Be close to the bathroom—the ideal is ensuite—to move easily from the shower to lovemaking and vice versa.

● Use several small dimmer lights or candles to give atmosphere.

● Have a space heater so that you can quickly boost background heat.

● Choose the largest bed you can afford, with the mattress at a height level with your partner's pubic bone when he is kneeling for comfortable penetration and firm enough that your pelvis doesn't sink in. A comforter is easier to maneuver than blankets during lovemaking; have extra pillows to slide under your buttocks to give height.

● For off-the-bed lovemaking, leave space for a soft rug on the floor and provide a stable chair without arms.

● Add a television and video for erotic films, a large mirror, and a drawer (lockable if children use the room) for sex toys, erotica, massage oil, and contraceptives.

Case history

"When we first met, we lived at opposite ends of the country, so we had phone sex. We'd exchange fantasies—often developed over several days. We'd tell each other exactly what we'd like to do to one another. We'd masturbate—separately or together, listening to each other's breathing getting heavier and heavier. Usually, it was in bed—late at night just before we slept, or as we woke; sometimes I took the mobile into the bath. We'd play games, I'd start masturbating, then pretend I was tired and make him beg me to carry on. Or he'd 'control' it, telling me to stop and start to order, keeping me just on the edge of climax until eventually I couldn't hold back."

SARAH

OUTDOOR SEX *is obviously best in a warm climate, although in temperate regions forests may provide enough privacy and good shelter from climatic extremes. Making love in the surf* (right)— *particularly at dusk or in the moonlight—is classically romantic, and in the sea or a swimming pool (if you have it to yourselves), you can use positions that are impossible on dry land.*

FANTASIES AND SEX

ENHANCING SEX BY STEPPING OUTSIDE REALITY

Women have often been wary of sexual fantasy. It can seem unfaithful or disloyal to our partners and is often far removed from real life. And some fantasies may seem risky, aggressive, or even submissive in ways that worry us.

Yet in surveys, most women say that they do fantasize. We dream of sexual experiences totally outside reality, arouse ourselves by images of sex when we masturbate, and enhance lovemaking by imagining that an unknown lover is pleasuring us.

Our minds are powerful: mental stimulation alone can create physiological responses. The mind allows us to fill a gap, whether created by the lack of a partner while he (or she) is away, or of good sex when none is available. And it allows us to experiment, playing through scenarios that we could never experience in real life because they are not possible, or ones that we would never allow in real life because they are too frightening. In fantasy, we are always in control. (Studies show, for example, that women who fantasize about forced sex make a clear distinction between this and actual sexual submission; in the fantasy, the woman is in total control, even of being desired.)

Attitudes are changing. The latest research shows that most women who fantasize see themselves as neither unfaithful nor disloyal to their partners, but report a more fulfilling sex life than those who do not. We are starting to appreciate fully that our mind is as capable of creating sexual pleasure as our bodies.

LEARNING TO FANTASIZE

● Make time and space to be undisturbed. Begin by relaxing, breathing deeply, and becoming aware of your body—imagine warm fluid slowly filling you from toes to head, particularly flowing into your sexual parts.

● Think back to a good sexual experience. Run it through like a film in your mind, hearing the sounds, feeling the feelings, seeing the pictures—or glimpses of them. Then run the film again, this time making the setting different, the sensations stronger, and the words or actions more elaborate.

● With practice, be more experimental. Develop an everyday incident into a sexual encounter, or take your favorite piece of erotica and cast yourself in the leading role.

● To enhance partnership lovemaking without letting the "perfect" fantasy diminish reality, integrate the two. Imagine, for example, that you are both in a fantasy setting, then blend what your partner is really doing with the story inside your head.

EROTIC DREAMS

Fantasies may seem under your control. But night dreams spring from your unconscious, do not seem controllable, and so can be much more worrying.

• Be reassured about dreams that worry or disgust you; they are part of an unconscious process to alert you to danger, rather than persuade you into it.

• Don't worry about erotic dreams that arouse you, but learn from them. What do they show about your desires, or about unexplored sexual possibilities?

• If a sexual nightmare wakes you, get up and walk around, flood the room with light, switch on the radio or television. Move the focus from inside your head to the outside world.

SEX WITH A DIFFERENT PARTNER *comes with no strings attached. The fantasy involves sex with someone it would be unwise to have sex with—a best friend's husband, for example (far left)—or someone it's impossible to have sex with, such as a film star. This is the only way sex is ever going to be possible with this person, and there is no emotional aftermath.*

SEX IN AN EVERYDAY SETTING *with someone you might typically meet during a normal day, such as the plumber or gardener (left), blends the boredom of real life with good sex to make it bearable. This fantasy often includes a partner as a kind of "director" to the proceedings to give permission to an incident which otherwise might feel wrong because it is all too possible.*

SEX IN AN UNUSUAL SETTING, *perhaps in a car (left) or airplane, on a rug in front of a roaring fire, in a medieval castle, or on top of a high mountain, is a safe fantasy, usually involving a current partner, which gives a new dimension to a relationship. It may have the added attraction that sex in public places is risky, forbidden, and therefore more exciting.*

FANTASIES AND SEX
ENHANCING SEX THROUGH UNREAL PARTNERS AND SITUATIONS

SHARING FANTASIES

Some partners feel threatened when they hear fantasies. They may believe that if you need to dream, they must be lacking in some way. Others may simply not understand the attraction. And what happens if the image that turns you on proves to turn him (or her) off? Remember that once a partner knows your fantasy, he can't unknow it.

● Take things slowly. Be particularly wary of sharing fantasies likely to stir up jealousy (such as wanting to make love with a mutual friend) or anxiety (such as those involving dominance). Hint at a scenario first, perhaps jokingly, perhaps while leafing through erotica, to test your partner's reaction.

● Once fantasies are shared, whisper key phrases during sex. Let one of you tell a story while the other pleasures. Free associate just before orgasm. Dream up fantasies for a few days before a special lovemaking session, then use them as foreplay.

● Always remember that real life is different from the imagination, so don't try to recreate a whole scenario. Instead, take key elements—the cushions and feathers from the harem scene, the key words from the sex-in-an-airplane script—and weave them into your lovemaking.

Finally, for safety:

● Never put pressure on a partner to fulfill your fantasies or submit to pressure from a partner to fulfill his or hers; acting out fantasies needs to be genuinely enthusiastic or it won't work.

● Never refer to fantasies later in anger; fantasies are only one part of someone's personality and shouldn't be used as evidence in partnership conflict.

SEX WITH MORE *than one partner* (right)—*or with an anonymous and unknown group—at an orgy or party has the lure of multiple sensations, the thought of being overcome with pleasure, and the uncertainty of who will be next and what he (or she) will do. It also offers the sort of extended, unpredictable sensation often missing from real-life lovemaking.*

ORAL SEX *is a favorite fantasy* (left), *particularly among heterosexual women and perhaps especially if they want more oral sex than their men give them, or want it differently. In this fantasy, it is possible to lie back and enjoy receiving pure sensation from a partner who is willing to pleasure you for hours on end without needing any quid pro quo.*

"OTHER GENDER" *fantasies* (below), *that is making love with the gender you're not normally attracted to, is popular, perhaps for its forbidden element. Heterosexual women may also be attracted by the thought of making love with someone who understands their sexual needs, and someone with whom they don't have to compromise.*

MALE FANTASIES

Men tend to fantasize differently from women. He will focus on images rather than words; single events rather than a storyline; sexual incidents rather than relationships. His early vulnerabilities are likely to have been about getting a partner, with the result that he may fantasize about sex being easily available or about partners finding him sexually irresistible. And because his sexuality is focused more on his genitals, his fantasies may involve direct, undiluted sex that quickly results in climax.

These differences are generalized, and many different-gender partners are remarkably compatible in their fantasies. But there can be gaps in understanding. You may need words and scene setting, while he may need only images and action; you may find his fantasies too blunt and straightforward, while he may find yours unnecessarily lengthy and vague. Don't go along with fantasies that genuinely disgust, but where there is simply difference, be prepared to compromise and take turns.

OVERCOMING A PARTNER *with passion* (left) *is a new fantasy for many women, perhaps a reflection of the fact that we are feeling more in charge during sex. In this fantasy it is possible to be all a partner ever needs, as a lover or even as a comforting—if sexual—mother figure. Occasionally, there is a measure of your forcing a partner to have sex, particularly if you need to feel in control in order to get aroused.*

BEING FORCED *to have sex* (left), *perhaps imprisoned in a dungeon, on the kitchen table, tied to a four-poster bed, or taken by a gang of Hell's Angels, is a scenario with certain specifications: the dungeon is clean, the Hell's Angels are handsome. Various interpretations of this fantasy have been suggested, including that it gives sex without responsibility; that it explores power roles; and that it frees you from having to please or to love.*

EROTICA

CHOOSING AND USING AROUSING SEXUAL MATERIAL

When the Kinsey Institute carried out one of the first sex surveys of the postwar years in 1953, it was claimed that women didn't like erotica: it was unnecessary, we didn't respond to it physiologically, nor did we want it.

Kinsey was wrong and the Institute has since realigned its views. Women love erotica, but only when it is arousing to women. Now that we are more able to have what we want, rather than what men want or what men say we want, we are proving to have just as much of an appetite for sexual material as men do.

What do we like? Physiologically stimulated more by sound than other senses, we may like words rather than pictures, so an erotic novel may turn us on much more than a pin-up poster. We may demand relationship and

OVER THE PAST *10 years, erotica has become much more available— in magazines, books, films, and videos. Much, however, is still male orientated. But increasingly, makers and distributors are realizing that there is a female market for such material and catering especially for it.*

JAPANESE "PILLOW BOOKS" (left) *were sex manuals designed to be kept by the bedside as sources of inspiration. Such manuals typically feature the penis— which is always larger than life and permanently erect — and pubic hair—in Japanese culture judged to be highly erotic. Often the accompanying text describes the thoughts and sexual fantasies of lovers, with the intention of arousing the reader.*

158

context—not necessarily romance, but some build-up to the act and resolution from it, some mental foreplay and afterplay. And we need erotica that respects us, shows us in control and powerful; even in erotica that describes a woman overpowered by passion, we need to know that she is willingly overpowered and ultimately triumphant.

The result is that women's erotica—books, magazines, and videos—is on the increase. As we gain more confidence in sex, and more power in the sexual arena, we are becoming better able to admit, and then fulfill, our need for arousing material.

IS IT HARMFUL?

As a woman, should you be opposed to erotica? When does it become pornography? Research has shown that material which demeans women or shows them suffering violence leads to sexual aggression, both in individuals and in society as a whole. But pure sexual explicitness, particularly in the context of a loving relationship, doesn't seem to have such negative side effects; men and women who use erotica of this nature are no more likely to stereotype the opposite gender, exploit them or see them as sex objects than those who don't.

A useful guideline seems to be that if the erotica is simply overtly sexual, there is no harm in using it. But if it shows women (or men) being dehumanized or degraded, as objects of violence or unwanted sexual attention, then you should avoid it, and object to a partner using it. Even if it turns you on, it perpetuates positive views of negative acts and, as such, works against all of us.

PERHAPS THE MOST FAMOUS *work of erotic literature, the* Kama Sutra *was not simply a collection of seemingly impossible positions. Its aim, quite openly, was to build good relationships through improving sexual fulfillment for couples. In particular, the* Kama Sutra *stresses the importance of women: it does not see them as sexual temptresses (as many cultures did and still do), but as sources of erotic pleasure. It criticizes men for not knowing what arouses their partners, and judges a man's success as a lover largely on how much pleasure he gives his bedmate.*

GETTING AND USING EROTICA

Heterosexual sex books are often available in retail bookstores, and most video rental stores have an "adult list." Women's "sex" magazines contain erotic pictures and stories and also often have an advertising section listing mail-order sources aimed at women's tastes. You can try sex stores, but you may need to plow through a great deal of male-orientated material to find something that turns you on. For lesbian erotica, you may have to visit a specialist bookstore.

If all else fails—or if the erotica you find doesn't stimulate your imagination—create your own. Take photos or videos of yourself naked and use them to turn you on. Write storylines based on your fantasies, and read them silently or aloud, as foreplay to couple sex or self-pleasuring. Record your own sounds of pleasure as you masturbate and play them back as an accompaniment to passion.

Partnership erotica—allowing a partner to take photographs, or setting the camcorder on automatic when making love—is the ultimate sign of trust and can be highly arousing. But take care: once the emotional involvement has ended, your trust can backfire. Always keep the negatives or master tapes yourself and destroy everything personally if you split up.

USING SEX TOYS
INTRODUCING AN ELEMENT OF FUN INTO YOUR SEX LIFE

The key to enjoying sex toys lies in the second word of the expression—toys. We often tend to approach them too seriously, worrying that if our sex life was perfect, we wouldn't need them. In fact, like children, we should give ourselves permission to use our toys lightly, enjoy them, and experiment with them, without guilt or self-blame.

We can use sex toys for pure physiological enjoyment, to add kinds of stimulation the human body simply is not capable of. But they can also help us learn—teaching ourselves to reach an orgasm with a vibrator, for example, can work where trying with a partner hasn't. Very often, we put sex toys to one side in favor of simple skin-to-skin contact. But we should allow ourselves, without concern, to pick them up again when we are ready to play.

CLOTHES AND COSTUMES *are the biggest selling group of toys after vibrators. They can be solely a male turn-on, so make sure you are happy to wear them and don't simply agree because a partner gets aroused. Many women like "second skin" costumes, such as silk underwear or leather pants, or gender enhancers like high heels and uplift bras.*

SEX STORES *and mail-order companies offer a wide range of toys.*

• Clitoral stimulators fit around the base of a man's penis and nudge your clitoris. If the "fit" is right, these can work but they often promise more than they deliver—and are less effective than a skillfully used hand or tongue.

• Vaginal balls fit in your vagina where their movement stimulates. Try inserting them in the morning so arousal builds through the day, or use them for extra sensation when masturbating.

Penis extension

Dildo

Clitoral stimulators

Vaginal balls

Novelty condoms

• A dildo is an artificial penis. Some have built-in vibrators. For woman-to-woman sex, you can buy double-ended dildos or ones that strap on.

• Condoms in varying colors, flavors, and shapes can be fun. Read the notes on the package carefully — many novelty condoms do not act as a barrier to sperm or STDs.

• Penis extensions, in a variety of designs, offer added stimulation.

160

PLEASURE ALONE 54–55
ENHANCING MASTURBATION 166–67

VIBRATORS

Specialist sex stores and magazine mail-order services offer a wide variety of vibrators. In addition, some regular electrical goods stores sell "massage aids," although these may be too big for accurate clitoral stimulation. Don't feel you have to opt for a penis-shaped one: an egg-shaped vibrator will fit inside your vagina and an angled one will stimulate sensitive areas like the G spot, although many women use vibrators only on the clitoris. Choose a battery model if you don't mind the noise, or an electric one if you're happy to plug it in or recharge it. Make sure the vibrator doesn't heat up uncomfortably, and that it has more than one speed for variety.

Use a vibrator to stimulate as you would use your fingers, although with more care. Lubricate your clitoris, apply gentle pressure, then build up to as much stimulation as you want. If the sensation overwhelms as you near an orgasm, finish off with your fingers. (Using the vibrator on the tip of a male partner's lubricated penis gets good results, too.)

Vibrator with "floating" head, suitable for men as well as women

● Don't use a vibrator near your vagina if it's been near your (or your partner's) anus.

● Don't share it without cleaning with disinfectant or diluted dishwashing liquid after use, to protect against STDs and HIV.

Case history

"I love sex toys. They're daring, they add spice and interest. I don't need them for passion—I get aroused very easily—but they are such fun. When I was with H, we would bring them home as presents for each other, instead of flowers or wine. The best was the balls—I used to walk around all day in a constant state of excitement until H came home. The next best was the vibrator; up until then we'd been using my electric toothbrush, nonbristle side, of course! I introduce sex toys to a partner very carefully, but actually if they're turned off, the relationship usually doesn't last."

EMMA

Vibrator with ridged sides

Vibrator with flexible head can be plugged into mains and recharged

"Handbag" vibrator with case

VIBRATORS *are the biggest-selling sex toy, and come in a variety of sizes. Although many are still made with a penile shape and flesh tone, manufacturers are increasingly* *realizing that many women don't in fact want a penis substitute for masturbation purposes and different shapes and colors are becoming more widespread.*

Sensual Massage
TREATING THE WHOLE BODY TO A SENSUOUS EXPERIENCE

All too often, sex is about genitals. We think of sex and imagine clitoral orgasms or intercourse. We move toward sex and make a leap for the most erogenous zones. Because of this, the rest of the body can be forgotten or ignored until it cries out for the sensation it never receives, or switches off from sensation because it has been deprived for so long.

Massage pays attention to the entire body. When we receive a massage, we allow ourselves to connect with each area of our body. It is a rounded experience, one that may lead to sex, but equally one that may simply increase our sensuousness and so make us more able to enjoy lovemaking.

PREPARATIONS

● Create a setting for massage as you would for any lovemaking session, with a well-heated, dimly lit, sensuous room. If your bed doesn't have a firm mattress, use a deep rug on the floor so that the person being massaged doesn't "sink."

● Choose oil that isn't absorbed into the skin too soon, such as almond, sunflower, or coconut oil; warm it before you start by putting the bottle in a bowl of warm water.

● Take time to wind down before you start; you'll give and receive a better massage if you're relaxed rather than tense or stressed. Perhaps sit quietly together for several minutes listening to background music or nature sounds before taking up your positions and getting ready to begin.

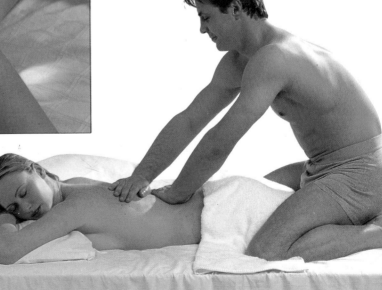

A GOOD PLACE to start is the back, a part of the body where tension builds up, and where even beginners can work wonders. Get your partner to kneel astride you, with his weight off your body. He can press down each side of your spine with his thumbs (above), or rest his hands flat and work outward.

DOS AND DON'TS

The more receptive you are to the signals your partner is giving you, and the more spontaneous you are, the better the massage will be. But there are some basic ground rules.

● Keep clear of vulnerable body parts: Infected skin or bruising; scars; varicose veins; his testicles; her abdomen if she's pregnant. Don't massage anyone who is ill or has a medical condition without checking with a doctor first.

● Never put firm pressure on places where skin stretches over bone, such as the spine, or on organs near the skin, such as the eyes.

● Once you've started massaging, it is vital not to break the touch. Even when you are replenishing oil, keep one hand on your

partner. Turn it palm uppermost and pour the oil into it with your other hand; alternatively, use a bottle of oil with a dispenser.

● Keep movements balanced; if you work on one side of the body, work on the other side in the same way for approximately the same amount of time. (Equally, although you may not always want to give and receive a massage in the same session, make sure that in general you take equal turns, so that one partner isn't always giving, the other always receiving.)

● It's more relaxing if you steer clear of genitals, although at the end of a session you may want to begin genital touching as a prelude to lovemaking.

A HEAD MASSAGE (above) can be very intimate. Use fingers and thumbs to massage the forehead outward in long strokes. Then stroke the cheeks, trace little circles along the jaw line, and work gently down the muscles of the neck into the shoulders.

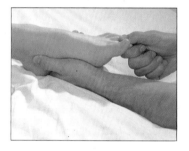

WHEN MASSAGING the front of the body (below), start from the neck and shoulders and work slowly downward— breasts, in particular, need gentle handling. Using both hands make gentle circular movement or long, firm, slow strokes on the abdomen to avoid tickling.

TOUCH FEET confidently to avoid tickling. Stroke along the top of the foot, then use thumbs to knead the sole—beware of too much pressure, which can hurt. Finally, pull gently on each toe, before holding the whole foot in both hands for a few seconds of prolonged contact.

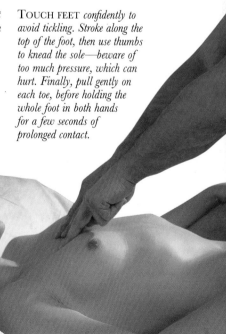

SENSUAL MASSAGE

HOW TO MASSAGE A PARTNER

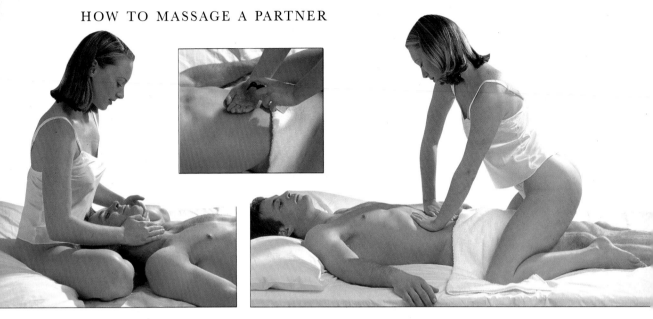

USING FEEDBACK

The massage suggestions on these pages are not to be followed slavishly. Rather, be aware of what your partner likes and be guided by his (or her) reactions.

● He may tell you what's good and what's not. Encourage him to use a "nonword" code, such as a murmur—words may stop him from relaxing fully.

● He may signal that something isn't pleasurable by a flinch, a sudden wriggle, a sharp intake of breath, a tensing of muscles.

● He may visibly relax and his muscles soften. The stiller he becomes and the more you need to "carry" his limbs, the more he's enjoying the massage.

● His unconscious physical signals may indicate contentment: his breathing may slow down, his skin warm to your touch. You may even notice his heart rate falling.

● He may signal that something is particularly pleasurable by a slight opening of his mouth, a slow outgoing breath, fluttering eyelids, a sudden heaviness of limbs.

RECEIVING A MASSAGE *doesn't simply mean lying there passively. You can help turn the massage into a two-way experience by being active: by actively relaxing, consciously clearing your mind of day-to-day intrusions and concentrating fully on your sensations and emotions. This makes it more likely that you will appreciate the experience. Such appreciation will show in your body language, and your partner will feel that his (or her) efforts are valued.*

WORKING UPWARD *from your partner's chest to his face can be particularly good if you rest his head in your lap (above left). Lean down over him to run your hands from his stomach upward in long, slow strokes. Trace circles around his nipples, then use overlapping movements of your palms up his neck to his face. Make sure that you maintain contact at all times, even when adding more oil (top).*

HIS STOMACH *(above) may be ticklish, so work cautiously with both hands placed firmly—but not heavily—on his abdomen, perhaps moving in overlapping circles.*

164

MASSAGE VARIATIONS

You can add variation to the basic process suggested here by:
Varying the way you massage...lick...kiss...bite very gently...use light finger movements (called pattes d'araignée *or* spiders' legs*)...use deep, high-pressure finger movements into the muscles.*

Varying what you massage with...use thumbs only ...use fists into big muscles such as the buttocks...use your eyelashes...use feathers, velvet gloves, flowers...use a vibrator...use a hairdryer (though never into body orifices)...use ice (not supercooled or dry ice; test on your tongue first to make sure it's not cold enough to burn).

A GREAT DEAL *of tension is often stored at the top of the back (far left).* Try *massaging the muscles across the top of the shoulders and around the shoulder blades with deep firm movements.*

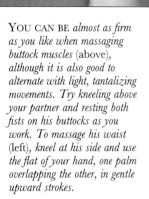

YOU CAN BE *almost as firm as you like when massaging buttock muscles (above), although it is also good to alternate with light, tantalizing movements. Try kneeling above your partner and resting both fists on his buttocks as you work. To massage his waist (left), kneel at his side and use the flat of your hand, one palm overlapping the other, in gentle upward strokes.*

CUP YOUR HANDS *around thigh and calf muscles (above), then press in firmly with your thumbs, working down in slow movements.*

ENHANCING MASTURBATION

USING HAND AND MOUTH TO BRING EACH OTHER TO CLIMAX

However much we love pleasuring and being pleasured, if we're in a relationship, masturbation can become the Cinderella of our sex life. Masturbation in private can feel disloyal and in front of a partner can be too risky. And masturbating each other can feel wonderful as part of foreplay, but if time and energy are limited, heterosexual couples at any rate may quickly develop the habit of deprioritizing it in favor of the "real thing" of intercourse.

But in fact, the knowledge we gain about ourselves and our partners from masturbation is the foundation on which really skillful sex is built.

MUTUAL MASTURBATION is often called "sixty-nine" because the shape of the numbers reflects the shape of your bodies as you do it. There are disadvantages: different speeds can distract; it's difficult to concentrate on giving oral sex when you're really aroused by receiving it; you may be wary of injury if either of you climaxes while licking the other. But as extended foreplay—perhaps taking turns when you're nearly at orgasm—it's a lovely, mutual thing to do.

FOR MASTURBATION by hand, try lying side by side on your backs (above), or top to toe on your side, using each other's knees as a pillow for your head. If you want vaginal stretching at the same time, he (or she) can put his arm through your nearest knee and bend it outward.

MASTURBATION BY MOUTH works best with one of you on your back and the other leaning over. Be sure to get the right angle so that as you work, you are reaching the most sensitive part of the glans (or clitoris). If your partner is male, you should be on top; otherwise, you may feel you are about to choke as he thrusts.

POLARITY SEX

For heterosexual couples, different timings can be a problem. A recent suggestion by American writer John Gray is polarity sex: taking it in turns to masturbate each other until you are both at roughly the same level of arousal, before moving on to the sort of mutual stimulation intercourse provides.

● Begin with about five minutes of strong, focused hand and mouth stimulation for him. Don't worry if you're not aroused; concentrate on him for the moment. When he's almost at climax, he should signal so and shift his attention to you.

● Now you relax and enjoy yourself. You get a lot longer than he does, perhaps 20 minutes of whatever stimulation you need. He, in turn, should put all his efforts into pleasuring you. When you're on the edge, you can again swap over and pleasure him.

● Swap as many times as you want, with each of you coming close to orgasm and then holding back several times; this approach physically increases your ability to feel more and more sensation.

● The process can end in intercourse. In classic polarity sex, however, he brings you to orgasm first with hand or mouth. Then, either you return the favor, or he penetrates you and goes for his orgasm in his own time. You, of course, already lubricated and aroused because you've climaxed, may climax again while he's thrusting.

WATCHING

If you feel secure masturbating alone, and comfortable about your partner masturbating you, you may want to combine the two—by masturbating "solo" in front of your partner. Some women feel anxious or embarrassed at the thought of "performing" in this way, but those who like it say that it not only helps a partner learn what you like, but also has its own excitement. The entire focus is on you, with your partner giving you all his (or her) attention; you don't have to worry about his pleasure; and any emotion you have about being watched can make you even more turned on.

In return, try watching your partner masturbate. He may need to feel particularly safe, so learn what he wants from you, perhaps for you to hold him in a certain way. Also, show by your reactions and your words when his passion arouses you; many people think that they look ugly during sex, particularly when climaxing, and being told that he looks desirable may be the reassurance he needs.

MUTUAL MASTURBATION *does not have to be about stimulating each other. If you prefer, lie entwined and masturbate yourselves, either all the way to climax, or until you want to move on to try a different position or variation.*

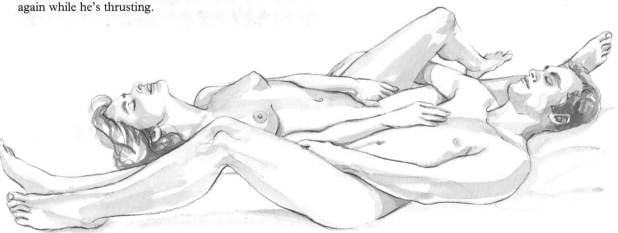

167

ENHANCING INTERCOURSE
VARYING POSITION TO GAIN MAXIMUM MUTUAL PLEASURE

Perhaps the key way women can enhance intercourse is to start joining in. All too often intercourse is male-led: he enters, moves, climaxes, and withdraws. We need to get involved, by knowing what we want and taking action to get it. Studies have shown that the more women experience sex as active participants, the greater their physical and emotional pleasure. So if sex is disappointing because of lack of stimulation, it may help if we identify and instigate appropriate movements, positions, and rhythms. If we lack the sense of relationship so important to us during intercourse, taking the initiative by looking, kissing, and talking may help.

Of course, there needs to be a balance of involvement between the genders. But this can only happen when we are prepared to be as as proactive as our male partners.

CREATING RELATIONSHIP

If you feel intercourse lacks a sense of real contact...

● Look: Choose positions that let you see each other—eye contact heightens sensation as well as closeness.

● Synchronize: Matching movement often happens naturally during good intercourse; if you find your movements are mismatching, try to breathe at the same rate as your partner, which may gradually coordinate your body language.

● Kiss: Kissing is one of the most personal of all sex acts because of the added intimacy of mouth and tongue, and the added information of smell and taste.

● Talk: Turn moans into words, and encourage words in return; while talking during sex can be distracting, it is also a shared experience and so creates contact.

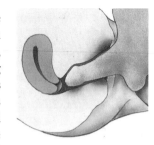

MOST MEN *naturally move into positions that give their penis the kind of stimulation they like, such as man on top* (left). *But if that doesn't reach the right parts of you, identify which position achieves the type of penis contact you need, then adjust position accordingly.*

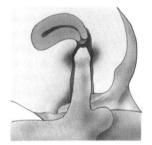

● *In positions in which you are on top* (left) *his penis can stimulate the entrance to your vagina, small deep areas on its front and back walls, and—if you like deep penetration—it can nudge your cervix.*

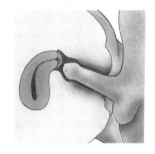

● *In rear entry positions* (left), *the penis stimulates most of the front and back walls of the vagina, and may also reach the G spot.*

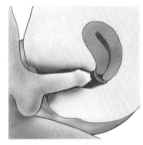

● *When you sit in your partner's lap* (left), *his penis stimulates all around the entrance to your vagina, and may also reach your clitoris.*

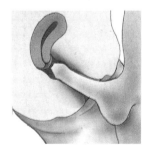

● *If you are both standing* (left), *the outer two-thirds of the back wall of your vagina and inner two-thirds of its front wall receive the most stimulation from your partner's penis.*

THE FACE-TO-FACE position of "woman on top" is a particularly active one for you, allowing control in movement and sensations. You can lean back and forward to get variations of pressure, your clitoris and breasts can be touched, you can kiss and talk. Use your vaginal muscles to pull upward with each thrust to add extra sensation. Try it on the floor or astride a stool; a rocking chair gives a disorientating but arousing feeling. This position needs a stiff erection, and is one of the few where you can injure him if you move clumsily.

Case history

"I've only just realized, with men I've slept with since the divorce, that men don't resent it if you start intercourse. Partners 20 years ago would get more threatened, I think. Maybe men are more relaxed now; perhaps they're tired of having to take the lead. But if I want intercourse, I go for it. I kiss, touch, work him up from cold if necessary. As long as I don't push when it's obvious nothing's going to happen, men are really into it. I think they find it as flattering as I do to be jumped by a lover."

PENNY

SOME WOMEN dislike being entered from behind (below) because it seems impersonal, so avoid this position if it makes you feel controlled. But it does give you different sensations and is erotic for a partner who finds female buttocks arousing. In this variation, kneel at the edge of the bed and support yourself firmly with your forearms tight into your body and your legs straight out behind; he then lifts your legs and enters you from behind. Be aware that in any rear-entry position, his penis can slip out quite easily; that air trapped in your vagina may noisily pop as he moves; and that his penis may hit an ovary if he thrusts strongly.

STANDING VARIATIONS are fun and experimental, especially if you're light or agile enough to wind your legs around his waist and be "carried" (right). They're particularly good for a partially clothed quickie, or at the start of a more-extended session before collapsing on to the bed or floor for more conventional positions. To get him inside you to begin with, lift one of your legs bent at the knee, turn it sideways to allow entry, then wind it around him to keep you joined. If height differences really do make the whole thing impractical, try doing this with one of you below the other on a flight of stairs.

169

ENHANCING ORGASM

DERIVING THE MAXIMUM PLEASURE FROM ORGASM

Unlike the climax of men, which typically depends on a build-up of semen, the muscular responses of female orgasm can happen again and again, with little or no recovery time in between. So some women have sequential orgasms, one following the other but with a clear break between contractions, while others report multiple orgasms—in which one set of contractions blends into the next with no break—or extended orgasms where the sensations, if not the contractions, last and last.

Some women have the capacity to orgasm without direct genital touching. The entire body can be a climax zone; many women report being able to orgasm through stimulation of breasts, buttocks, feet, or even ear lobes. Others say that fantasy alone can bring them to climax, with perhaps just one or two light touches to tip them over the edge.

Women report different kinds of orgasm: climaxes focused and experienced totally in the clitoris; those centered on the vagina; "whole body orgasms" in which the sensation starts in the feet and builds upward to the head.

The lesson seems to be that our orgasms may on occasion be less reliable than those of our male counterparts—but they may also be much more unexpected and extraordinary.

SIMULTANEOUS ORGASM used to be seen as a sign of love, or at the very least compatibility. Now, the emphasis is off such "goal-oriented" sex which may distract you from pleasure because you are worrying about timing.

For heterosexual couples, it may also create a difference of emotion. After orgasm, a man loses his arousal quickly and his pleasure hormones disperse, while yours stay high for much longer. As a result, he may be "coming back to reality" and withdrawing from intimacy while you are still at a peak. Many experts now suggest you orgasm separately, preferably woman first.

PELVIC FLOOR MUSCLES

Your pelvic floor muscles, surrounding the vagina, urethra, and anus, are the ones that contract when you climax. (Stop the flow next time you pass water; to do that, you use your pelvic floor muscles.) They can be strengthened to give you vaginal awareness, stronger orgasms, and a more active role during intercourse. These strengthening exercises are based on those begun by gynecologist Arnold Kegel nearly 50 years ago and developed by psychologist Sheila Kitzinger.

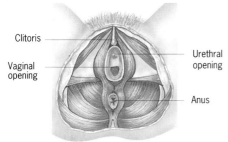

Clitoris
Vaginal opening
Urethral opening
Anus

Pelvic floor muscles

● Insert a finger into your vagina and contract your muscles until you can feel them squeezing your finger. Practice, then take your finger out and keep practicing.

● Imagine you have a small piece of fruit in your vagina. Squeeze it, chew it, swallow it.

● Now imagine you are lifting the piece of fruit up slowly, step by step, through your body. Pull up from your vagina, but push down with your shoulders.

● Practice any or all of these exercises several times a day—at the bus stop, at your desk, while cleaning your teeth. Aim for 20 squeezes each time, as fast as you like.

● Then try using them during masturbation for extra arousal, and during intercourse to grip your partner's penis even more pleasurably.

G SPOT, U SPOT, A SPOT?

Over the past 15 years, researchers have identified certain sensitive points in the vagina. Some women say they simply can't find these points, others that they lead to fail-safe orgasm. To find them, first empty your bladder, then explore with two fingers inside your vagina on the upper side; you may find it easier if you press on your stomach with your other hand. All these spots can be stimulated by your partner's finger or a gently used dildo or penis-shaped vibrator.

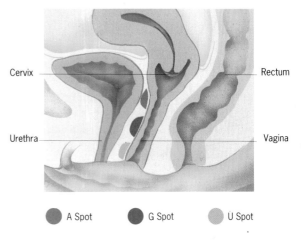

Cervix
Urethra
Rectum
Vagina

● A Spot   ● G Spot   ● U Spot

A spot: a fairly recent discovery, this is situated midway between the G spot and the cervix. It can be stimulated directly or by rubbing around the vaginal walls to each side. During intercourse, try sitting on the end of the bed while your partner enters you from in front.

G spot: first noticed by Ernst Grafenberg in 1944, this was "rediscovered" in a bestselling book of 1982. It is a bean-shaped area about 2 inches (5 cm) from the vaginal entrance. Good intercourse positions to stimulate it are woman on top, and rear entry with firm contact from your partner's penis.

U spot: situated about (1 inch) 2.5 cm into the vagina, this is often confused with the G spot. Touching it makes you want to pass water, and stimulation seems to work particularly well when combined with clitoral stimulation.

8 LIFETIME SEXUALITY

IT'S BECOMING CLEAR THAT A WOMAN'S sexuality is lifelong, an integral part of our experience and a deep foundation for everything we do. Women may, in the past, have believed that sex was not as consistently important to them as it was to men, that it was primarily only relevant in the context of childbearing and that above a certain age they shouldn't feel or behave sexually. But these beliefs were purely cultural, they were not founded in reality. In fact, barring injury or illness, we are naturally capable of pleasurable lovemaking throughout our lives.

The difference is that now we know it. Through women talking together, through female role models, through films and television, books and magazines, we are beginning to learn the truth. We are starting to realize that we have a lifetime of sexuality to enjoy.

Of course, this is in many ways a self-fulfilling prophecy. The more we learn that women are sexual from cradle to grave, the better able we feel to admit to our sexuality whatever our age. And the more we acknowledge that it is natural—and wonderful—to make love at every stage in our lives, the more essential to our womanhood we consider such lifelong lovemaking.

A LOVING RELATIONSHIP—*perhaps built over a lifetime, perhaps a new discovery late in life—is often the motivation and the basis for keeping sexuality alive. How can any human being not value her (or his) own ability to give and receive pleasure when someone else values it, too?*

SEXUAL STAGES
THE IMPACT OF LIFE EXPERIENCES ON SEXUALITY

We experience a number of shifts in the course of our sexual lives. We pass from the uncertain exploration of childhood through to the confident passion of maturity. At the peak of our fertility, we bear our children, then move to the postfertile years of the climacteric. We undergo different life experiences which, although not sexual in themselves, affect our attitude to lovemaking.

Being aware of these shifts is crucial: without this knowledge we cannot adapt individually, perhaps by preparing for a rise or fall in desire or expecting to take on a different approach or alter our views. We can also cope better with the impact these changes might have on our relationships, as our different perceptions of sexuality cause us to rethink, recommit, or decide that, sexually, a particular partner is now no longer who we need.

In fact, we constantly redefine ourselves sexually as the years go by and a new phase of our life succeeds the previous ones. It is only by being fully aware of this constant redefinition of our sexual role that we can hope to experience all our sexual possibilities.

LIFE STAGES

LIFE STAGES are individual and variable: not every woman will experience all these stages, in this order, or at about these times, but most of us experience most of them in our lifetime.

2 PHYSIOLOGICAL MATURITY
With the menarche and fertility we experience a positive desire for sexual arousal, fantasizing, masturbating, and even actively experimenting.

4 SEXUAL INDEPENDENCE
We begin to take our own sexual decisions, such as who to sleep with; often this decision-making power increases our capacity for pleasure.

6 SEXUAL COMMITMENT
We usually do not make our first statement of fidelity to a single partner for reasons of sex alone, but real sexual compatibility is essential.

1 SEXUAL BEGINNINGS
We explore childhood, sometimes unaware of our sexuality for a few years, but increasingly conscious of it.

3 SEXUAL PARTNERSHIP
Our first significant sexual experiences start to bring an appreciation of just how powerful sexuality can be.

5 PLAYING THE FIELD
By taking a number of partners, we start to learn what does and doesn't work for us sexually and emotionally.

7 SEXUAL DEVELOPMENT
We reach a point of sexual confidence, when we know our preferences and when our orgasms are often controllable and reliable.

SEX AND KEY LIFE EVENTS

Single crucial events—crisis or celebration, promotion or pregnancy, illness or attack—may change your outlook to everything, including sex.

● YOU MAY HAVE RENEWED ENERGY FOR LOVEMAKING
This is particularly likely after a positive event such as getting married. But if it happens in the wake of a tragedy, such as a miscarriage, don't feel guilty—you are reaffirming life. If your partner reacts differently and doesn't want sex, don't pressurize. Find your own resolution through fantasy and masturbation.

● YOU MAY LOSE INTEREST IN SEX
This is particularly likely when you are recovering from a crisis or rejection, such as losing your job or divorce, but also when putting your energy into a new project, such as moving house. Look after yourself, both physically—by eating well, exercising, sleeping, and relaxing—and emotionally, getting support from family, friends, or a counsellor. Reassure your partner you still care. In time, this phase will pass and your sexuality will come back into balance.

8 SEXUAL ITCH
Between five and nine years into a committed relationship, we may experience a crisis of sexuality, feeling restless and tempted to have an affair or change partners.

10 CHILD REARING
Sex often becomes less important as we focus our energies on our children, but as they become increasingly independent, we may reclaim our sexuality.

12 CLIMACTERIC
As fertility declines and we pass through the menopause we may feel either that our sex life is over, or, alternatively, freer to be more uninhibitedly sexual.

14 RETIREMENT
When we stop work—or a partner does—there may be readjustment as we both realize this is now likely to be our only sexual partnership for the remainder of our lives.

9 SEX FOR A FAMILY
We often undergo a change of attitude to sex because of pregnancy, failure to become pregnant, or taking the decision not to have a family.

11 REACHING A PLATEAU
The belief that life has peaked may turn passion off or mean we need the reassurance of better sex, within or outside our prime relationship.

13 RELEASE FROM CHILD CARE
As the last child leaves home, we reestablish our prime relationship; a second honeymoon, or disillusion and perhaps commitment to another partner, may follow.

15 OLD AGE
Illness, perceived loss of looks, the death of a partner, and cultural expectations may all erode sexuality. But if we can overcome these challenges, we can continue to be sexual until the end.

SEX AND WORK
HANDLING SEXUALITY IN THE WORKPLACE

One of the major changes in cultural norms over the past half century is that women now expect to work outside the home—hardly any of us will never have a job. As a result, it's unsurprising that work has become the largest single source of sexual contact for women today: 60 percent of us at some point will have sex with a colleague; 30 percent of us will marry one. The large, flexible pool of possible partners, the regular day-to-day contact, and the forging of cooperative links all make the workplace a most effective arena for sex.

Case history

"We didn't have sex immediately. The whole thing just grew on us, particularly as I knew Ben was married. Then we worked together on some exam schemes and I really respected how he handled things. I had trouble with my boyfriend, and Ben helped me kick him out; almost immediately we slept together.

"It was difficult then; I found it a strain never being able to touch him in the staff room. But we managed without anyone suspecting until we were ready to make our move. We waited until the last day of term, then he simply went back home, packed, and came to me. The next six weeks were terrible, as he worked things out with his family. But it meant we started back at school the following term with everything sorted. The other staff were a bit sniffy; I don't think it went down well that I'd 'stolen' him. But in the end, they accepted it."

PAT

AS WOMEN GAIN MORE POWER *at work they may increasingly be judged on factors that are irrelevant to a man's career. Depending on the culture of the workplace, women who dress in a sexually attractive way can be seen as high fliers or lightweight, while those who dress androgynously are either serious contenders or neutered low achievers. In the same way, women who smile attractively may be called "teasers," those who display neutral body language can be deemed "unfeminine," and those who are assertive or aggressive can be termed "ball breakers."*

There are no simple solutions. Following company norms in dress, behavior, and body language will get you an easy

life. Challenging them may give you grief in the short term. But in the long term it makes a useful statement: that women at work are as competent as men and that their sexuality is, in fact, irrelevant.

HANDLING WORK SEXUALITY

An intimate relationship that begins at work has a good chance of succeeding: you will have fewer illusions about each other, so can build your passion on real understanding. But there are disadvantages which you will need to offset.

• *Institute a "shifting gears half hour" when you first arrive home to prevent work intruding into your lovemaking. Spend time apart so your interests become broader than just work and sex.*

• *Don't let physical intimacy creep into work – your efficiency may suffer and colleagues resent what is happening and make trouble. (One rule of thumb is not to speak about personal matters or touch intimately once either of you is in work clothes.)*

• *Be prepared, even if you handle your work situation impeccably, for one of you to be "transferred" or asked to leave once the relationship is known. Many companies consider that a sexual bond threatens corporate loyalty. Plan ahead: what will you do if given an ultimatum by the management?*

• *If the affair ends, steel yourself for even more of a kickback than normal after a break-up. Having to continue working alongside each other will be difficult; you may want to move jobs, or at least avoid meeting for a while.*

COPING WITH HARASSMENT

Up to 90 percent of women suffer sexual harassment in the workplace. This can take the form of pressure for sexual activity, suggestive remarks, or offers of promotion in return for favors. Such incidents are less about sex than about power; the harasser wants to feel that he (or she) has control. Justice is not always done. A 1992 study suggests that most incidents are never reported. Even when they are, more than 50 percent of offenders are not disciplined, and often it is the complainant who is reprimanded. But these tips will help.

● Never give an impression of availability at work, through dress, body language, or words.

● Don't flirt; discourage those who try to flirt with you.

● If you are harassed, avoid being alone with the harasser from that point on.

● Keep a record of what happens: when, where, and who was present.

● Face your harasser, with a witness. Tell him (or her) calmly but without apology: what you object to; the behavior you expect in future; what you will do if you are harassed again. Put it in writing.

● If harassment continues, file a complaint with your manager or personnel officer.

● If you are not satisfied with management response, go to the Equal Employment Opportunities Commission [EEOC]. Your company may be legally responsible if they allow harassment to continue.

● If you are in the management level, discourage harassment on the part of your staff, from either gender.

WHEN A RELATIONSHIP ENDS
FACING THE FUTURE AFTER A BREAK-UP

Our grandmothers expected their sexual relationship to be for life, and our mothers expected their marriage to be for life, even if that marriage wasn't their only sexual relationship. We, by contrast, expect the majority of our sexual relationships to come to an end. Such endings always shock. Symbolically, a sexual parting can often seem a rejection or a failure, whatever its cause. Practically, such a break-up probably means the loss of other things—cuddles, comfort, commitment, financial support, or joint parenting.

But even though we regret endings, we are increasingly capable of positively choosing them and making the best of them. Typically, we realize that a bad relationship is worse than no relationship at all. In many Western countries, women sue for divorce more often than their male partners, and after a break-up, we are more likely than they are to feel that the ending was for the best. We also appear to be better than men at finding a new partnership which is more successful than our previous relationship.

RE-ENTERING THE SEXUAL ARENA

● If you feel nervous or pessimistic, unattractive, or lacking in confidence, remember that everyone in your situation feels equally unsure; concentrate on helping them to relax.

● If you are uncertain of the "ground rules"—particularly if they seem to have changed since last time around—talk them through with friends and prospective partners. Admitting you don't know is not a sin. Swapping notes often solves a problem.

● Never be persuaded into doing something you don't want to. It may seem a more sexually liberated age than before, but in many ways, there's less pressure to have sex immediately. It is typical now to get to know someone before you sleep with him (or her).

● Conversely, don't expect that making love necessarily means involvement—as it did, by definition, with your previous partner. Wait until you are sure your agendas are mutual before intimacy, otherwise, you may be disappointed.

● If you have a family, it's probably best not to have many short-term partners. If Dad has just left, children can feel doubly betrayed if subsequent "uncles" come and go. But when you do make a commitment, be clear with children that your sex life is your affair and that they can't dictate or veto it, just as—when the time comes—you can't make their sexual decisions for them.

BEREAVEMENT

Heterosexual women are likely to lose a partner through death. One woman in two is widowed, compared to only one man in five.

Sexually, the impact of bereavement is traumatic. As your body moves through the normal bereavement stages of disbelief, grief, anger, and depression, it may lose its hormonal rhythm, so your menstrual periods may stop and sexual desire die away. You may find that you stop climaxing for a while. It is also normal to feel a need for comfort, and so to long for a sexual relationship, only to feel that this longing is a betrayal of your dead partner.

The secret of survival is to allow yourself to mourn. The more you cut off emotionally, the less likely you are to recover fully. Cry, rage, howl when you need to. Write or talk, as if to him. Keep a diary about your mourning process.

If you never married or are lesbian, your role may not be recognized by society. Talk to others about their positive memories of your partnership—celebrating your partner and your sex life together as fully as you can is a major step on the road to recovery.

PARENTING is hard work even for two. If a relationship breakdown also leaves you with sole—or major—responsibility for child care, there may be very real practical reasons, as well as emotional ones, for postponing new sexual intimacy. In addition to being stressed and fatigued, you may wish to offer your children stability they may feel is lacking.

RECOVERING FROM A BREAK-UP

At the end of a sexual relationship, women often report passing through a sequence of "recovery" phases. You may not experience them all, and some may have more impact on you than others, but these are the phases that are most commonly cited.

● Taking time alone, or withdrawing from the world, in order to give mind and body a rest. While at first sexual desire may be low, with time there may be a rush of sexuality.

● Making contact again, often with people with whom there's little chance of a sexual relationship so that they don't complicate matters, either by making sexual demands or by offering comfort only to withdraw it later.

● Resisting all attempts by friends and family to pressurize you into a new sexual relationship; they will often think you are ready before you actually are. One year's recovery time is normal, two years is typical, though everyone has her own recovery timetable.

● Realizing that you are ready for sex— whether in the context of a casual or committed relationship. Key signs are: when you are no longer emotionally connected to your old partner; when you feel that you are valid as a single person; when you see the old relationship clearly and are determined not to make the same mistakes again.

CLIMACTERIC
UNDERSTANDING MENOPAUSE

As we get older, our ovaries no longer produce estrogen and progesterone, and they lose their ability to ripen eggs. We stop having monthly cycles, and as our body adjusts, it responds with varying symptoms. This time, when a woman ends her child-bearing years, is known as the climacteric. It used to be seen as the last phase of a woman's life. After this, she was no longer fertile, hence no longer sexual, and often unhealthy. In any case, life expectancy was such that she probably had only a short time to live.

Nowadays, sex doesn't have to result in conception, and childbearing may cease 20 years before the climacteric. Sex is seen more for pleasure than procreation, and having offspring is not essential for survival, so there is less significance in being fertile. With medical advances, both traditional and complementary, midlife changes are more bearable, allowing an active lifestyle. We may not even notice menopause, apart from being glad that we no longer bleed.

The climacteric, however, still needs to be understood and managed, both physically and emotionally. With the average female life expectancy at 80-plus years, we may be only halfway through our allotted span when we have our last menstrual period. The climacteric is no longer a final phase, merely a transition between the first and second half of our life.

CHARTING THE CHANGES YEAR BY YEAR

The climacteric lasts about 15 years between the ages of 40 and 60. The first stage, perimenopause, starts when your hormones begin to fluctuate between the ages of 35 and 45, and as a result your menstrual periods become erratic. The final stage, menopause, is marked by your last period, so it is only obvious after the event. It can happen at any age from 45 to 58. (A menopause that happens before the age of 35 is considered premature. This happens because of ovarian problems or after a hysterectomy, particularly one that removes your ovaries.) In the post-menopause years, which begin between ages 55 and 65, your body gradually adjusts to shifting hormone levels, although it will develop some longer-term vulnerability as a result.

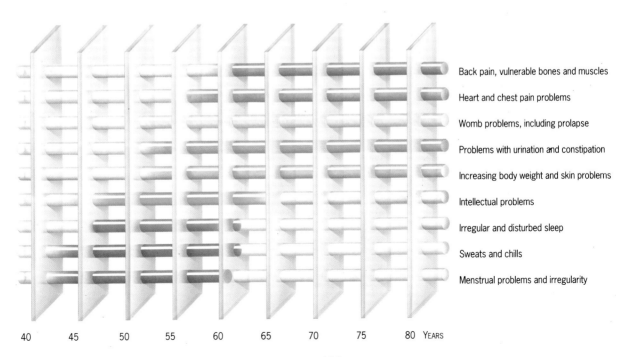

Back pain, vulnerable bones and muscles

Heart and chest pain problems

Womb problems, including prolapse

Problems with urination and constipation

Increasing body weight and skin problems

Intellectual problems

Irregular and disturbed sleep

Sweats and chills

Menstrual problems and irregularity

40   45   50   55   60   65   70   75   80   YEARS

BECOMING A WOMAN 14–15
KNOWING YOURSELF 26–27
WHEN SEX CREATES PROBLEMS 40–41
CLIMACTERIC 182–85

CLIMACTERIC SYMPTOMS

Every woman's response to the climacteric is individual to her. Not all women have noticeable symptoms, although 85 percent of Western women do.

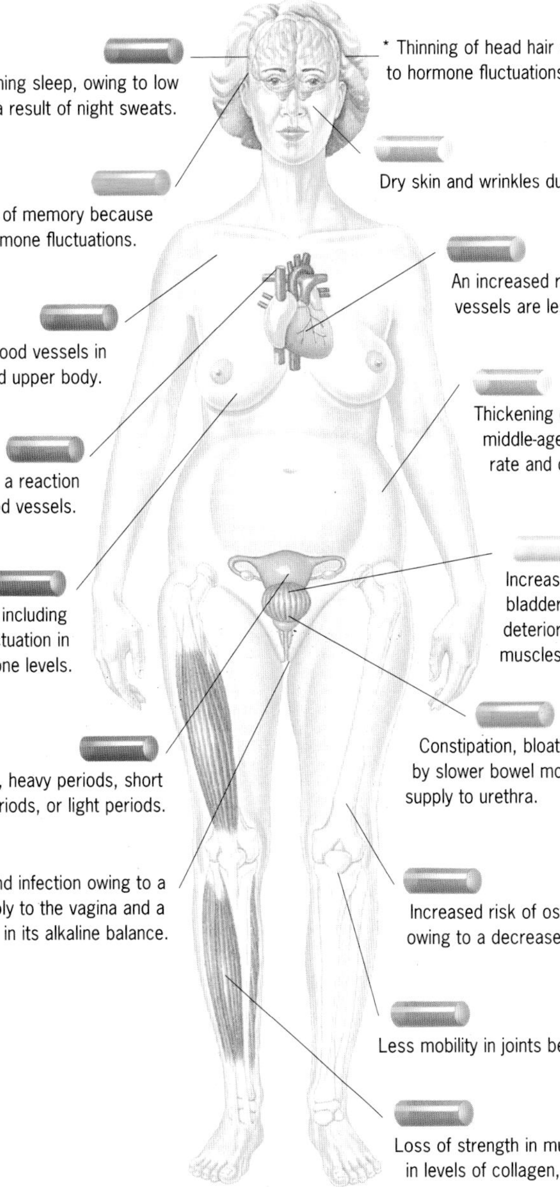

Climacteric symptoms
Long term side-effects
Insomnia and lack of dreaming sleep, owing to low estrogen or as a result of night sweats.
* Thinning of head hair and thickening of facial hair owing to hormone fluctuations.
Dry skin and wrinkles due to a decrease in estrogen.
Mood swings, anxiety, and loss of memory because of hormone fluctuations.
An increased risk of heart disease as blood vessels are less able to dilate.
Hot flushes caused by dilating blood vessels in your face and upper body.
Thickening of body shape and weight gain—middle-age spread—due to lower metabolic rate and decline in estrogen levels.
Night sweats and cold chills as a reaction to dilating blood vessels.
Increased symptoms of PMS, including breast tenderness, owing to fluctuation in hormone levels.
Increased risk of infection in womb, bladder, and bowel as a result of deterioration of organs, nerves, and muscles in pelvic area.
Constipation, bloating, and urgency urination caused by slower bowel movements and decrease in blood supply to urethra.
Missed menstrual periods, heavy periods, short periods, or light periods.
* Vaginal dryness, itching, and infection owing to a decrease in the blood supply to the vagina and a change in its alkaline balance.
Increased risk of osteoporosis (bone vulnerability) owing to a decreased ability to process calcium.
Less mobility in joints because of hormone decline.
Loss of strength in muscles and ligaments due to a drop in levels of collagen, a protein.

** These symptoms can first appear in perimenopause and continue throughout the climacteric.*

CLIMACTERIC

SOLVING THE PROBLEMS ASSOCIATED WITH MENOPAUSE

The climacteric affects most women. Some barely notice the symptoms, others find their whole life influenced for the worse. The good news is that there are several possible solutions to both short-term symptoms during the climacteric itself and its long-term effects. We can supplement our hormones chemically or try more "natural" complementary methods. Debate rages about which option is best, which gives most immediate relief, and ultimately which is most helpful or least harmful. But beyond this debate, the important thing is that remedies exist. There is a vast fund of scientific knowledge and self-help wisdom to support us in remaining physically fit, emotionally healthy, and sexually fulfilled.

Long-term measures

There are various self-help methods of tackling the long-term effects of the climacteric.

Help your adrenal glands—the main source of estrogen—to function by avoiding nicotine, caffeine, alcohol, sugar, and processed foods; eat an organic low-fat diet. Avoiding high-cholesterol foods helps to minimize the risk of heart disease, and eating calcium-rich foods reduces the risk of osteoporosis. Supplements of vitamins B, C, D, and E, with at least 1,500 mg of calcium daily, will help support your adrenal glands and offer protection against osteoporosis and heart disease.

Take at least 20 minutes of brisk exercise daily. Walking or cycling regularly helps to build bone density, and yoga or stretching offsets middle-age spread and loss of mobility and muscle strength. In addition, do regular pelvic floor exercises.

Stress influences hormone levels, so actively trying to reduce the stress you are under is another way to offset menopausal symptoms. Exercise can be beneficial, as are relaxation and mental approaches such as meditation and autogenic training.

Complementary health approaches, such as aromatherapy, homeopathy, herbalism, and acupuncture, can also support self-help measures.

Finally, a support group for women approaching menopause can keep you in touch with current developments and remind you that you're not alone.

SELF-HELP FOR SYMPTOMS

• *Varying menstrual periods: Take iron supplements to prevent anemia; if periods are both irregular and heavy, have a medical check-up in case there is something wrong.*

• *PMS: Use the remedies outlined on pp. 26–27.*

• *Insomnia: Avoid mental activity before bedtime, take physical exercise, a lukewarm bath, a hot milky drink; try relaxation exercises or herbal remedies.*

• *Vaginal symptoms: Use vaginal moisturizers; masturbate and have intercourse to keep tissues strong and lubricated; follow the guidelines for vaginal health on pp. 38–39.*

• *Hot flashes: Keep a diary to trace any pattern; try avoiding alcohol, caffeine, sugar, chocolate, and spicy foods; stop smoking; take exercise; use vitamin E supplements; wear layered cotton clothing; breathe with a flash when it happens in full, slow, relaxing breaths.*

• *Night sweats: Put a large towel under the sheet; have bedclothes that are easy to kick off; keep spare bedding, ice water, a perfume spray, and an electric fan near the bed.*

SOME EXPERTS *claim that exercise is as beneficial as hormone replacement therapy (HRT), since it increases the amount of estrogen circulating* in the blood. Exercise can also reduce stress and increase strength and suppleness. If you are unused to exercise, don't push yourself too hard at first.

HORMONE REPLACEMENT THERAPY

HRT has had a mixed press. Those who use it happily swear it keeps them looking young and sexually active; it also seems to protect against osteoporosis, heart disease, and ovarian, colonic, and cervical cancer.

Those who are suspicious of HRT say it creates the symptoms of PMS, increases the risk of breast and endometrial cancer (particularly if you are taking mainly estrogen rather than a mixture of estrogen and progesterone), and may worsen fibroids, gallstones, and endometriosis.

Before starting HRT, make sure that you are thoroughly screened for vulnerability to problems. And be prepared to experiment to find a blend of hormones that suits you. Consult your doctor if you have unexpected bleeding, which could signal gynecological cancer.

● Pills: One tablet a day, most commonly estrogen for perhaps 16 days plus progesterone for 12 days a month. You have to remember to take them, but can stop at any time.

● Implants: Tiny estrogen pellets inserted under the skin of your abdomen or buttocks which last for six to nine months—you usually take added progesterone. Implants are convenient, but any negative side effects last for a while even after the implants are removed.

● Patches: Need to be replaced every few days; longer-lasting ones are being researched. They have the advantages and disadvantages of pills, but because they bypass the liver, may avoid some of the side effects.

● IUS: A new interuterine system to give you progesterone (see p. 111) seems to have fewer side effects, but you still need to take estrogen in pill form.

● Estrogen cream and suppositories and the vaginal ring: Inserted in the vagina to help combat vaginal soreness and dryness. As there is no progesterone added, these are usually used only as short-term measures.

Implant

Vaginal ring

Pills

Skin patches

Pills

Estrogen cream

Estrogen suppositories

Applicator

ESTROGEN *is produced by eggs in the ovary. Production is erratic during menopause, when an egg may not be released every month; after menopause, it is only present in small amounts. Progesterone is produced in response to ovulation, so is absent after menopause.*

Normal menstrual cycle

During menopause

After menopause

Progesterone

Estrogen

Menstruation

0   7   14   21   28 DAYS OF CYCLE

CLIMACTERIC

CHALLENGING THE MYTHS SURROUNDING THE MENOPAUSE

A woman facing the menopause can be tempted to believe that she faces not only a shift in her hormones, but also a shift in her ability to live effectively, significantly, and influentially. But increasingly, the middle years are seen as a positive time for women. And the more we can do to add to this, the more successful we will become. Celebrating other women, fulfilling our own potential, developing our sexuality—all these will challenge the myth of the menopausal monster.

FAYE DUNAWAY (below) *continues to enjoy an acting career that has spanned several decades.*

LAUREN HUTTON (left) *is still modeling in her fifties.*

Case history

"When I was 49, I fell in love for the first time ... with Fiona. I'd always wondered why I'd never remarried after David died; I'd just never been around lesbian women and realized what I felt. My children thought I was just going through the change; one of them said 'but now we're out of the way, Mom, you can have a proper boyfriend.' Aaargh!!! The thing that makes me angry is that it's taken me over half my life to find out what I really wanted."

LESLEY

THE NEED FOR CONTRACEPTION

You are still able to conceive until you have not had a menstrual period for 24 months (if you are under 50) or 12 months (if you are over 50). Since there is a much greater chance of a baby conceived after the age of 40 having—or causing—health problems, it is important to use totally reliable contraception during this time.

● The rhythm method isn't suitable because, during the climacteric, your periods are irregular and fluctuating hormone levels make the mucus and temperature methods of gauging the fertile period unreliable.

● The lower reliability of barrier methods may well be offset by the fact that you are less fertile as you approach menopause. Using a condom (or female condom) may cause problems if you suffer from vaginal dryness, or if your (male) partner has started to need strong sensation to get an erection.

● The lower reliability of the IUD may make it more suitable as your fertility declines; and the associated risks of infection decrease if you are in a stable relationship.

● Estrogen-based contraception such as the combined pill can provide perfectly good "hormone replacement" as well as protection. If you don't smoke and are in good general health, try the lowest dose pill available.

● The progesterone-only pill, injectables, or implants are useful if you can't take estrogen. But if you have irregular bleeding while taking them, see your doctor immediately; this can be a symptom of cancer of the womb, the risk of which increases with age.

ISABELLA ROSSELLINI (left) *was in her forties when she was awarded a lucrative modeling contract for a cosmetics company.*

TINA TURNER (below), *in her fifties, is a sexual icon, admired by men and women for her energetic performances live and on record.*

Case history

"For two years after my husband left, I felt like dying. I was 52, well into the change of life, and felt and looked awful. It seemed like the end of everything. Then I was with friends one day and Steven walked in. He's 15 years younger than me. I told him I was too old; he said nonsense. I've never had sex like it; I've discovered oral sex, vibrators, and multiple orgasms. It probably won't last, but I've got my confidence now. There will be someone else if it's not Steven."

BREDA

SEX AS YOU AGE

CHALLENGING THE MYTH THAT THE OLD DO NOT MAKE LOVE

The message is spreading that old age does not kill sexual desire but can even enhance it. Although looks and health undeniably decline and physiological changes may affect sexual potential, these disadvantages are often offset by the mental and emotional developments that come with age. In a series of studies, 95 percent of the elderly reported they liked sex, 75 percent stated an orgasm was essential to good sex, and 50 percent said they had sex at least once a week—a higher frequency than some of their 30-something counterparts. In addition, 75 percent of those who were sexually active said their lovemaking had become more, not less, rewarding over the years. One Australian doctor tells of a patient who at 72 began to have extramarital sex and at 74 had her first orgasm.

If we really nurture our sexual selves, old age can be a supremely sexual time. Lovemaking may become more important, as career and family responsibilities fade in significance. And, older, we may develop the confidence to state our sexual preferences clearly and to be more adventurous. And if we move into our final years within the context of a stable relationship, we may also move into a new phase of sex, where over time we become able to sense intuitively what is wanted and so make sex a reflection of deep love.

BODY SHIFTS

Over time, aging may affect your sexuality in the following ways. Unless you are injured or ill, the most effective way of offsetting them is to keep making love—to yourself or with a partner—thereby keeping your sexual organs strong and healthy.

● You may begin to feel "unsexual" because your skin, hair, and figure do not fit an ideal, but remember in sex, passion and experience easily outperform surface attractiveness.

● Your vagina may shorten and narrow and continue the vulnerability to soreness and dryness which began with menopause. Use plenty of lubrication and extended foreplay. Be reassured: 80 percent of women do not experience any problems.

● Your breast tissue and nipples may respond less during arousal so you may need to use different kinds of foreplay.

● Your clitoris may become less engorged when aroused, but it may be even more sensitive.

● Orgasms may not be quite as intense; pelvic exercises to strengthen your muscles may help retain the depth of contractions.

● Your cervix may lose sensitivity; experiment with different sexual positions.

● Some women notice a drop in desire with age, but this by no means typical; if you do, go for a check-up.

● If you have had a prolapse, in which the pelvic muscles weaken and the womb drops, sex may be painful. Medical solutions include a surgical repair or a support ring fitted around the cervix; pelvic exercises may also help.

ENJOYING SEX AND RETAINING SEXUALITY INTO OLD AGE

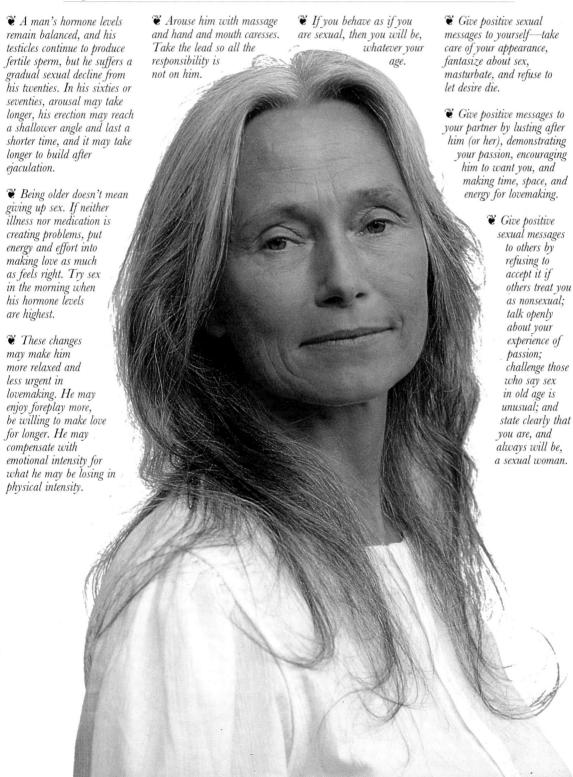

❦ *A man's hormone levels remain balanced, and his testicles continue to produce fertile sperm, but he suffers a gradual sexual decline from his twenties. In his sixties or seventies, arousal may take longer, his erection may reach a shallower angle and last a shorter time, and it may take longer to build after ejaculation.*

❦ *Being older doesn't mean giving up sex. If neither illness nor medication is creating problems, put energy and effort into making love as much as feels right. Try sex in the morning when his hormone levels are highest.*

❦ *These changes may make him more relaxed and less urgent in lovemaking. He may enjoy foreplay more, be willing to make love for longer. He may compensate with emotional intensity for what he may be losing in physical intensity.*

❦ *Arouse him with massage and hand and mouth caresses. Take the lead so all the responsibility is not on him.*

❦ *If you behave as if you are sexual, then you will be, whatever your age.*

❦ *Give positive sexual messages to yourself—take care of your appearance, fantasize about sex, masturbate, and refuse to let desire die.*

❦ *Give positive messages to your partner by lusting after him (or her), demonstrating your passion, encouraging him to want you, and making time, space, and energy for lovemaking.*

❦ *Give positive sexual messages to others by refusing to accept it if others treat you as nonsexual; talk openly about your experience of passion; challenge those who say sex in old age is unusual; and state clearly that you are, and always will be, a sexual woman.*

BIBLIOGRAPHY

General

Women on Sex, Susan Quilliam, Barricade Books, New York 1994

The Kinsey Institute New Report on Sex: What You Must Know to be Sexually Literate, J. Reinisch, St. Martin's Press, New York 1990

The Hite Report, Shere Hite, Dell Publishing Company Inc., New York 1982

Chapter 1

ABUSE
The Courage to Heal, Ellen Bass and Laura Davis, Harper Collins US, New York 1989

Chapter 2

GENERAL HEALTH
American Medical Association Guide to Women's Health, Ann Furedi and Mary Tidyman, Random House, New York 1996

The New Our Bodies, Ourselves, The Boston Women's Health Book Collective, Touchstone, New York 1996

DIET, SMOKING, ALCOHOL, EXERCISE
The general health books mentioned above include advice on these issues.

BODY IMAGE
The Beauty Myth, Naomi Wolf, Bantam Doubleday Dell Publishing Group Inc., New York 1996

GYNECOLOGICAL PROBLEMS
The general health books mentioned above include advice on gynecological issues, but the following more specific resources may also be helpful.

You Don't Have to Live with Cystitis! Larian Gillespie, Avon, New York 1995

Alternatives for Women with Endometriosis, Ruth Carol, Third Side, New York 1994

STDS
Living with Herpes, D. Langston, Doubleday & Co., New York 1994

Sexually Transmitted Diseases, K. K. Holmes, McGraw-Hill, New York 1990

Terrific Sex in Fearful Times, B. Peters, St. Martin's Press, New York 1988

SEXUAL MIND
The Mirror Within, Anne Dickson, Salem House Publications, New York 1986

SEXUAL DECISION MAKING
A Woman in Your Own Right, Anne Dickson, Salem House Publications, New York 1983

CELIBACY
The New Celibacy, Gabrielle Brown, McGraw-Hill, New York 1980

UNWELCOME SEX
I Never Called It Rape, R. Warshaw, Harper Row, New York 1988

MASTURBATION
Sex for One, Betty Dodson, Crown Trade Paperbacks, New York 1996

Chapter 3

The New Joy of Sex, Alex Comfort, Crown Publishing Group, New York 1991

Sexual Happiness for Men, Maurice Yaffe, Elizabeth Fenwick, and Raymond Rosen, Henry Holt and Company Inc., New York 1989

Sexual Happiness for Women, Maurice Yaffe, Elizabeth Fenwick, and Raymond Rosen, Henry Holt and Company Inc., New York 1989

Chapter 4

BODY LANGUAGE
Body Language, Susan Quilliam, Random Value Publishing 1996

Sexual Body Talk, Susan Quilliam, Carroll and Graf, New York 1992

Women's Experience of Sex, Sheila Kitzinger, Viking Penguin, New York 1985

Chapter 5

CONTRACEPTION AND TERMINATION
Contraception – A User's Handbook, Anne Szarewski and John Guillebaud, Oxford University Press, New York 1994

INFERTILITY
Give us a Child: Coping with the Personal Crisis of Infertility, L. Stephenson, Harper & Row, New York 1987

Challenging Conceptions, Lisa Saffron, LPC Inbook, Chicago, Illinois 1994

Infertility, Roger Neuberg, Harper, San Francisco 1994

PREGNANCY
The Well Pregnancy Book, M. Samuels and N. Samuels, Harper & Row, New York 1986

BRINGING UP SEXUAL CHILDREN
The What's Happening to My Body? Book for Girls: A Growing Up Guide for Parents and Daughters, L. Madras, New Market Press, New York 1983

Talking with your Child About Sex, M. S. Calderone and J. Ramsey, Random House, New York 1982

Chapter 6

GENERAL
Love is Never Enough, Aaron Beck, Harper & Row, New York 1988

ORGASMIC PROBLEMS
Becoming Orgasmic: A Sexual and Personal Growth Program for Women, J. Heinman and J. LoPiccolo, Prentice Hall, New Jersey 1988

MALE SEXUAL PROBLEMS
Male Sexual Health: A Couple's Guide, R. F. Spark, Consumer Reports Books, Mount Vernon, New York 1991

Men and Sex, Bernie Zilbergeld, Harper Collins, New York 1980

Chapter 7

FANTASY
Women on Top: Women's Sexual Fantasies, Nancy Friday, Pocket Star Books, New York 1993

Forbidden Flowers, Nancy Friday, Pocket Star Books, New York 1991

My Secret Garden: Women's Sexual Fantasies, Nancy Friday, Pocket Star Books, New York 1991

MASSAGE
The Joy of Sensual Massage, Roger Hicks and Victoria Day, Sterling Publishing Company Inc. US, New York 1994

The Complete Book of Massage, Clare Maxwell-Hudson, Random House Inc., New York 1988

Chapter 8

MENOPAUSE
Vogue Futures, Deborah Hutton, Crown Publishing Group, New York 1995

AGEING
Living, Loving and Ageing, S. Greengross and W. Living, State Mutual Book and Periodical Service Ltd., New York 1989

Love and Sex After 60, R. Butler & M. Lewis, Harper & Row, New York 1988

USEFUL ADDRESSES

Chapter 1

ABUSE
Child Abuse Listening and Mediation (CALM), PO Box 90754, Santa Barbara, CA 93910-0754. Tel: (805) 965-2376. 24-hour hotline: (805) 569-2255.
Incest Survivors Resource Network (ISRNI), PO Box 7375, Las Cruces, NM 88066. Tel: (505) 521-4260.

Chapter 2

GENERAL HEALTH
The following are national organizations which can give you lists of practitioners in your area.
American Acupuncture Association (AAA), 4262 Kissena Blvd, Flushing, NY 11355. Tel: (718) 886-4431.
American Foundation of Traditional Chinese Medicine, 505 Beach St, San Francisco, CA 94133. Tel: (415) 776-0502.
American Phyto Aromatherapy Association, 7436 SW 117 Ave, Ste 188 Miami, FL 33183. Tel: (305) 460-3392.
International Foundation for Homeopathy (IFH), 2366 Eastlake Ave E, No 301, Seattle, WA 98102. Tel: (206) 324-8230.
National Women's Health Resource Center (NWHRC), 2440 M St NW, Ste 325, Washington DC 20037. Tel: (202) 293-6045.

DIET, SMOKING, ALCOHOL
Action on Smoking and Health (ASH), 2013 H St NW, Washington DC 20006. Tel: (202) 659-4310.
Alcoholics Anonymous World Services (AA), 475 Riverside Drive, New York, NY 10163. Tel: (212) 870-3400.
Narcotics Anonymous (NA), PO Box 9999, Van Nuys, CA 91409. Tel: (818) 780-3951.

BODY IMAGE
American Anorexia/Bulimia Association (AA/BA), 425 E 61st St, New York, NY 10021. Tel: (212) 891-8686.
National Eating Disorders Organization (NEDO), 445 E Granville Rd, Worthington, OH 43085. Tel: (614) 436-1112.

GYNECOLOGICAL PROBLEMS
Endometriosis Association (EA), 8585 N 76th Pl, Milwaukee, WI 53223. Tel: (414) 355-2200. Toll-free no: (800) 992-3636.

WOMEN'S CANCERS
Breast Cancer Advisory Center (BCAC), PO Box 224, Kensington, MD 20895. Fax: (305) 949-1132.
Burger King Cancer Caring Center, 4117 Liberty Ave, Pittsburgh, PA 15224. Tel: (412) 261-2211.
Cancer Care (CC), 1180 Avenue of the Americas, New York, NY 10036. Tel: (212) 221-3300.
National Alliance of Breast Cancer Organizations (NABCO), 9 E 37th St, 10th Fl, New York, NY 10016. Tel: (212) 719-0154.
Y-ME National Breast Cancer Organization (Y-ME), c/o Sharon Green, 212 W Van Buren, Chicago, IL 60607. 24-hour hotline: (708) 799-8228.

STDs AND AIDS
American Social Health Association (ASHA), PO Box 13827, Research Triangle Park, NC 27709. National AIDS hotline: (800) 342-2437. National STD hotline: (800) 227-8922.
Herpes Research Center, PO Box 13827, Research Triangle Park, NC 27709. Tel: (919) 361-8488.
National Association of People With AIDS (NAPWA), 1413 K St NW, Washington DC 20005. Tel: (202) 898-0141.
People With AIDS Coalition (PWA), 50 W 17th, 8th Fl, New York, NY 10011-1607. Tel: (212) 532-0568.

UNWELCOME SEX
National Coalition Against Sexual Assault (NCASA), 912 N 2nd St, Harrisburg, PA 17102. Tel: (202) 483-7165.
Women Against Rape (WAR), PO Box 02084, Columbus, OH 43202. Tel: (614) 291-9751.

Chapter 5

GENERAL
American Academy of Natural Family Planning (AANFP), 615 S New Ballas Rd, St Louis, MO 63141. Tel: (712) 279-2048.
Association for Childbirth at Home International (ACHI), PO Box 430, Glendale, CA 91209. Tel: (818) 545-7128.
National Abortion Federation (NAF), 1436 U St NW Ste 103, Washington DC 20009. Tel: (800) 772-9100.
National Association of Childbearing Centers (NACC), 3123 Gottschall Rd, Perkiomenville, PA 18074. Tel: (215) 234-8068.

National Family Planning and Reproductive Health Association (NFPRHA), 122 C St NW, Ste 380, Washington DC 20001. Tel: (202) 628-3535.

INFERTILITY
National Infertility Network Exchange (NINE), c/o Ilene Stargot, PO Box 204, East Meadow, New York, NY 11554. Tel: (516) 794-5772.
Resolve Inc., 1310 Broadway, Somerville, MA 02144-1731. Tel: (617) 623-0744.

DEATH OF A CHILD
National SIDS Resource Center (NSRC), 8201 Greensboro Dr, Ste,600, Maclean, VA 22102. Tel: (703) 821-8955.
Pregnancy and Infant Loss Center (PILC), 1421 E Wayzata Blvd, No 30, Wayzata, MN 55391. Tel: (612) 473-9372.

POST-NATAL ILLNESS
Depression After Delivery (DAD), ,PO Box 1282, Morrisville, PA 19067. Tel: (215) 295-3994.

BRINGING UP SEXUAL CHILDREN
Parents Anonymous (PA), 675 W Foothill Blvd, Ste 220, Claremont, CA 91711-3416. Tel: (909) 621-6184. Stressline: (800) 421-0353.
Sex Matters, PO Box 9207, SOuth Burlington, VT 05403-9207. Tel: (802) 863-1400.

Chapter 6

SEX AND DISABILITY
Coalition on Sexuality and Disability (CSD), 122 E 23rd St, New York, NY 10010. Tel: (212) 242-3900.

SEX THERAPY AND RELATIONSHIP COUNSELING
American Counseling Association (ACA), 5999 Stevenson Ave, Alexandria, VA 22304-3300. Tel: (703) 823-9800. Toll-free no: (800) 347-6647.

Sex Information and Education Council of the US, 130 W 42nd St, Ste 350, New York, NY 10036. Tel: (212) 819-9970.

Chapter 8

SEX AT WORK
WIC (Women In Crisis), 360 W 125th St, New York, NY 10027. Tel: (212) 665-2018

BEREAVEMENT
International Association for Widowed People (IAWP), PO Box 3564, Springfield, IL 62708. Tel: (217) 787-0886.

MENOPAUSE
North American Menopause Association (NAMA), University Hospitals of Cleveland, Dept of Ob/Gyn, 11100 Uleed, Cleveland, OH 44106. Tel: (216) 844-3334.

INDEX

ACKNOWLEDGMENTS

Photographic credits

1 Stefan May/Tony Stone Images; 2–3 Trevor Watson/
Akehurst Bureau; 5 Trevor Watson/Akehurst Bureau;
6 Stewart Cohen (left) Ken Fisher (center) Daniel Boster (right)
Tony Stone Images; 7 Andy Cox (left) Ken Fisher (center)
Tony Stone Images, ZEFA (right); 8–9 Paul Venning;
11 Bubbles (top) Nancy Durrell McKenna/The Hutchison
Library (bottom); 12 Richard Open/Camera Press (top left),
J. Fisher/Bubbles (top right) M. Goodacre/S.I.N. (bottom left)
Jennie Woodcock/Reflections (bottom right); 16&17 Laura
Wickenden; 18 Graeme Harris/Tony Stone Images;
19 L.J. Thurston/Bubbles; 20 ZEFA; 21 Tony Souter/The
Hutchison Library; 22 ZEFA; 24–25 Paul Venning; 27 Nancy
Durrell McKenna/The Hutchison Library; 28 Dominic
Sansoni/Panos Pictures; 29 Laura Wickenden (left), ZEFA
(right); 30 Christopher Bissell/Tony Stone Images;
30–31 Peter Myers; 32 Laura Wickenden (top) Nancy Durrell
McKenna/The Hutchison Library (bottom); 33 Laura
Wickenden; 34 Nancy Durrell McKenna/The Hutchison
Library; 43 ZEFA (top, center left, center), Tony Souter/
The Hutchison Library (center right) Overseas/
The Hutchison Library (bottom left), Laura Wickenden
(bottom right); 44 Peter Correz/Tony Stone Images;
45 David Harry Stewart/Tony Stone Images; 48–49 Elyse
Lewin/The Image Bank; 51 Laura Wickenden; 52 Paul
Winch-Furness/Camera Press; 56–57 Paul Venning;
58–59 Laura Wickenden; 60 Walter Bibikow/The Image
Bank; 60–61 ZEFA; 64 Dr Ray Clark & Mervyn Goff/
Science Photo Library; 67 Camera Press; 69 Paul Venning;
74–75 Laura Wickenden; 81 Elke Selzle/Tony Stone Images;
82–83 Paul Venning; 84–85 Paul Venning; 86 J. Bourboulon/
Tony Stone Images; 88–89 Laura Wickenden; 92 Paul
Venning; 94–95 Paul Venning; 96 Peter Sylent/Bubbles (left),
Penny Tweedie/Tony Stone Images (right); 97 Jean Michel
Turpin/Frank Spooner Pictures (left), Bruce Ayres/Tony
Stone Images (right); 98 Bruce Ayres/Tony Stone Images;
100–101 ZEFA; 104 Peter Sylent/Bubbles; 106–107 Laura
Wickenden; 109 Laura Wickenden; 111 Laura Wickenden;
114 ZEFA (top), Laura Wickenden (bottom); 117 L.J. Thurston/
Bubbles (top), John Greim/Science Photo Library (bottom left)
Custom Medical Stock/Science Photo Library (bottom right);
119 A. Dawton/Bubbles; 124–125 T. Bevan/Bubbles;
128–129 Laura Wickenden; 130 ZEFA; 132–133 ZEFA;
136 ZEFA; 146 The Lister Hospital (top, bottom) St. Georges
Hospital (center); 148 Zigy Kaluzny/Tony Stone Images;
150–151 Laura Wickenden; 152 Laura Wickenden (top)
Johnny A. Ready (bottom left) Infocus Intl (bottom right) The
Image Bank; 153 W. Behnken/The Image Bank; 154 Trevor
Watson/Akehurst Bureau; 154 Trevor Watson/Akehurst
Bureau; 155 Trevor Watson/Akehurst Bureau; 156 Trevor
Watson/Akehurst Bureau (top), Rex Features (center), Paul
Rider/Camera Press (bottom); 157 Trevor Watson/Akehurst
Bureau; 158 Laura Wickenden (top), E.T. Archive (bottom);
159 Nitin Jhaveri/TRIP; 160 Laura Wickenden;
161 NoNoYes (left), Laura Wickenden (right); 162–163 Laura
Wickenden; 170 ZEFA; 172–173 Laura Wickenden;
174 ZEFA (left, right), David Hanover/Tony Stone Images
(center); 175 Dan Bosler/Tony Stone Images (left), Eliane
Sulle (center) Elyse Lewin (right) The Image Bank; 176 Walter
Hodges (top), Howard Grey (bottom left) Tony Stone Images,
ZEFA (bottom right); 177 ZEFA; 179 Jon Gray/Tony Stone
Images; 182 Camera Press; 183 Laura Wickenden;
184 Camera Press; 185 Rex Features; 186 Nancy Durrell
McKenna/The Hutchison Library; 187 IMS/Camera Press.

Illustration credits

Debbie Hinks 78, 79, 87, 123, 143, 147, 166, 167
Kevin Jones 14–15, 34, 35, 65, 99, 101, 115, 180, 183
Sally Launder 40, 66, 67, 76, 77, 120, 121, 134, 135
Ruth Lindsay 26, 27, 36, 38, 39, 62, 63, 70, 71, 72, 73, 108,
110, 138, 142, 181
Michael Saunders 10, 15, 17, 23, 53, 112–13, 168, 171
Kathy Wyatt 54, 55, 139, 140, 141, 144–45, 169

With thanks to

Elizabeth Arden, Condomania, The Dental Implant Centre,
Dreams Bed Superstores, Margaret Pyke Family Planning
Clinic.